Elements of General Linguistics

ELEMENTS
OF GENERAL LINGUISTICS

by
ANDRÉ MARTINET

With a Foreword by
L. R. PALMER

Translated by
ELISABETH PALMER

Phoenix Books

THE UNIVERSITY OF CHICAGO PRESS

Translated from: *Éléments de Linguistique Générale*
© 1960 by Max Leclerc et Cie
Published by Librairie Armand Colin 1960

THE UNIVERSITY OF CHICAGO PRESS, CHICAGO 60637
FABER AND FABER LIMITED, LONDON, W.C. 1, ENGLAND

English translation © 1964 by Faber and Faber Limited
Published 1964. Third Impression 1967
Printed in the United States of America

Foreword

During the last few decades the science of linguistics has made great strides, and it is now the concern not merely of 'philology' in the old sense, but of those engaged in communications engineering, machine translation, to say nothing of sociology, psychology and other approaches to the study of man in society. This vigorous development has had one unfortunate result: the different linguistic schools have developed their own special terminologies so that mutual communication is impeded. Further, those who continue to study language on more traditional lines—the great bulk of teachers and taught in our universities—have in the main been unaffected by these new developments. Recently a distinguished professor of Classics, trained in the old school of comparative philology, has been heard to declare that nothing made him feel so old as reading works of modern linguistics.

In this situation Professor Martinet, an outstanding theoretician with close acquaintance of the major linguistic schools on both sides of the Atlantic, is especially well qualified to write a work of introduction to modern linguistics. Tracing the beginnings of a completely autonomous science of language to Ferdinand de Saussure's famous *Cours*, he initiates the reader into the concepts and procedures of descriptive and structural linguistics and deals successively with its main branches: phonetics, phonemics and morphemics. A further chapter on the variety of linguistic usage is concerned with what may be termed the sociology of language. The final chapter poses in new and stimulating terms the problems of the causation of linguistic change.

L. R. PALMER

University of Oxford

Contents

9

Preface

If we reflect how natural and advantageous it is for man to identify his language with reality, we shall appreciate how high a degree of sophistication had to be reached before he could dissociate them and make of each a separate object of study. There is a well-known story about a Tyrolese who on his return from a visit to Italy sang the praises of that country but added that the inhabitants must be quite idiotic to call *cavallo* the animal which every reasonable man knows to be a *Pferd*. This identification of word and thing is perhaps the condition of a smooth and unconscious functioning of language. But it is a view which must be superseded if we are to proceed from practical usage to scientific observation of language. The first efforts in this direction led to the identification of language and reason: 'logic' in Greek originally meant 'the art of speaking'. This meant, of course, either that a reasonable and logical character had to be discovered in the worst inconsistencies of language or that corrective law must be laid down when usage seemed not to conform to reason. It was the comparison of languages, usually engaged in for historical considerations, which revealed the variety of linguistic structures. Henceforth, if human reason were a universal phenomenon, then the different forms of language could not be identified with it. Language thus now had to be regarded as a reflection of thought, a thought believed to be determined by social structures rather than obedient to the laws of logic. Hence linguistics took a psychological and sociological turn, and this lasted as long as its task was regarded as the study of the facts of evolution and not of the constitutive features of language as such. Only a strictly synchronic approach could isolate the purely linguistic facts independent of the changing needs of man which at every moment require adaptations of the linguistic tool.

The legitimacy of a completely autonomous general linguistics was put beyond challenge by the publication of the *Cours* of Ferdinand de Saussure, in which synchronic analysis is presented as the first and fundamental step in this discipline. However, de Saussure's doctrines bore real fruit only when grafted on other scions. It was the task of the various structuralist schools which followed to eliminate what proved less acceptable in de Saussure's exposition: a more or less explicit psychologism which prevented according a fully linguistic status to phonematic articulation and obscured the fact that everything that counts in language is represented, in one guise or another, at every point in the circuit of speech.

Modern 'structuralists' are at one in insisting on the priority of synchronic analysis and in rejecting introspection in its entirety. This apart, methods and approaches differ widely from one school or movement to another, and terminological similarities often conceal fundamental divergencies. It will not, therefore, be possible to present within the covers of a single book the totality of doctrines current among contemporary linguists. It need hardly be said that any attempt at syncretism would be doomed to failure. The principles and methods which are expounded in the present work are characterized, vis-à-vis their competitors, by a greater degree of realism and by less formalism and *a priori* argumentation. If the author may venture to make this claim in all modesty, it is because docility to fact is not always recommended by the theoreticians of today. Emphasis will be put as much on the function of linguistic units as on the structures which they constitute. Over and above the synchronic approach, diachronic matters will be considered, although we shall be careful to ensure that the two points of view are not confused.

The different parts of this work doubtless reflect the preferences and the personality of the author, but in very different degrees. The principles of phonological analysis have long become common property. On the other hand, what is offered in Chapter IV apropos of syntax is new, perhaps too new to form part of a manual like this. The necessity of presenting a method of description which will cover in a coherent way the totality of linguistic facts has compelled me to anticipate the completion of a collective, although inadequately coordinated effort, which sought to establish for the significant units something analogous to what phonology represents for the distinctive units. What is said in Chapters V and VI about the variety of human speech and the dynamics of languages is certainly less original. All this has in one form or another been previously expounded. But this does not mean that what will be found in this part of the book is universally accepted.

Few read prefaces. If, however, a beginner has ventured to peruse these preliminary pages, he ought to be told that they were not written with him in mind. It is to be hoped that he will find the body of the book proper less remote and that if he returns to re-read the preface once his study is completed, he will be in a better position to see what place the doctrines of the author occupy in the framework of linguistic researches.

CHAPTER I

Language and Languages

1.1 Linguistics—a non-prescriptive discipline

Linguistics is the scientific study of human language. A study is
said to be scientific when it is founded on the observation of facts
and refrains from picking and choosing among the facts in the
light of certain aesthetic or moral principles. Thus 'scientific' is
opposed to 'prescriptive'. In the case of linguistics it is particularly important to insist on the scientific and non-prescriptive
character of our approach: the object of this science being a form
of human activity, there is a great temptation to forsake the
domain of impartial observation in order to recommend certain
modes of behaviour or conduct, in other words to cease to
observe what is in fact said and to make pronouncements on
what ought to be said. The difficulty felt in making a clear
distinction between scientific linguistics and normative grammar
recalls the similar difficulties in distinguishing between morals
and a true science of ethics. History teaches us that until a very
recent date those who engaged in the study of language in general
or of particular languages have done so with prescriptive intentions, whether tacit or explicit. Even today the general public,
however highly educated, remains virtually unaware of a science
of language as distinct from school grammar and the normative
activities of popular journalism. But the modern linguist, faced
with sentences such as *la lettre que j'ai écrit, occasion à profiter,
la femme que je lui ai parlé* feels neither the virtuous indignation
of the purist nor the fierce joy of the iconoclast. For him such
phenomena are simply facts which he must note and explain

15

within the framework of the customs and usages wherein they are manifested. He will not depart from his role of scientific observer if he records the protests and mockery aroused in certain circles by such utterances or the indifference of others; but *qua* linguist he will refuse to take sides.

1.2 The vocal character of language

The language which is the proper object of study for the linguist is human language. It should not be necessary to make any further distinction, for the other applications of the word 'language' are almost always metaphorical: the 'language of animals' is an invention of the story-tellers; the 'language of ants' must be regarded as a hypothesis rather than a datum of observation. The 'language of flowers' is nothing more than a code, one of many such codes. In ordinary parlance 'language' properly designates the faculty which human beings have of making themselves understood by means of vocal signs.

It is worth stressing this vocal character of language. In civilized countries we find that for millennia use has been made of pictorial or graphic signs corresponding to the vocal signs of language. This is what is called writing. Until the invention of the gramophone every vocal sign was perceived immediately or lost forever. On the contrary, a written sign lasted as long as its basis, whether of stone, parchment or paper and the traces left on this basis by the chisel, stilus or pen. This fact was summed up in the dictum *verba volant, scripta manent*. This permanent character of the written document has endowed it with great prestige. It is in a written form that those works of *literature* (so called precisely because of their written form) have been transmitted, which still constitute the basis of our culture. Alphabetic scripts present for each sign a succession of letters, clearly separated in printed texts, which one is taught to recognize in school. Any educated Frenchman knows what are the components of the written sign *temps*, but he would have difficulty in distinguishing the components of the corresponding vocal sign. Thus everything conspires to identify in the minds of educated people the vocal sign with its graphic equivalent and to establish this latter as the sole valid representative of the complex.

This should not obscure the fact that the signs of human language are primarily vocal; that for hundreds of thousands of years these signs were *exclusively* vocal; and that even today the majority of human beings speak without being able to read. Reading comes as a reflection of spoken usage: the reverse is never true. The study of writing is a discipline distinct from linguistics proper, although practically speaking it is one of its dependencies. Thus the linguist in principle operates without regard for written forms. He takes them into consideration only in so far as they may on occasion influence the form of vocal signs.

1.3 Language as a human institution

We often speak of language as one of the human faculties. We ourselves used this term above but without giving it a strict definition. It is probable that the relationships between man and his language are of too peculiar a character for it to be possible to situate it precisely within a more extensive type of definite functions. What can not be asserted is that language is the result of the natural function of some organ, like breathing or walking, which are so to speak the *raison d'être* of the lungs and the legs. We speak, it is true, of the organs of speech, but we usually add that the primary function of each of these is quite a different thing. The mouth serves for the ingestion of food, the nasal fossae for respiration, and so on. The convolutions of the brain which have been regarded as the seat of speech, because lesions of the cortex are frequently accompanied by aphasia, probably have something to do with the proper functioning of language. But nothing proves that this is its primary or essential function.

Consequently we are tempted to rank language among human institutions, and this angle of approach has many incontestable advantages. Human institutions are the result of life in a society. This is certainly true of language, which is conceived essentially as an instrument of communication. Human institutions imply

17

the exercise of the most diverse faculties. They can be widespread and even, as is the case with language, universal, without being identical from one community to another. The family, for example, is perhaps characteristic of all human groups, but it presents itself in different guises in different places. Similarly language, while identical in its functions, differs from one community to another to such an extent that it cannot function except among the members of a given group. Institutions, not being primary phenomena but the products of social life, are not immutable. They are liable to change in response to different needs and under the influence of other communities. Now we shall see that this is no less true of the particular languages such as French, English, German, etc., which are merely different modalities of language as a universal human phenomenon.

1.4 The function of language

Nevertheless, to say that language is an institution gives but an imperfect notion of the nature of this phenomenon. Although it is metaphorical, the designation of a given language as an instrument or tool focuses attention on what distinguishes language from many other institutions. The essential function of this instrument, if we regard any given language as such, is communication. Thus French is primarily the instrument which enables French-speaking people to establish contact, to enter into relations with one another. We shall see that if, as is the case, every given language changes in the course of time, it does so essentially because of the need to adapt itself in the most economical way to the needs of communication of the community which speaks it.

We must, however, not forget that language has other functions than that of ensuring mutual understanding. In the first place language serves, so to speak, as an aid to thought. Indeed, this is so far true that we may wonder whether mental activity that lacks the framework of a language really deserves the name of thought at all. But it is for the psychologist, not the linguist, to make pronouncements on this point. On the other hand, man

18

uses language frequently to express himself, that is to say in order to analyse what he feels without overmuch concern for the reactions of possible listeners. At the same time he finds in language the means of asserting himself in his own eyes and those of others without really having anything of consequence to communicate. We might also speak of an aesthetic function of language which it would be difficult to analyse, so closely is it bound up with the functions of communication and expression. In the final analysis it is certainly communication which must be singled out as the central function of the instrument which any given language represents. In this connection it is noteworthy that society represses soliloquy by mockery, soliloquy being the use of language for purely expressive ends. A person who wishes to express himself without fear of censure must find a public before which he can act the comedy of linguistic exchange. There is, besides, every indication that everybody's language would suffer rapid corruption without the necessity of making oneself understood. It is this permanent necessity which maintains the instrument in good working order.

1.5 Are languages nomenclatures?

According to an extremely naive but fairly widespread notion a language is simply a catalogue of words, that is to say of vocal or graphic products, each of which corresponds to a thing. Thus a particular animal, say a horse, is matched in the French language with a particular vocal product which the orthographer presents in the form of *cheval*. For those who regard languages in this light the differences between languages are reduced to differences of designation: for the same animal the English say *horse* and the Germans *Pferd*. To acquire a second language, all we have to do is to learn off a second nomenclature which is parallel at all points to the first. The few cases where a rupture in the parallelism is undeniable are classed under the heading of 'idioms'. The vocal products themselves, in this view of language, are normally composed, in all languages, of the same sounds, the only difference lying in the choice and arrangement of the sounds for each word. This is confirmed, if we think simply in terms of writing rather than of sounds, by the use of the same alphabet for a wide variety of languages. The labels *cheval*, *horse*, *Pferd*, and so on, in fact use the letters of one and the same alphabet, the *e* in all three words, the *h* in *cheval* and *horse*, the *r* in *horse* and *Pferd*. It is true that for the ear everything cannot be reduced to the choice and arrangement of the same elements. Then we speak of an 'accent'; but an accent is regarded as an extremely marginal thing, something superimposed on the normal articulation of the sounds of the language which it would be slightly absurd and almost improper to attempt to imitate when we learn another language than our own.

1.6 Language is not a copy of reality

This notion of language as a catalogue is based on the naive idea that the whole world is ordered, prior to its perception by man, into perfectly distinct categories of objects, each of which necessarily receives its appropriate designation in each language. This is true up to a certain point, for instance in the case of different species of living creatures; but it does not hold good in other domains. We might regard it as natural to distinguish between still and flowing water. But within these two categories there are subdivisions whose arbitrary nature is clearly apparent: oceans, seas, lakes, ponds on the one hand and rivers, streams, brooks and torrents on the other. It is doubtless our common western civilization which determines that the Dead Sea is a sea and the Great Salt Lake is a lake. But this does not prevent the French from being the only ones who distinguish the *fleuve* which flows into the sea from the *rivière* which discharges its water into another river. In another domain French uses the same word *bois* for a place planted with trees, for wood as a material in general, for timber and for wood used as fuel, to say nothing of such special expressions as *bois de cerf* (stag's antlers). Danish, however, has a word *træ* (our *tree*) which designates the tree as well as wood as a material and also, and here in competition with *tömmer* (our *timber*), wood as a constructional material. But for a place planted with trees it uses instead *skov* while wood for fuel is called *brænde*. For the main senses of the French word *bois* Spanish distinguishes between *bosque*, *madera* and *leña*, Italian between *bosco*, *legno*, *legna*, *legname*, German between *Wald*, *Gehölz*, *Holz*, Russian between *les*, *dérevo*, *drová*, each of the words being capable of application to things which French would designate by other words than *bois*. German *Wald* is usually a *forêt*; Russian *dérevo* is, like the Danish *træ*, the normal equivalent of the French *arbre*.

In the solar spectrum a Frenchman, in common with most occidental people, will distinguish between violet, blue, green, yellow, orange and red. But these distinctions are not found in the spectrum itself, where there is a continuum from violet to red. This continuum is divided up differently from language to language. Without having to leave Europe we may note that in Breton and Welsh a single word *glas* is applied to a segment of the spectrum which coincides roughly with the French zones of blue and green. We frequently find that what we call green is divided up between two units, one including a part of what we call blue and the other the main part of our yellow. Some languages content themselves with two basic colours corresponding broadly to the two halves of the spectrum.

This holds good also for the more abstract aspects of human experience. It is known that words like English *wistful*, German *gemütlich*, Russian *ničevó* have no exact French equivalents. But even words like French *prendre*, English *take*, German *nehmen*, Russian *brat'*, which are regarded as equivalent, are not always used in the same circumstances, or in other words, they do not cover exactly the same semantic fields. In fact, to each language there corresponds a particular organization of the data of experience. Learning a new language does not simply involve putting new labels on known objects. It requires new modes of analysing what is referred to in linguistic communications.

1.7 Each language has its own sounds

Much the same is true apropos of the sounds of language. The vowel of the English sound *bait* is not a French *é* pronounced with an English accent; nor is the vowel of *bit* a French *i* distorted for the same reasons. It must be understood that within the phonetic zone where French distinguishes between *i* and *é*, English makes a threefold distinction: the vocalic types exemplified respectively in the words *beat, bit* and *bait* which are irreducible to the *i* and *é* of French. The consonant represented in the Spanish spelling as *s* and which is pronounced in Castilian in a way which resembles to some extent the first sound of the English *ship*, is neither an *s* nor a *sh*. In fact, whereas in a certain articulatory zone English distinguishes two types, those of the initial sounds of *sip* and *ship*, Spanish uses only one which cannot be identified either with the first sound of *sip* or *ship*. What is called a foreign accent proceeds from the erroneous identification of the phonetic units of the two different languages. It is just as dangerous and mistaken to see variants of one and the same type in the initial sounds of French *tout*, English *tale*, German *Tat*, Russian *tuz*, as to consider French *prendre*, English *take*, German *nehmen*, Russian *brat'* all as corresponding to one and the same aspect of reality existing prior to these various designations.

1.8 The double articulation of language

We often hear it said that human language is articulate. Those who express themselves in this way would probably find it difficult to define exactly what they mean by it. But there is no doubt that this term corresponds to a feature which characterizes effectively all languages. It will be well, however, to give a closer definition of this concept, the articulation of language, and to note that this is manifested on two different planes. Each of the units which emerges from a first 'articulation' is in fact articulated in its turn into units of a different type.

The first articulation of language is that whereby every fact of experience to be communicated, every need that one wants to make known to another, is analysed into a succession of units each of which is endowed with a vocal form and a meaning. If I am suffering from pains in my head I can make this known simply by screams. This may be involuntary: in that case they are the concern of physiology. But they may be more or less willed and designed to make my disposition known to my environment. Still, this would not suffice to make my shouts and screams into a linguistic communication. Each of my cries is unanalysable and corresponds to the totality, likewise unanalysed, of my feelings of pain. The situation is quite different if I pronounce the sentence *j'ai mal à la tête*. Here none of the successive units *j'*, *ai*, *mal*, *à*, *la*, *tête* corresponds to any particular feature of my indisposition. Each of them may recur in quite different contexts in order to communicate other facts of experience. *Mal*, for instance, appears in *il fait le mal* and *tête* in *il s'est mis à leur tête*. It is easy to see how economical this first articulation is: we might imagine a system of communication in which a special cry would correspond to each given situation or fact of experience. But if we think of the infinite variety of such situations and these facts of experience, it will be clear that if such a system were to serve the same purposes as our languages, it would have to comprise so large a number of distinct signs that the memory of man would be incapable of storing it. A few thousands of such units as *tête*, *mal*, *ai*, *la*, freely combinable, enable us to communicate more things than could be done by millions of unarticulated cries. The first articulation is the way in which experience common to all the members of a given linguistic community is organized. It is only within the framework of this experience, necessarily limited to what is common to a considerable number of individuals, that linguistic communication is possible. Originality of thought can be manifested only in the form of an unexpected manipulation of the units. Personal experience, incommunicable in its uniqueness, is analysed into a succession of units, each of slight specificity and known to all the members of the community. A greater degree of specificity will be attained only by the addition of new units, such as attaching adjectives to a noun, adverbs to an adjective, or in general terms determinants to a determined.

Each of these units of the first articulation presents, as we have seen, a meaning and a vocal (or phonic) form. It cannot be analysed into smaller successive units endowed with meaning. The totality *tête* means 'head' and we cannot attribute to *tê* and to *te* a different meaning, the sum of which would be 'head'. But the vocal form itself is analysable into a series of units each of which makes its contribution to distinguishing *tête* from other units such as *bête*, *tante*, or *terre*. This is what we propose to call the second articulation of language. In the case of *tête*, these units are three in number. We may represent them by the letters t e t which it is customary to enclose in slants /tet/. It is easy to see how great a degree of economy is achieved by this second articulation. If we had to match each minimum significant unit with a particular unanalysable vocal product, we should have to invent thousands of such distinct units, which would be incompatible with the articulatory capacity and the auditory sensibility of human beings. Thanks to the second articulation language can make do with a few dozen distinct phonic products which are combined to achieve the vocal form of the units of the first articulation. *Tête*, for example, uses in two places the phonic unit which we represent by means of /t/, a second unit with the notation /e/ being inserted between the two occurrences of /t/.

1.9 Basic linguistic units

A sentence such as *j'ai mal à la tête* or a part of such an utterance which makes sense, such as *j'ai mal* or *mal*, is called a linguistic sign. Every linguistic sign comprises a significatum, its meaning or value, which we place between quotation marks ('I have a headache', 'I am unwell', 'bad') and a significans through which the sign is made manifest. This we represent between slants (/ž e mal a la tet/, /ž e mal/, /mal/). In current usage the word sign is reserved for the significans. The units produced by the first articulation, with their significatum and their significans, are signs, and minimal signs, since none of them can be further analysed into a succession of signs. There is no universally accepted term to designate these units. We shall refer to them as monemes.

Like every sign the moneme is a unit with two facets, one the significatum, its meaning or value, and the significans itself in its phonic forms. The latter are composed of units of the second articulation, to which we give the name phoneme. In the sentence which we are using as an illustration there are six monemes which are identical with what in ordinary usage we call words. *j'* (for *je*), *ai*, *mal*, *à*, *la*, and *tête*. But we should not draw the conclusion that moneme is merely a technical substitute for 'word'. In a word like *travaillons* there are two monemes *travaill-* /travaj/, which denotes a certain type of action, and *-ons* /õ/ which indicates the person speaking along with one or more persons. It is not unusual to draw a distinction between *travaill-* and *-ons* by saying that the former is a semanteme and the latter a morpheme. This terminology has the drawback of implying that only the semanteme is endowed with meaning, which the morpheme lacks. This, however, is inaccurate. In so far as the distinction is useful at all, it would be better to use the term lexeme for those monemes which are listed in the lexicon and not in the grammar and reserve the term morpheme to designate those, such as *-ons*, which figure in the grammar. We note that a lexeme like *travaill-* is normally listed in the lexicon in the form *travailler*, that is to say it appears with the infinitive morpheme *-er* attached.

1.10 The linear form and vocal character

Every language is manifested in the linear form of utterances which represent what is sometimes called the 'spoken chain'. This linear form of spoken language derives in the last resort from its vocal character: vocal utterances are necessarily produced in time and are necessarily perceived by the ear in succession. The situation is quite different when communication is of the pictorial type and perceived by the eye. It is true that the painter paints the elements of his composition successively, but the spectator perceives the message as a whole or he may concentrate his attention on the elements of the message in this order or that without the content of the message thereby being affected. A visual system of communication such as that represented by the road signs is not linear but has two dimensions. The linear character of utterances explains the serial nature of monemes and phonemes. In such series the order of the phoneme has distinctive function no less than the choice of this or that phoneme. The sign *mal* /mal/ comprises the same phonemes as the sign *lame* /lam/, yet there is no confusion between the two. The situation is rather different as regards the units of the first articulation. It is true that *le chasseur tue le lion* has a different meaning from *le lion tue le chasseur*, but quite often a sign may change its position in the utterance without any appreciable modification of the sense: *il sera là, mardi* and *mardi, il sera là*. On the other hand it often happens that lexemes are combined with morphemes which indicate their function in the sentence, that is to say their relations with the other signs; and this enables them to figure in different positions without any appreciable effect on the sense of the whole. This is often the case, for instance, in Latin where the word *puerum*, adequately characterized by the segment *-um* as the object of the verb, may appear indifferently before or after the verb: *puer-um videt*, or *videt puer-um*.

1.11 The double articulation and the economy of language

The type of organization which we have just sketched exists in all languages which have been described up till now. It seems to have imposed itself on human communities as best adapted to the needs and resources of man. It is only the economy that results from the two articulations which secures an instrument of communication of general applicability, capable of transmitting so much information in so economical a way. Apart from the extra measure of economy achieved by the second articulation, it has the additional advantage of making the form of the *significans* independent of the value of the *significatum* and thus confers greater stability on the linguistic form. It is clear that in a language in which a particular grunt corresponded to each separate word nothing would prevent people from modifying this grunt in whatever way each individual thought fit to make it more exactly descriptive of the object designated by it. But since it would be impossible to bring about unanimity in such matters, the final result would be a chronic instability prejudicial to the maintenance of mutual understanding. The existence of the second articulation guarantees this maintenance in linking the fate of each component of the significans, each of the phonic segments /m/, /a/, /l/ *mal* not with the sense of the corresponding significatum 'bad' in our example, but with that of the components of other significantia of the language, the /m/ of *masse*, the /a/ of *chat*, the /l/ of *sale* etc. This does not mean that the /m/ or the /l/ of *mal* will be incapable of changing in the course of centuries but if it changes it will not be able to do so without a simultaneous and similar change with the /m/ of *masse* and the /l/ of *sale*.

1.12 Each language has its own proper articulation

Although it is true that all languages agree in exhibiting this double articulation, they differ in the manner in which their speakers analyse the data of experience and the way in which they exploit the possibilities offered by the organs of speech. In other words, each language articulates in its own way both its sentences and its significantia. In a situation where a French-man would say *j'ai mal à la tête*, an Italian will use *mi duole il capo*. In one case the subject of the sentence is the person speaking, in the other the head that aches. The expression for the pain is nominal in French but verbal in Italian and the pain is attributed to the head in the first case and to the patient in the second. It makes no difference that the Frenchman may also say *la tête me fait mal*. What is decisive is that in a given situation it is natural for French and Italians to employ completely different analyses. We may similarly compare and contrast the equivalents Latin *poenas dabant* and French *ils étaient punis*, English *Smoking prohibited*, Russian *kurit' vospreščáetsja* and French *défense de fumer,* German *er ist zuverlässig* and French *on peut compter sur lui.* We already know that the words of one language have no exact equivalents in another. This naturally ties up with the different modes of analysing the data of experience. It may well be that differences of analysis entail a different way of regarding a phenomenon or alternatively that a different conception of a phenomenon entails a different analysis of a situation. In fact it is not possible to make a definite choice between these two alternatives.

As regards the articulation of the significantia we must beware of basing our judgment on the written forms, even when we have to do with transcriptions and not orthographic forms. If we make a start with /ž e mal a la tet/ and /mi duole il kapo/ we should not delude ourselves into thinking that the /a/ of /kapo/ represents the same linguistic reality as that of /mal/. In French where we distinguish between the /a/ of *mal* and the /â/ of *mâle*, the first sound is restricted to an articulation of limited depth, whereas the /a/ of *capo* enjoys a much wider latitude. It is only for reasons of economy that the phonemes of two different languages are transcribed by means of the same characters.

1.13 The number of monemes and phonemes

The number of possible sentences in each language is theoretically infinite, for there is no limit to the number of successive monemes which a given sentence may comprise. The list of the different monemes of a language is an open list. It is impossible to determine precisely how many distinct monemes a language presents because in a whole community new needs constantly make themselves felt and these new needs give rise to new designations. The words employed or understood by a civilized person today may amount to tens of thousands. But many of these words are comprised of monemes which may appear as independent words, (e.g. in *farmyard, highway*) while others are restricted to compounds (e.g. *thermostat, telegraph*). This means that monemes, even if we count inflections such as *-ed* and suffixes like *-ish*, are much less numerous than words.

As for the list of phonemes in any given language, this is a closed list. Castilian, for instance, distinguishes 24 phonemes, neither more nor less. What causes difficulty in giving an answer to the question 'How many phonemes does such and such a language possess?' is the fact that civilized languages which are spoken over huge areas do not exhibit perfect unity but vary somewhat from one region to another, or from one class or one generation to another. These differences do not prejudice intelligibility on the whole but they may entail some differences in the inventory of units, both the distinctive units (the phonemes) and the significant units (monemes or more complex signs). Thus Spanish as spoken in America exhibits 22 phonemes instead of 24. The variety of French spoken by the author comprises 34 phonemes. But among Parisian speakers born since 1940 a system of 31 phonemes is no rarity. We use the latter simpler system in the transcription of our French examples.

1.14 What is a language?

We may now attempt to formulate what we understand by a 'language'. A language is an instrument of communication in virtue of which human experience is analysed differently in each given community into units, the monemes, each endowed with a semantic content and a phonic expression. The phonic expression is articulated in its turn into distinctive and successive units. These are the phonemes, of limited number in each language, their nature and mutual relations varying from one language to another.

This implies (1) that we must reserve the term language to describe an instrument of communication with this twofold articulation and vocal manifestation; (2) that outside this common basis there is nothing linguistic in the proper sense which may not differ from one language to another. It is in this sense that we must understand the assertion that the facts of language are 'arbitrary' or 'conventional'.

1.15 Marginal phenomena

All languages exhibit the type of organization just described. But this does not mean that languages do not have recourse to procedures which fall outside the framework of double articulation. In French, for instance, the interrogative character of the utterance is frequently denoted by a rise in pitch of the voice with the last word. In this way there is a clearly marked distinction between the statement *il pleut* and the question *il pleut?* This is tantamount to saying that the raising of the voice in *il pleut?* plays the same role as the sign /esk/=*est-ce-que*. We may say therefore that this melodic curve is a sign just like *est-ce-que*, with a significatum 'interrogation' and audible significans, the raising of the pitch. But whereas the significans *est-ce-que* conforms to the second articulation with its series of three phonemes /esk/ and to the first in the sense that it takes its place in a succession of monemes, the significans of the melodic curve does nothing of the kind. In fact the significans does not occupy any given position in the spoken chain but is superimposed, so to speak, on the units of the twofold articulations and we are not in a position to analyse it into a succession of phonemes. The linguistic facts which fall outside the articulation into phonemes are often called 'suprasegmental' and they form a chapter entitled prosody distinct from phonematics, which treats of the units of the second articulation.

1.16 The non-discrete character of intonation

There is a fundamental opposition between the melodic difference which distinguishes the statement *il pleut* from *il pleut?* and the difference between two phonemes. The physiology of speech organs normally brings it about that the voice is raised at the beginning of an utterance corresponding to a progressive tension and is lowered towards the end of a sentence corresponding to a progressive relaxation. If this lowering does not come about, the hearer will have the impression that the sentence is not finished, that he is asking, for example, for a complement in the form of a reply to a question. This fact is utilized to make *il pleut?* into an equivalent of *est-ce-qu'il pleut?* But this is not to say that the raising of the voice here has a definite function opposed to that of the lowering of the voice. The exact meaning of the sentence will vary according to the degree to which the voice is raised or lowered. A very low pitch level marks a blunt and emphatic statement, and the categorical nature of the assertion is toned down if the descent of the melodic curve is made less steep. If we raise the curve we pass gradually to statements tinged with doubt, and as doubt increases, to questions which are progressively more 'dubitative'. It is not that the ascent is made in definite steps so that the choice of a given level will result in an utterance radically different; the situation is rather that any modification, whatever it may be, of the melodic curve brings about a parallel and proportional modification of the sense of the utterance.

1.17 Discrete units

The situation is quite different when we consider two phonemes and not two different directions of the melodic curve. The words *pierre* /pier/ and *bière* /bier/ are distinguished only by the use of the phoneme /p/ in the one and /b/ in the other. We can pass imperceptibly from the characteristic articulation of /b/ to that of /p/ by a progressive reduction of the vibration of the vocal cords. Physiologically, then, we find the same unbroken continuity that we have observed in the raising of the voice. But whereas every change in the raising of the voice brings about some real, if only slight, modification of the message, nothing of the kind is produced with regard to the vibrations which characterize /b/ vis-à-vis /p/. As long as they remain perceptible the word pronounced will be understood as 'beer'. But once a threshold is reached, which incidentally may vary according to the context and situation, the hearer will understand 'stone', that is to say the initial sound will no longer be interpreted as /b/ but as /p/. The sense of the message will then be entirely changed. If the speaker articulates badly or if there is noise and the situation does not help my work as a hearer, I may hesitate between interpreting what I hear as *c'est une bonne bière* or *c'est une bonne pierre*. However, I shall have no option but to choose one or the other. There will be no sense of speaking of an intermediate or compromise message. Just as one could not conceive of a thing which would be rather less *bière* and a little more *pierre*, so one could not envisage any linguistic fact which would be not quite /b/ or almost /p/. Every segment of an utterance recognized as French is necessarily identifiable *either* as /b/ or as /p/, or as one of the 32 other phonemes of the language. We sum all this up by saying that the phonemes are discrete units. This discrete character of phonemes was naturally implied in the remark made above that the phonemes are fixed in number in any given language. Our alphabetic writing, which in its origin reflects a phonematic analysis, has preserved its discrete character. In a manuscript text we may hesitate whether to interpret a letter as *u*, or *n* but we know that it must be one of the two. Reading implies the identification of each letter as one of a limited number of units for each of which the printer's compositor has a separate case; it does not concern itself with the subjective interpretation of the details of the shape of each individual letter. A well-printed text is one in which the differences between individual occurrences of *a* are so slight that they do not interfere with the identification of all *a*'s as specimen of the same graphic unit. The same is true of sentences and phonemes. A sentence will achieve clarity in proportion as the successive manifestations of one and the same phoneme are immediately identifiable as the same phonic unit. This links up with what was said above of the solidarity which unites the *m* of *masse* with the *m* of *mal*. The same unit is involved, as is indicated by the identical transcription, and speakers have an interest in reproducing it in the same way if they wish to facilitate the understanding of what they say.

Thus discrete units are those whose value is in no way affected by variations of detail determined by the context or by other circumstances. They are indispensable to the functioning of every language. Phonemes are such discrete units. Such prosodic features as the phenomena of intonation described above are not discrete units. But other prosodic facts characterized as such because they do not enter into phonematic segmentation are discrete no less than phonemes. Such are tones, a definite number of which exist in certain languages. There are none in French or in the majority of European languages. Two are numbered in Swedish, four in northern Chinese and six in Vietnamese.

1.18 Language and speech, code and message

When we say that a language has or comprises 34 phonemes, we mean that it is from among 34 units of the second articulation that a speaker must make his choice at each point of his utterance in order to produce the significans which corresponds to the message that he wishes to transmit; /b/ and not /p/ or /t/ or any other French phoneme at the beginning of *bière* if I want to say *c'est une bonne bière*. But when we say that an utterance comprises 34 phonemes, we mean that it exhibits 34 successive segments each of which is identifiable as a particular phoneme without however implying that the 34 successive units are all different units. The sentence *c'est une bonne bière* /s et ün bòn bier/ comprises 12 phonemes in the sense that it exhibits 12 successive segments each identifiable as a given phoneme. But it twice uses the phoneme /n/, twice the phoneme /b/, twice the phoneme /e/, so that it utilizes only 9 different phonemes. What has been said of the phonemes applies also to more complex linguistic units, with the difference that we are not in a position to state how many monemes or words a language comprises. In *le garçon a pris le verre* there are 6 successive monemes but only 5 different monemes.

It is essential to make a careful distinction between the linguistic facts of every kind which are presented in utterances and the linguistic facts conceived as belonging to a repertory or catalogue at the disposal of the person wishing to make a communication. It does not fall to the linguist as such to determine precisely where the speaker stores the linguistic facts on which he draws; nor is he required to explain by what processes the speaker makes the choice adequate to the needs of his communication. But we must necessarily suppose the existence of some psycho-physiological organization, which, during the process of learning a language in infancy, or later, in the case of a second language, has been conditioned in such a way as to permit the analysis of the experience to be communicated according to the norms of the given language and to offer the necessary choices at each point of the utterance. It is this conditioning which is properly called 'a language'. Such a language, it is true, manifests its existence only through speech, or more concretely, through utterances. But speech, the audible acts of speech, are not the same as language. The traditional opposition between speech and language may also be expressed in terms of code and message, the code being the organization which permits the composition of the message. It is to this code that each element of a message is referred in order to elicit its sense.

This extremely useful distinction between language and speech may lead one to think that speech has an organization independent of that of language, so that one could imagine, for instance, a linguistics of speech distinct from a linguistics of language. Yet it should be clear that speech merely gives concrete expression to the organization of language. It is only by the examination of speech and the behaviour it determines among hearers that we can attain to a knowledge of language. To carry out this task we must disregard in speech everything that is non-linguistic, such as the tone of voice peculiar to an individual. In linguistics we pay attention only to the collective habits acquired in the process of learning a given language.

1.19 Each unit implies a choice

Among linguistic facts are some which are revealed by the simple examination of an utterance and others which are identified only by a comparison of different utterances. Both sets are facts of language. Take an utterance such as *c'est une bonne*

bière /s et ün bòn bier/; if we assume that the analysis into monemes and phonemes, as represented in our transcription, has
been carried out, this utterance provides information about
important features of the structure of this language. /bòn/ can
appear after /ün/ and before /bier/, the phoneme /r/ can appear
at the end of the utterance and the phoneme /n/ at the end of a
moneme, and so on. All these permissive features form part of
the rules according to which human experience is analysed in
French and belong to the language (*langue*). They have some
advantage for the linguist over other points in that they are
revealed by simple examination of the arrangement of the units
in an utterance. However, if we are in a position to say something about the permissible combinations of /bòn/, this presupposes that this segment of the utterance has been recognized as
constituting a particular unit distinct from /ün/ and /bier/. To
attain this result it was necessary first to establish that /bòn/ in
this context corresponds to a specific choice between a certain
number of possible epithets. A comparison of other French
utterances has shown that in the context where /bòn/ appears
we also find /ekselät/ (*excellente*) /mòvez/ (*mauvaise*) etc. This
indicates that the speakers, whether consciously or not, have
avoided all the competitors which could appear between /ün/
and /bier/ but were found unsuitable in the event. To say of a
hearer that he understands French implies that he identifies by
experience the successive choices made by the speaker, that he
recognizes /bòn/ as a choice distinct from that of /ün/ and that
of /bier/, and that it is quite possible that the choice of /bòn/
instead of /mòvez/ will influence his behaviour.

The same holds good as regards phonemes. If we are in a
position to say anything about the 'combinatory latitudes' of
/n/ in /bòn/, it is because /n/ has been recognized as a particular
distinctive unit, different in particular from the /ò/ which
precedes it in /bòn/. Here, too, it has been established that /n/
corresponds to a specific choice, for the speaker, doubtless
unconsciously, must have rejected /t/, which would have produced /bòt/, that is to say the word *botte*, /s/, which would have
produced *bosse*, /l/ which would have given /bòl/ or /f/ which

would have resulted in the pronounceable but non-existent /bòf/.

It is clear that all the choices made by the speaker at each point of his utterance are not arbitrary choices. It is evidently the nature of the experience to be communicated which leads him to choose /bòn/ rather than /mòvez/, /bier/ rather than /limònad/. It is because the sense demands /bòn/ that he must choose the final /n/ instead of /t/, /s/ or /l/. But are there choices which are not so determined? We must not suppose that the choice of monemes is 'freer' than that of phonemes.

1.20 Contrasts and oppositions

We have seen that linguistic units, whether signs or phonemes, exhibit two distinct types of relationship. We have on the one hand the relationships in the utterance, which are called syntagmatic and are directly observable. Such are, for instance, the relationships of /bòn/ with the neighbouring /ün/ and /bier/ those of /n/ with the /ò/ which precedes it in /bòn/ and the /ü/ which it follows in /ün/. It will be well to reserve the term contrasts to designate this kind of relationship. On the other hand we have the relationship which we conceive as existing between units which may figure in a given context and which, at least in this context, are mutually exclusive. Such relationships are called paradigmatic and we designate them as oppositions. *Bonne, excellente, mauvaise,* which may appear in the same contexts, are in the relationship of opposition. The same holds good of adjectives denoting colours which can all appear between *le livre* . . . and . . . *a disparu.* There is also opposition between /n/, /t/, /s/ and /l/ which can all appear in the final position after /bò/.

CHAPTER II

The Description of Languages

2.1 How a given language functions

Human language (*langage*) which is the object of linguistics, exists only in the form of particular languages (*langues*). The first task of the linguist therefore is to study these languages. These appear to us primarily as instruments of communication. It will thus be appropriate to study and describe them first and foremost in their functioning. Our first task will be to make clear, for each given language, in what way it analyses human experience into significant units and how it exploits the range of possibilities offered by the so-called organs of speech.

2.2 Synchrony and diachrony

Anyone who begins the study of linguistics today without preconceived ideas would regard it as normal to begin the study of an instrument in its functioning before inquiring how and why this instrument undergoes changes in the course of time. It is however the case that the scientific study of languages, for nearly a century, was practically confined to problems of evolution. We shall come back to these problems later. For the present we shall merely note that languages change constantly, without of course ever ceasing to function, and that it is likely that any language which we approach to describe its functioning is in the process of modification. A moment's reflection will serve to convince us that this holds good of all languages at every moment. This being the case, we may wonder whether it is

37

possible to dissociate the study of functioning from that of evolution, but the existence of modifications in progress is revealed only by the comparison of the reactions of different generations face to face. Of a few hundred Parisians born before 1920, forming a random assemblage, all possess two distinct vowels in *patte, pâte*. Of a few hundred Parisian girls born after 1940, more than 60 per cent have one and the same vowel /a/ in these two words. We could disregard all aspects of evolution by limiting our observation to the usage of a particular generation. But nothing prevents us in our description from taking into account the linguistic behaviour of two generations in contact. I know from repeated experience and observation that the differences in question do not hinder the functioning of French as an instrument of communication between adults of more than 40 years and young persons of less than twenty. Even if I were to confine my observations to the usage of the youngest, I should have to take into account the fact that a minority of them preserve the traditional distinction and so present a picture which would not exclude the usage of adults. In fact our description must be strictly synchronic, that is to say based exclusively on observations made over a period of time so short as to be considered in practice a point on the axis of time. A study is said to be diachronic when it involves the comparison of different usages of one and the same language with the intention of drawing conclusions of an evolutionary nature. The facts noted above as regards the vowels of *patte* and *pâte* may either be the object of a synchronic formulation (the opposition /a/–/â/ is not universal in contemporary usage) or a diachronic formulation (the opposition /a/–/â/ is tending to disappear in Parisian speech).

2.3 Variety of usage

Languages, we know, are not necessarily identical over the whole territory in which they are spoken; the differences may be so great as to jeopardize efforts at communication. In this case we say that the language has a number of dialects and every description will have to specify that it is dealing with such and such a dialect. But less profound differences may exist which do not affect mutual intelligibility; such are the differences between the French of a speaker from Toulouse and a Parisian. The Southern Frenchman, on the whole, does not distinguish between *piqué* and *piquait*. Here, too, the linguist who is describing contemporary French will have a choice; he can exclude southern usage from his description; or note that the distinction between /-é/ and /è/ is not universal. No linguistic community of any great size is homogenous. But the describer, once he has delimited his field at his discretion, will have to present the differences which he establishes as variants of the same usage; he cannot speak of two distinct usages.

2.4 The 'Corpus'

Synchronic description is not limited to contemporary languages which we can hear and record. Nothing prevents the linguist from attempting a description of the Latin of Cicero or the Old English of Alfred. His task will be more complex, in such a case, because he will have to discover a system of phonemes behind the writing which reflects it only to an imperfect degree. On the other hand his work may be facilitated by the fact that the extant works of Cicero or Alfred form a well-defined whole which can easily be submitted to statistical procedures, enabling us to draw precise conclusions. Doubtless the literary works of a given period necessarily give only an imperfect idea of the language thus attested. But if there is no other means of access to this language, then we may without misgivings regard these documents as fully representative. These conditions of work present such advantages that one is tempted to recreate them in dealing with a contemporary language, by setting up a 'corpus', that is to say a collection of utterances recorded on a tape or taken down from dictation. Once this collection has been made, it is regarded as inviolable and no additions are permitted, the language being described as a function of what the corpus contains. The theoretical objection one may make against the 'corpus' method is that two investigators operating on the same language but starting from different corpuses, may arrive at different descriptions of the same language. The practical objection is that at any given moment the investigator may feel the need to supplement or verify his information and that if he refuses to satisfy the need when it makes itself felt, he deliberately eliminates certain aspects of reality, not because they are irrelevant, but because they eluded him in the first instance.

2.5 Relevance

Every description implies a selection. Every object, however simple it may appear at first sight, may be revealed as of infinite complexity. Now a description is necessarily finite, which means that only certain features of the object to be described can be taken note of. Those selected by two different persons may well turn out to be different. Contemplating one and the same tree one observer will note the majesty of its bearing and the imposing character of its foliage, another will note the cracks in the trunk and the shimmer of the leaves; another will try to give precise figures; a fourth will indicate the characteristic form of each organ. Every description will be acceptable provided only that it is coherent, that is to say, made from one particular point of view. Once this standpoint has been adopted certain features, which we call relevant, are to be singled out. Others, which are irrelevant, are firmly disregarded. It is clear that from the point of view of the pit-sawyer the colour or shapes of the leaves are irrelevant, just as the calorific properties of the wood are to the painter. Each science presupposes the choice of a particular point of view. In arithmetic the only relevant things are numbers, in geometry shapes, in calorimetry temperatures. The same holds good of linguistic description. Take any segment of a spoken chain. We may consider it as a physical phenomenon, a series of vibrations which the acoustician can record by means of his machines and which he will describe in terms of frequency and amplitude. A physiologist will be able to examine its production;

he will note that such and such an organ comes into play and in this and that manner. In so doing the acoustician and the physiologist will probably make their contribution and facilitate the task of the describer. But not for one moment will they have begun the task of the linguist.

2.6 Choice and function

The task of the linguist begins only at the moment when, from among all the physical and physiological facts, we sort out those which contribute directly to the establishment of communication from those which do not. The elements selected are those which, in the context where they occur, could *not* have appeared, that is to say those which the speaker has used *intentionally*, to which the hearer reacts because he recognizes therein a communicative intention on the part of his dialogue partner. In other words, only those elements are relevant in linguistics which are vehicles of information. If in the utterance *prends le livre!* the linguist distinguishes three units of the first articulation, it is because he establishes three choices in it: *prends* instead of *donne, jette, pose* etc., *le* instead of *un, livre* instead of *cahier, canif, verre*. If we distinguish three phonemes in *mille* /mil/, it is because we observe three successive choices: /m/ instead of /b/ (which would give *bile*), /p/ (which would give *pile*), /v/ (which would give *ville*) etc., /i/ instead of /a/ (*mal*), /ò/ (*molle*), /u/ (*moule*) etc., /l/ instead of /z/ (*mise*), /r/ (*mire*), /š/ (*miche*), or even zero (*mie*).

The Spanish word *mucho*, which physically would be correctly analysed as [oštum] if we produced a recording backwards, will be analysed into four and not five distinct successive phonemes, for in Spanish the sound [š] necessarily entails a preceding [t], so that [tš] represents a single choice and not two successive choices. Linguistically speaking, then, the sole relevant elements of the spoken chain are those whose presence is not automatically secured by the context in which they appear, and this is what confers on them their function of information. It is in virtue of its function that an element of utterance is considered as linguistic and, as we shall see, it is according to the nature of this function that it will be classed among the other elements singled out. It would be a mistake to believe that the linguist is not interested in the physical reality of sounds. What he disregards is what normally eludes the control of speakers, such as the peculiar timbre of his voice, or the overlapping which results from the inertia of organs which do not adapt themselves promptly enough to distinct successive requirements. In *longuement* /lõgmã/ the nasal resonance relevant to /õ/ joins up with that of /m/, which is equally relevant, and so nasalizes the intermediate segment /g/ which, despite this, does not cease to be the phoneme /g/.

2.7 Is it possible to eliminate meaning?

Certain linguists have set before themselves as an ideal the elaboration of a method of description which dispenses with the meaning of the significant units. This would confer greater rigour on linguistics by eliminating a domain in which, as experience has shown, it is not easy to bring order into the facts. A certain amount of ingenuity would in fact enable us to proceed quite far along these lines. Let us suppose that French is known only from an extensive corpus recorded on tapes and suppose further that the analysis into phonemes has already been achieved. The describer will soon have noted certain segments which recur in different contexts, for example /kaje/ (*cahier*) in the contexts /œ̃kajever/ (*un cahier vert*) and /lekaježõ/ (*les cahiers jaunes*). Once this basic analysis of the text into successive monemes has been carried out, we can classify together those which appear in the same contexts. We should have, for instance, the class of monemes which are frequently followed by /è/, /ré/, /ra/, /rõ/ etc. . . . (i.e. *-ais, -ait, -aient, -rai, -ras, -rons, -ront*, etc.) such as /dòn/ (*donn, donne-*) /kur/ (*cour-*) /revej/ (*réveill-, réveille-*), etc. In this we would have isolated what we regard as the verbal stems of the language, and statistical considerations would probably permit us to attribute to them the predicative function which we know belongs to them. In this way we should arrive at a total analysis of the language which would enable us to establish its grammar and perhaps even a lexicon which would lack only the definitions of our dictionaries. But in fact no linguist seems to have attempted to analyse and describe a language of which he understands nothing. In all probability such an enterprise would demand for its successful completion such an outlay of time and energy that it has repelled even those who see in this method the sole theoretically acceptable method. When we know that /kaje/ in *le grand cahier* denotes a certain object and that /kaje/ in *le lait caillé* indicates a particular state of certain liquids, we shall not waste time in investigating whether /lè/ (*lait*) is a unit belonging to the same class as /grã/ (*grand*), i.e. an adjective, which would enable us to identify /kaje/ in the two contexts. One cannot therefore recommend a method which wholly disregards the meaning of the significant units, but no less must we be on our guard against the dangers which arise from an incautious approach to the domain of semantics.

2.8 Form as a guarantee of linguistic character

The dangers which beset the investigator who operates within his own language are those inherent in the employment of introspection. Since I speak French and the word *maison* is a French word, I have only to ask myself what the word *maison* represents and in this way I shall determine the meaning of the word. Unfortunately when I try to see what it evokes in me, an image appears which is more or less composite and I am sure, from certain of its features, that it is not the same as that which the word will evoke in other persons. It is thus clear that this image, which incidentally varies from moment to moment, cannot be considered as the 'meaning' of the word, certainly common to all persons of French speech. All that I know of the meaning of '*maison*' is that with me a certain type of experience is associated with the significans /mezõ/ or with its graphic substitute *maison* and that this same association exists with other persons of French speech. The proof is provided by their behaviour, including their linguistic behaviour, whereby *maison*

appears in exactly the same contexts in which I would situate it
myself. It should be noted that the sight of a house does not
automatically evoke the linguistic process associated with it;
similarly the use of the word *maison* does not necessarily evoke
some experience undergone. Indeed, it is even probable that
in the majority of cases nothing of the kind takes place and that
an utterance is not, in general, accompanied by a series of
reactions or states of awareness corresponding to each of the
significant units. This would scarcely be compatible with the
rapidity of speech. But it is not for the linguist to make pronouncements on this point. He will confine himself to saying
that nothing can be recognized as forming part of the language which is not common to several speakers. This holds good
of meaning as of everything else, and it excludes introspection
as an admissible method of observation, since it can affect only
one person, who incidentally, being both observer and observed,
finds himself in the most unfavourable conditions for carrying
out impartial research. What, in fine, is common to several
individuals and directly observable are their reactions, linguistic
and non-linguistic, to the phonic messages which establish
communication. Thus there will be no 'meaning' in linguistics
which is not formally implied in the phonic message. To each
difference of meaning there corresponds necessarily a difference
of form somewhere in the message. The cases of homonymy
might be offered as objection. But a segment such as *cousin*
/kuzẽ/ has strictly no meaning outside formally different
contexts (*mon cousin Charles m'a écrit*) (*les cousins ne résistent
pas au fly-tox*) which establish its value either as a kind of
relative or as an insect.

This has important consequences which we must never lose
sight of: on the one hand a linguistic element has, strictly speaking, meaning only within a context and a given situation. In
itself a moneme or a more complex sign only contains semantic
possibilities, certain of which are actually realized in a given act
of speech. To take once again the example of *maison*, in the acts
of speech *Madame n'est pas à la maison, il représente une maison
de commerce, il lutte contre la maison d'Autriche* the context

brings out in each case certain potentialities and suppresses others. On the other hand, no category, grammatical or lexical, can be attributed to a language if it does not correspond to phonic differences which characterize it and contrast it with categories of the same type. Thus we could not speak of a subjunctive in a language which does not possess subjunctive forms that are distinct from those of the indicative, such as *ie sache* and *je sais*.

2.9 Dangers of translation

When we operate on a language which we know imperfectly, we become aware of the meaning of its significant units only by translating them into 'our own language'. The danger in such a case is that we may be tempted to interpret the language under description in terms of the one into which we are translating. If for one and the same form of the other language I have in French 'je sais' in one case and 'je sache' in another, I may be misled into speaking of the indicative in one case and the subjunctive in the other, that is to say I shall attribute to the foreign language features of the language which I use for the description. However, if the first always offers identical forms to match the indicatives and subjunctives of French, it would be as misguided to attribute a subjunctive to it as if a German insisted on distinguishing in French between a nominative and accusative *l'homme* on the grounds that in one case he says *der Mann* and in the other *den Mann*. In the same way we should not be justified in speaking of singular and plural in a language where there is no formal distinction between the numbers of the noun. We must therefore bear in mind the dangers to which we are exposed through the necessity, for understanding another language, of translating each utterance into our own, that is to say, of re-articulating a foreign mode of experience to conform to the model which is familiar to us. We ought, in the first instance, to state as a general principle that we are not bound to find in the language under examination any of the distinctions and categories, either phonological or grammatical, to which our previous linguistic experience has accustomed us. On the other hand we must expect to encounter, formally expressed, distinctions which we could not have imagined. We must not be astonished at the absence of any grammatical expression of time, at indifference to active and passive voice, at the non-existence of genders, nor at the necessity the speaker may feel of distinguishing between 'we' which includes the person spoken to and a 'we' which excludes him, or between verbal forms denoting what is visible and others which are employed with reference to what goes on outside the field of vision. We must not lay it down as a fundamental principle that every language operates with a subject of the proposition, possesses adjectives, and distinguishes the verb from the noun. In short, since we have agreed to bestow the name 'language' on everything that satisfies a certain definition (cf. 1.14), we must not postulate, in a given language, the existence of something which does not figure, either explicitly or implicitly, in our definition.

2.10 We shall begin with the second articulation

When we envisage language in its functioning as an instrument of communication, it is normal to designate as the first articulation that whereby the experience to be communicated is analysed. The second articulation will be the analysis of the significantia into successive phonemes. But it should not be forgotten that in linguistic communication we 'signify' something which is not manifest by means of something that is. It is therefore normal for the describer who proceeds by examination of observable facts, to start with what is manifest, i.e. the significantia and to approach what is not so manifest from this angle. Now significantia will necessarily be described in terms of their phonic component phonemes and other possible distinctive features. This is why it is normal for the description of a language to begin with an account of its phonology, i.e. what appears in the first place is what we have called the second articulation. We shall therefore first examine the conditions and methods of phonological analysis.

2.11 Articulatory phonetics

Below we shall identify the relevant phonic features and describe the various types of phonological units by reference to the way in which they are produced by the 'organs of speech'. We could utilize for the same purpose the sound waves produced by the action of these organs. But articulatory or motor phonetics remains more familiar to the majority of linguists, and in general it gives us a clearer insight into the causality of phonetic changes. In order to facilitate comprehension in what follows it will be useful to recall briefly the functions of the organs which contribute to the production of the sounds of speech. We shall lay stress only on what is of direct use for the readers of this book.

2.12 Transcriptions

The sounds of language are symbolized by means of letters and various signs to which a conventional value is attached. There are numerous systems of phonetic transcription, which are in general addressed to different audiences. The symbols used in this work are for the most part those recommended by the International Phonetic Association. A phonetic transcription is usually placed between square brackets: [oštum]. A phonemic transcription notes only the features which analysis of the language has shown to be distinctive, or in more general terms, endowed with linguistic function. Such a transcription is placed between oblique strokes /mučo/.

2.13 The glottis

The sounds of speech result for the most part from the action of certain organs on a column of air coming from the lungs. The first of these organs, the glottis, is situated at the level of the 'Adam's apple'. It is formed by two muscular membranes called the vocal cords. The closing or abrupt opening of this organ (such as comes about at the commencement of a cough) is rendered [ʔ] and called the glottal stop. The glottal stop may accompany the production of other sounds. The rubbing sound between the walls of the glottis is symbolized by [h] and is called the aspirate. What is heard when the vocal cords vibrate under the action of the air current is called voice. Voice normally forms part of the articulation of vowels. It also characterizes the vocal products described as 'voiced' such as the [z] of *zone*. A sound like the [s] in *saute*, which is not accompanied by glottal vibrations, is called voiceless. The pitch of the voice, high or low, depends on the length of the vocal cords and their degree of tension. This is what constitutes the speech melody.

2.14 Vowels

Vowels represent voice modified in various ways by the shape of the oral cavity. This shape, and consequently the nature of the vowel, is determined largely by the position of the lips and that of the tongue. A vowel such as that of *cou* [u], that of *beau* [o], that of *lu* [ü] or that of *peu* [ö], which is articulated with rounded, pouting lips, is called a rounded vowel. The vowel of *riz* [i] or that of *ré* [e] is articulated on the contrary with retracted lips. The vowels of *cou* [u], *beau* [o] and of *cor* [ɔ] are pronounced with the mass of the tongue pushed towards the rear of the mouth; hence they are called the back vowels. In the production of the vowel of *riz* [i], of *lu* [ü], of *ré* [e] and of *peu* [ö] the mass of the tongue is pushed towards the front of the mouth. These vowels are thus called front vowels. Those French speakers who distinguish between *patte* and *pâte* usually have a front [a] in the former and a back [â] in the latter. The vowels [i], [u] and [ü] are articulated with the tongue raised towards the roof of the mouth, the palate; such sounds are called closed or high vowels. The vowel of *passe*, for which the mouth is opened wide, is said to be open or low. The vowel of *rat* is more open (lower) than that of *raie* [ɛ]; this in its turn is more open (lower) than the vowel of *riz* [i]. Thus [a], [ɛ], [e] and [i] represent four different degrees of opening or closure. Similar relationships hold good between the [ɔ] of *cor*, the [o] of *beau* and the [u] of *cou* on the one hand and between the [œ] of *peur*, the [ö] of *peu* and the [ü] of *lu* on the other. The neutral vowel denoted by [ə] is neither very open nor very closed; it is neither front nor back, neither retracted nor rounded. Some French persons pronounce the *e* 'mute' of *brebis* or *dis-le* in this way. Others employ in these words a vowel which approximates to [ö] or [œ].

The palate is divided into two zones. The front portion is called the hard palate while the soft hinder part is called the velum. The velum ends in a kind of little tongue called the uvula, which may be raised or lowered. When raised it serves to shut off the nasal passages. Vowels are usually articulated with the velum raised. If it is lowered so as to open up the nasal passages, nasal resonances are produced which are added to the buccal resonances. Such vowels are said to be *nasal*. The vowels of *banc* [ã], of *pont* [õ] ,of *vin* [æ̃] and of *brun* [œ̃] (in those speakers who distinguish the vowel from the preceding) are nasal vowels. Vowels may be short or long according to their duration. Many French people make the [ε] of *maître* longer than that of *mètre*; the length of the vowel is indicated by a macron (a horizontal stroke) above the phonetic symbol, but also by a raised point or a colon placed after the symbol. A long [ε] will thus be denoted variously as [ε̄], [ε·] or [ε:].

2.15 Consonants

The name consonant is given to those sounds which are difficult to observe without the support of a preceding or following vowel. A consonant which is produced by a closure of the air passage with an explosion before a following vowel is called a stop or plosive. A consonant resulting from a narrowing or restriction of the air passage is called a fricative if the 'friction' of the air is clearly perceived and a spirant in the contrary case. A consonant is (bi)labial if it is articulated with the lips as the [p] of *pont* and the [b] of *bon*. It is apical if it is pronounced with the tip of the tongue (apex) like the [t] of *touche* and the [d] of *douche*. It is dorsal if it is produced by means of the upper surface (*dorsum*) of the tongue, like the [k] of *car* and the [g] of *gare*. A further distinction could be made between the pre-dorsals, which use the front part of the dorsum, and the post-dorsals, which bring the back part into play. According to the point of application an apical consonant will be dental (apico-dental) with the point of the tongue placed against the upper teeth (as in the case of [t] in French *touche*) or alveolar (apico-alveolar), with the apex of the tongue against the alveoli, the ribbed part of the gums just behind the front teeth, this being the mode of articulation of [t] in the English *touch*. A dorsal may also be alveolar (dorso-alveolar) with the front part of the dorsum pushed towards the alveoli, as is the case with the [s] of French *souche*; pre-palatal, articulated with the dorsum against or close to the velum; or finally post-velar or uvular as in the initial sound of *rouge* in the Parisian pronunciation.

A fricative, which is articulated by placing the upper teeth on the lower lip, is called a labio-dental. Such are the [f] of *fou* and the [v] of *vous*. The sibilants [s] and [z] in *sou* and *zone* and the 'hushing' sounds ([š] and [ž] in *chou* and *jaune*) are strong fricatives with an alveolar articulation, distinguished from one another by different positions of the lips. In French *seul* the sibilant is dorso-alveolar, in Castilian *solo* the sibilant is apico-alveolar and to the ear it approximates to the [š] of the French *chou*. A fricative (or spirant) produced with the point of the tongue between the teeth is symbolized by [θ], and the voiced variety by [ð]. Such are the sounds heard at the beginning of the English words *thin* and *this*. The voiceless post-velar dorsal fricative is denoted by [x]. This occurs at the beginning of the Spanish word *Juan* in the Castilian pronunciation and at the end of the German word *Buch*. The voiced equivalent of [x] can be heard in certain varieties of the Parisian pronunciation at the beginning of the word *rouge*.

Trills are produced by the vibration of one of the speech organs. Such a vibration takes the form of a rapid succession of beats. The apical trill is symbolized as [r] in what is called the trilled r. When the air passes on either side of an obstacle, the sounds thus produced are called laterals. The [l] at the beginning of *loup* is an apico-dental lateral, the closure which forms the obstacle being made with the point of the tongue against the upper teeth, whereas in English the corresponding sound has the closure against the alveoli. If a stop at any point of the mouth is combined with a relaxation of the velum, thus bringing about a resonance in the nasal passages, the consonants thus produced are called nasals. Such consonants are [m], the labial nasal [n], the dorso-palatal nasal [ñ] (e.g. the final sound of *pagne*) and the dorso-velar [ŋ] (e.g. the final sound of English *ring*). A sound which begins as a stop and continues as a fricative is called an affricate. The affricate in which the fricative part is a 'hushing' sound is denoted by [č] when it is voiceless and [ǧ] when it is voiced. More analytical versions are [tš] and [dž].

It is possible to combine the articulation of a consonant and a vowel; for instance, the bilateral stop [p] and the high retracted vowel [i] .In such a case we could speak of a [p] which has the timbre of [i]. Consonants of this character are called palatalized. Those which possess the timbre of [u] are called labiovelarized. Those consonants which may be regarded as having the timbre of [a] are those whose quality most closely approximates to that of ordinary consonants.

2.16 The syllable

In practice the boundary between vowels and consonants is not always clear-cut. If, while making the sound [i], the high or closed front vowel, we progressively raise the front part of the tongue, there comes a point at which we hear the friction of the air: in other words there is a transition from the vowel [i] to the fricative consonant [j], e.g. the first sound of the English *yoke*. The corresponding consonant produced by the analogous 'exaggeration' of [u] will be denoted by [w] (e.g. the first sound of the English *week*). Vowels being more perceptible than consonants, each vowel of an utterance will normally correspond to a peak in the curve of perceptibility or audibility, and as a general rule we perceive as many syllables as there are vowels. But a consonant like [l] when placed between consonants of lesser perceptibility or audibility such as [p] and [k], may function as syllabic peaks, while a vowel like [i] juxtaposed with a more open vowel like [ɑ] in such contexts as [iɑ] or [ɑi] does not necessarily constitute a distinct syllabic peak. In French the [iɑ] of *tiare* forms a single syllable with [ɑ] as the peak and it is commonly represented as [jɑ] but [ɑi] forms two peaks in *ébahi*.

CHAPTER III

Phonological Analysis

(i) THE FUNCTION OF PHONIC ELEMENTS

3.1 Three fundamental functions

The aim of phonological analysis is to identify the phonic elements of a language and to classify them according to their function in that language. Their function is distinctive or oppositional when they contribute to the identification, at one point of the spoken chain, of one sign as opposed to all the other signs which could have figured at that point if the message had been a different one. In the utterance *c'est une bonne bière* the sign /bier/ is identified as such by its four successive phonemes, each of which plays its part by the fact that it is distinct from all other phonemes which could have figured in this context. But in addition to this essential phonological function, the phonetic elements of a language may assume contrastive functions when they help the hearer in analysing the utterance into successive units. Such a contribution is made by the accent in general and particularly in a language like Czech, where the accent occurs regularly on the first syllable of every word. The same task is performed by the phoneme /h/ of English which, in addition to its essential distinctive function (*hill*, as distinct from *ill*, *bill*, *pill*, etc.), has also one of demarcation, since /h/ cannot, in traditional vocabulary, appear anywhere except at the beginning of a moneme. Another phonological function is the expressive function, which serves to inform the hearer about the state of mind of the speaker without recourse to the scheme of the double articulation. Thus in French, a lengthening and exaggeration of /p/ in *impossible* in *cet enfant est impossible* may be interpreted as an indication of irritation, whether real or feigned.

3.2 Non-functional characteristic features

We speak of the function of phonic elements only in so far as these result from a choice on the part of the speaker. But we may note the existence of phonic features which give information, whether the speaker wishes or no, about his personality, his position in society, or his place of origin. These may claim inclusion in a phonological description in so far as they possess such values only in a given linguistic community. In French, for instance, we may note the existence of two principal varieties of the phoneme /r/, the throaty [ʀ], characteristic of urban communities and the rolled [r] which is wide-spread in country districts, although it is on the way out. There would be no point of course in noting in a phonological description that men speak on a lower pitch than women, since this is the result of universal somatic differences and is not characteristic of a particular community. But when, as in certain languages of north-east Asia, we find that one and the same phoneme represented as /c/ is manifested as [tš] among men and as [ts] among women, this fact cannot be passed over in silence, since in another given language, say in Italian, both men and women agree in pronouncing [tš] at the beginning of *cinque* and [ts] at the beginning of *zucchero*.

3.3 Physical reality and linguistic function

The same phonic feature may possess a certain function in one language and have quite a different value in another. The glottal stop, which is a phoneme, for instance, in Egyptian Arabic, has no distinctive function in German, even though it has a contrastive value since it marks the beginning of roots with an initial vowel. Thus in *verachten*, composed of *ver* and *achten*, a glottal stop separates -*r*- from the following -*a*-. In Hottentot and Bushman a sound with full phoneme status exists which serves in English merely as a signal of slight irritation and is rendered as *tut tut*. In other words, a sound to which South African languages attribute a distinctive function, possesses in English only an expressive value. In Arabic, the rolled *r* and the throaty *r*, the latter being denoted as *gh* in the transcription of the word *Maghreb* for instance, represent two different phonemes, whereas in French the use of one or the other does not affect the sense of what is said, but merely gives some information about the personality of the speaker. There is no better illustration of the mutual independence of the objective physical character of a sound and linguistic function than the way in which different languages employ what is called melodic pitch. As we shall see later, the different degrees of pitch and the direction of the melodic curve may assume a distinctive function where they are opposed to each other as tones; a contrastive function when they contribute to accentual prominence; finally, an expressive function when they are to be considered as features of intonation.

3.4 Two conflicting criteria: function and segmentation

The linguist is interested in phonic facts only in so far as they possess a function. Thus what we expect from a phonological analysis is that it should group together facts which fulfil the same function even if they are physically different, and that it should separate those which have different functions even if in a material sense they are similar. In fact this principle conflicts with another whereby phonic facts are classified according to the dimensions of the segment of the chain in which they fulfil their function: the melodic rise which enables us to distinguish *il pleut?* from *il pleut* certainly has an oppositional function, no less than the degree of opening which enables us to distinguish *ré* from *riz*. But we know that such a melodic rise falls outside the double articulation, that it is not properly *distinctive* in the way that the difference between two phonemes is, but significant rather like the opposition between two monemes. On the other hand intonation is of such a nature that it is sometimes difficult to say whether the function is properly oppositional (the opposition of two different meanings) or expressive (an indication of the state of mind of the speaker). This is why segmentation is often preferred to function as a basis of classification. Needless to say, the facts for each type of segmentation are evaluated and classified on the basis of their function. This means in practice that we have to treat separately the phonemes, the units of the second articulation, and the prosodic facts, which by definition elude this second articulation.

(ii) PHONEMATICS

3.5 Potential pauses

Phonematics treats of the analysis of the utterance into phonemes, of the classification of these phonemes, and of the examination of their combinations in forming the significantia of the language. The significantia of the language under examination form the primary data which are the starting point for the linguist. These significantia, which are the observable face of the linguistic sign, may vary greatly in size and complexity. There is a significans /ž e mal a la tet/ corresponding to the sign *j'ai mal à la tête* and a significans /mal/ corresponding to *mal*. We might try, when carrying out the phonological analysis, to start with the significantia of complete utterances which form the primary data for the linguist without any interpretation or previous analysis into phrases or clauses, words or monemes. But this would cause considerable difficulties, both practical and theoretical. It is the case, for instance, that a given phoneme may be pronounced in quite different ways according to the context in which it is situated. The /l/ of British English is pronounced differently according as it precedes or follows a vowel, e.g. *lake* and *whale*. Parisians give a different pronunciation to the /ò/ of *joli* and that of *cor*. The absence of a following phoneme is also an element of the context: thus in French the /ɑ̃/ of *grand* /grɑ̃/ is often shorter than the /ɑ̃/ of *grande* /grɑ̃d/. This difference between the vowels of /grɑ̃/ and /grɑ̃d/, which is apparent when the two forms are pronounced in isolation, or in a final position, may be preserved when they appear in the middle of an utterance, for instance in /... ɑ̃ grɑ̃ dadè/ *un grand dadais* and /... la grɑ̃d adèl/ *la grande Adèle*, that is to say the pronunciation which is normal before a pause may be maintained even when the pause is, so to speak, potential but not actual. If we did not take into account such a 'potential pause', that is to say the segmentation into words, we should have to distinguish in French between a 'short' phoneme /ɑ̃/ and a 'long' phoneme /ɑ̃·/, since this difference of short or long would alone serve to distinguish between /... grɑ̃dadè .../ with short [ɑ̃] in *un grand dadais* and /... grɑ̃·dadè/ with long [ɑ̃·] in *grande Adèle*. It is therefore advisable to base our analysis on segments of the utterance not liable to be interrupted by a pause. This means in practice what are called words. In the transcription the potential pauses are, of course, indicated by spaces.

3.6 Internal junctures

In some languages the phonological behaviour observed generally before a potential pause recurs in a more marked form in the interior of what are called words, on the boundary of two monemes. In English the compound word *night-rate* /naitreit/ is not confused with *nitrate* /naitreit/ even though the series of phonemes and prosodic elements are the same in both cases. In the same way the last part of the single moneme *minus* /-ainəs/ is not identical with that of *slyness*, which comprises the adjective *sly* and the suffix *-ness*. It is thus apposite to register the existence of a type of potential pause, the effects of which are not necessarily identical with those of the type previously examined; it will be appropriate to indicate it in our transcriptions by means of a hyphen. This special treatment may extend to unexpected contexts, such as when, for instance, the German *Theater* is treated as though it was composed of *Tee* and a nonexistent *Ater* with a glottal stop before *-a-*. Such potential pauses are called junctures.

3.7 Which significantia form the basis of analysis?

For phonematic analysis we shall use, therefore, segments of the utterance which certainly do not contain potential pauses. It should not be forgotten that if there is an evident relation between the potential pauses and the points of segmentation into words and monemes, there is not necessarily an absolute coincidence. Consequently, in a phonological transcription, the blank space or the hyphen indicate, strictly speaking, the points of the chain where certain accidental features may occur which we have decided to disregard in the phonematic analysis. On the other hand, it will be necessary to group together only such segments which are sure to exhibit the same prosodic features: i.e. the accent must be in the same place in the case of an accentual language, while the same tones must lie on the same syllables in the case of a tone language. In the case of a language like French this last proviso is pointless, and we may use as a segment any word whatsoever. Finally, we shall disregard in a recorded word any element with an expressive function; this means that we shall not, for instance, set *impossible* with a lengthened and emphatic /p/ in opposition to *impossible* with a normal /p/, as though we had to do with two different units.

3.8 Phonematic segmentation

The words *chaise* and *lampe* are perfectly distinct in French: the behaviour of a hearer will not be the same if I say *apportez la chaise* or *apportez la lampe*. This confirms my own impression that *chaise* and *lampe* correspond to different aspects of experience and that *chaise* in its pronunciation is so distinct from *lampe* for any confusion to be improbable. On examination no segment of the spoken form of one of the words appears to be identical with any segment of the other. The position is quite different if the two words at stake are *lampe* and *rampe*. Here again the hearer's reaction will be different if I say *prenez la lampe* or *prenez la rampe*. But in comparing the two spoken forms I have the impression that they are almost identical and that the distinction which prevents the confusion of the two forms, and so uncertainty, on the part of the hearer, as to the behaviour expected from him, is located at the beginning of the two forms. The same holds good if my two words are *bûche* and *cruche*. Yet, if I compare *ruche* and *cruche*, I notice that what distinguishes *cruche* and *bûche* is analysable into two successive elements, the one that is found initially in *ruche* and another one before it. The spelling, of course, implies this result. But in the eyes of the phonologist the testimony of orthography is not valid. It is solely analysis by successive comparisons which enables us to determine linguistic units. To return to *lampe* and *rampe*, I should search in vain for a French word rhyming with the two which would permit me to carry the analysis a stage further, as proved possible in the case of *cruche* and *bûche*, where, thanks to *ruche*, the two successive elements were distinguished in the initial cluster which marked the word off from *bûche*. The initial features of *lampe* and *rampe* are therefore said to be minimal segments, in other words phonemes. It could be objected that it stands to reason that the initial of *cruche* is more complex than that of *bûche*, since it comprises two distinct successive sounds as opposed to the single 'sound' of *bûche*. But to this we shall rejoin that the difference in homogeneity between the initial of *cruche* and that of *bûche* only strikes us because the habitual use of forms like *cruche* and *ruche* have accustomed us to analyse the former into two successive units. We may add that it is a question of degree rather than of kind, and that it has nothing to do with phonological analysis since there are languages, such as Hottentot and certain Swiss dialects, which exhibit initial segments analogous to that of *cruche*, which cannot be analysed owing to the absence of words in *ru-*, *tru-*, etc., so that it must be regarded as a minimal segment, in other words a phoneme. The situation recalls that mentioned above (2.6.) apropos of the Spanish [tš] in *mucho*, which is a single phoneme since [š] does not exist in this language without a preceding [t], so that [tš] represents a single choice on the part of the speaker.

3.9 One sound for two phonemes and vice versa

Operations of the type just described enable us to carry out the phonematic segmentation of utterances and to establish how many phonemes are comprised in such and such a significans; thus there are three in *ruche* and *rampe*, four in *cruche* and five in *cruchon*. We may be tempted to believe that such operations may also enable us to determine what the phonemes of the language are, in the sense that once we have carried out the analysis of all the significantia, the segments thus obtained from the different significantia may be compared and those which resemble one another as much as the *-ampe* of *rampe* and *lampe* can be regarded as specimens of the same phoneme. In the same way the initial phoneme /r/ of *ruche* will be identified with that of *rouge*. However, when we compared *lampe* and *rampe* we noted a physical identity, namely what the orthographer renders as *-ampe* in both words, and this enabled us to locate the difference between the two significantia at the beginning. But we did not conclude that *lampe* and *rampe*, the initial sounds apart, were formed of the same phonemes, because we know that physical identity does not permit a conclusion as to linguistic identity. One and the same phoneme may be realized in different ways according to the environment, and one and the same sound may be the manifestation of different phonemes. In Danish, for instance, the phoneme /æ/ is manifested as [ɛ] in *net* 'pretty' but as [a] in *ret* 'correct, right'; the sound [a] which is the manifestation of the phoneme /æ/ in *ret* is the manifestation of another phoneme /ɑ/ in *nat* 'night'. If physical identity does not imply here linguistic identity, it is because the /r/ of Danish has the effect of opening (lowering) the articulation of front vowels in contact with it. Danish distinguishes phonologically between four degrees of opening for these vowels, and this holds good in contact with /r/. The phoneme of the first degree of opening cannot be characterized by the timbre, which varies between [i] and [e] according to the context, but by what distinguishes it, in all positions, from other front vowels, namely its minimal degree of opening. In the same way what constitutes the unity of the phoneme denoted /æ/ is the fact that there are, in the front of the mouth, two phonemes less open and one phoneme more open than it, i.e., it is characterized by the third degree of opening. This opposes it to the other front vocalic phonemes, its manifestation varying according to context between [ɛ] and [a]. This [ɛ] and this [a] are, in their respective contexts, in an identical relationship with the other vowels.

3.10 Segments are defined before comparison

It is now clear that we could not say that *ruche* and *rouge* begin with the same phoneme until it has been established that they are in an identical relationship with the various units which may appear in their respective contents, i.e. *-uche* and *-ouge*. The case is parallel with that of the [ɛ] of Danish *net* and the [a] of Danish *ret*, which are recognized as one and the same phoneme because both are defined relatively to the other units which may appear in the same contents as they, as being of the third degree of opening. Thus before proceeding to set up the inventory of phonemes it is necessary to define each phoneme by determining what, in a phonic environment, distinguishes it from all other units which could have appeared in its place. Once this procedure is completed, we shall be in a position to identify as manifestations of one and the same phoneme segments from different contexts which have an identical definition.

3.11 Operating with limited contexts

If we felt bound to respect *au pied de la lettre* what has been said above about the conditions which enable us to identify different minimal segments as manifestations of one and the same phoneme, we should soon encounter insuperable difficulties due to the fact that in all languages only a small fraction of the possible phonematic combinations are actually exploited to

61

form words as monemes. In the same total and precise context in which the /r/ of *ruche* appears, French uses no other phonemes than /b/ in *bûche* and /ž/ in *juche*. However, if we do not hesitate to utilize phonic environments which are only slightly different but which do not seem to affect the conditions under which sounds appear before *bûche*, we may add a good many other phonemes to the list: /l/ and /n/, for instance in *peluche* and *grenuche*. It would soon be clear that in French everything that can appear before *-u* can also appear before *-uche*. Further, we shall note that in that language the nature of the vowel carries no implications restricting the choice of the preceding consonantal phoneme, which of course will greatly simplify our task. But this is not what we find in all languages; this raises problems for the identification of phonemes to which we shall return later.

3.12 Relevant features

The identification of minimal segments, the necessary preliminaries to any identification of phonemes, implies the comparison of the phonetic nature of a given segment with all the other segments which may appear in the same context; in other words it is compared with other segments which are 'in opposition' to it. Take, for instance, the first segment of the word *douche*; it is in opposition with the first segment of the word *souche*. We note in the one case an explosion preceded by a closure of the expiratory passage produced by putting the point of the tongue against the upper teeth with simultaneous vibrations of the vocal cords. In the other case we observe friction of the air between the upper alveoli and the front part of the dorsum of the tongue, with no glottal vibrations. At this point of analysis we do not know whether these different characteristics are always concomitant. If it were confirmed later that in French the apico-dental plosive is always accompanied by voice and the pre-dorso-alveolar fricative is always voiceless, that is to say that both result from a single choice on the part of the speaker, we should have to consider each of these articulations complexes as a single relevant or distinctive feature.

But as soon as we bring into consideration the word *touche*, we note that its first segment is opposed to that of *douche* not by the apical articulation which is common to both words, but by the absence of concomitant glottal vibrations. In order to produce *douche* we must, for the first segment, make a choice (1) of the mode of articulation which closes the air passage by putting the point of the tongue against the upper teeth (this is common to *douche* and *touche*, (2) of a mode of glottal articulation (letting the vocal cords vibrate, which is what distinguishes *douche* from *touche*). If we now compare *mouche*, we note that *douche* differs from this word in that its initial closure is apical and not labial and that it is accompanied by a raising of the velum, which prevents the air from streaming out through the nasal passages, whereas the first segment of *mouche* requires an escape of air via the nose before the labial explosion. Nothing so far tells us that in French the voiced labial plosive (stop) is not always accompanied by an escape of air by the nose. But the example of *bouche* shows that the labial closure and nasal quality can be dissociated, while the *-nouche* of *Minouche* indicates that apical closure and nasal quality may be combined. This carries a further implication, namely that the pronunciation of the first segment of *douche* supposes a third choice—the raising of the velum which distinguishes it from the first segment of *-nouche*. If we now bring in the word *couche*, this does not impart any new element; the closure is in this case dorsal and not apical and there are no concomitant glottal vibrations, but this does not reveal any special feature in the articulation of the first segment of *douche*. The first sound of *louche* also presents an apical articulation but here the air escapes on both sides of the tongue (lateral articulation). This segment is therefore characterized as lateral, since we never find in French either before *-ouche* or anywhere else a lateral which is not apical. This means that in this instance there is a single choice and consequently a single relevant feature: the first segment of *louche* is opposed *qua* lateral to all other segments which are capable of appearing before *-ouche*. Since its apical character is not regarded as relevant, we have no occasion for dissociating,

63

in the case of the first segment of *douche*, a relevant feature which would be the 'non-lateral' characteristic. Thus we shall pick out three relevant features for the segment: (1) apical closure, (2) voiced sound, (3) non-nasal or oral articulation.

3.13 Proportionality in relations

If we determine in the same way the relevant features of the minimal segments which appear or may appear before *-ouche* and if we group together the segments characterized by a given relevant feature, we obtain the following classes: 'unvoiced' p f t s š k; 'voiced' b v d z ž g; 'non-nasal' b d j; 'nasal' m n ñ; 'lateral' l; 'uvular' r; 'bilabial' p b m; 'labio-dental' f v; 'apical' t d n; 'hiss' s z; 'hush' š ž; 'palatal' j ñ; 'dorso-velar' k g. The term chosen to designate each of the features is not intended to give an exhaustive description of the phonic product in question. The adjective 'voiced' is equivalent to the expression 'accompanied by glottal vibrations' in our previous analysis. But neither of these designations is intended to be descriptive. It has long been known that the glottal vibrations which accompany the pronunciation of certain buccal articulations are linked with other phonetic manifestations. What is implied here by voiced is the proportionality in the relationship of /p/ to /b/, /f/ to /v/, /t/ to /d/ etc. Whatever the phonetic realities are which distinguish /p/ from /b/, we maintain that they are the same as those which distinguish /f/ from /v/ with the sole differences entailed by the bilabial closure in one case and labio-dental friction in the other. The use of quotation marks for a term like 'voiced' points to its conventional character. It will be noted that a class such as /t d n/ is designated simply as 'apical' although analysis had revealed apical *closure* for these three segments. However, if we were to choose the description 'apical closure' instead of 'apical', we should run the risk of suggesting the existence of two distinct relevant features, although there are never two distinct choices, since 'apicals' are always stops in French. Since 'apicals' are not the only phonemes which are 'stops' we must naturally keep to the term 'apical', which alone is specific. It is likewise to be noted that before *-ouche* the segments /m n ɲ/ are not only nasal but also voiced. However, here voice cannot be dissociated from nasality since in this position there are no voiceless nasals. This is why /m n ɲ/ do not figure in the class of the 'voiced' elements, which are defined as such solely in virtue of their opposition to 'voiceless' partners.

3.14 Tabular representation of the proportions

We may illustrate the proportionality of the relationships denoted by the terms 'voiceless', 'voiced', 'nasal', 'bilabial', 'labio-dental', 'apical', 'hiss', 'hush', 'palatal', and 'dorso-velar' by arranging the units characterized by each of these features on the same lines and the same columns. It should be pointed out that not all the relevant features brought out by the analysis are represented; 'non-nasal' and 'lateral' are missing. These are the features which characterize phonemes which do not enter into proportions, such as /l/ and /r/ or those which would require certain phonemes (e.g. /b d/) to appear twice in the table.

	'bilabial'	'labio-dental'	'apical'	'hiss'	'hush'	'palatal'	'dorso-velar'
'voiceless'	p	f	t	s	š		k
'voiced'	b	v	d	z	ž		g
'nasal'	m		n			ñ	
						j	

3.15 From segment inventories to phonemes

In principle the preceding inventory is that of the distinctive units which appear or may appear before *-ouche*, and analysis, in other contexts, may result in inventories which may be either more or less extensive. The units of these new inventories will be identified with those elicited above not by bringing together units which sound the same but those which are characterized by the same relevant features. Only those units of different inventories represent one and the same phoneme which are in the same relationships with the other units of these respective inventories: the initial segments of *buche* and that of *bouge* will be identified as manifestations of the same phoneme /b/ because these two units are both defined as (1) 'bilabial' (2) 'voiced' (3) 'non-nasal'.

We can, of course, class the phonemes thus established, as was done above for the distinctive segments which occur before *-ouche*, and attempt to represent schematically the proportions of the system, by arranging in a 'grid' the sets of phonemes characterized by the same relevant feature. A class of consonantal phonemes characterized by the same feature such as French /p f t s š k/ which are produced at a series of points along the expiratory passage is called a *series*; consonants such as /t d n/ or /š ž/ which are articulated at the same point of the passage and by means of the same organ form what is called an *order*. In French we distinguish between a voiceless, a voiced and a nasal series; and between orders of bilabials, labio-dentals, apicals, sibilants, hushing sounds, palatals and dorso-velars. Two series such as /p f t s š k/ and /b v d z ž g/ form what is called a *correlation*. This term implies that each of the two series exists only in virtue of the fact that the other also exists. The relevant feature which distinguishes the two series is called the *mark*. In our example the mark is 'voice'.

3.16 Combinatory variants

The identification of the /b/ of *buche* with that of *bouge* would not present any difficulties within the framework of the operation described above. But things are by no means always as simple as this. On comparing two inventories we find in the most favourable case that we have the same number of units. But, even then, it is exceptional for the description of each one of these in one inventory to find its exact equivalent in the other. If we draw up the inventory for the distinctive units of Spanish in the context *na . . . a*, we shall establish in the word *nada* 'nothing' a unit which we shall describe as an apico-interdental spirant [ð], a spirant that has some resemblance to the fricative which appears in the English *father*. If we next draw up the inventory for the context *fon . . . a*, we find in the word *fonda* 'inn' a unit which will be described as an apico-dental stop [d]. But the spirant [ð] does not appear in this position any more than the stop [d] appears between two *a*'s. Since however the relationships of the apico-dental spirant with the units of its inventory are the same as those of the apico-dental stop with the units of its own inventory, we shall identify them as two variants of one and the same phoneme denoted /d/. A comparison of the two following tables shows that [ð] and [d] enter into the same system of proportions in their respective inventories.

Partial Inventory between Vowels			Partial Inventory between Nasal and Vowel		
p	t	k	p	t	k
β	δ	γ	b	d	g
f	θ	x	f	θ	x

We speak of combinatory or contextual variants when we take note of the difference in the manifestations of one and the same phoneme in different contexts; that is to say, when the difference is so striking that it could lead, as is the case in Spanish for [ð] and [d], to non-identical descriptions. We must however bear in mind that certain differences noticed by one person may escape the notice of another observer with a different linguistic background. A Spanish speaker who had to describe another language than his own in which [ð] and [d] are simply variants of one and the same phoneme, would not make a distinction between the two variants in that language. He has never been called upon to choose between the two and so he identifies them. In the same way the ordinary Parisian would not notice the difference between the /ò/ of *joli* and that of *cor*. But for an American who hears the /ʌ/ of his own word *sun* in the first and the /ɔ/ of *lord* in the second, they are well-defined variants, or 'allophones' as some linguists call them. To say that a phoneme has no variants or that it has two, three or more, is to make the mistake of transposing reactions peculiar to the describer into the system of the language under description.

A combinatory variant is, of course, not a chance product. It finds its explanation, at least to some extent, by reference to the phonic context. If the Spanish phoneme /d/ is manifested as a stop after /n/, this is because the buccal articulation of the latter requires a closure and it is simpler and more economical to maintain this closure for the following /d/. If it is manifested between two vowels as a spirant, this is because, in the framework of the Spanish system, it is more economical not to close the mouth completely between two vocalic articulations which are themselves manifested with the mouth wide open. The combinatory variants of a given phoneme are said to be in complementary distribution.

3.17 Other variants

There are other phoneme variants than combinatory variants. The French phoneme /r/ is 'throaty' with some speakers and 'rolled' with others. We then speak of individual variants. In the case of the actor who 'rolls' his r's on the stage but uses the 'throaty' pronunciation elsewhere, we may rather speak of 'optional' variants. But variations may also be conditioned. There are some French people who use the rolled /r/ in *très* and the throaty variety in *fer*, that is they exhibit individual variants with a combinatory conditioning.

3.18 Neutralization and archiphonemes

It often happens that the inventories drawn up for two different contexts do not comprise the same number of distinctive units. It may be, for instance, that a unit of one inventory, which has no equivalent in the other, does not enter into any of the proportions of the system. Such is the situation among French Creole speakers, where the sole unit defined as a uvular is attested at the beginning of a word such as *riche* but does not occur at the end of the word or syllable (*pour* or *perdu* pronounced without an r). In this case we may simply say that the phoneme in question shows gaps in its distribution. The situation is quite different when the units under consideration are in proportional relationships. Take for instance the consonants of Russian. The inventory, in the position before a vowel, comprises (generally in two distinct forms, palatalized and non-palatalized) a unit characterized as (1) bilabial (2) non-nasal (3) voiceless, and another as (1) bilabial (2) non-nasal (3) voiced, a third as (1) apico-dental (2) non-nasal (3) voiceless etc., that is to say a proportional system:

$$
\begin{array}{ll}
\text{p} & \text{t} \\
\text{b} & \text{d etc} \\
\text{(m} & \text{n)}
\end{array}
$$

For the final position the corresponding inventory is reduced to a unit which is (1) bilabial and (2) non-nasal and a unit which is (1) apico-dental and (2) non-nasal; i.e. we have a system which no longer distinguishes between /p/ and /b/ or /t/ and /d/. Physically speaking, the only sounds which occur as absolute finals are those which are voiceless [p] and [t]. But this voiceless character is not relevant, since it is automatically determined by the context and is no longer subject to choice on the part of the speaker. Thus whereas before a vowel we must distinguish, for the majority of stops and fricatives, between a voiced and a voiceless phoneme, this does not hold good at the end of a word, nor again at the end of a syllable where the presence or absence of glottal vibrations is determined by the context. In this case we have to do with a single distinctive unit which embraces the two corresponding units appearing in the pre-vocalic position; this common unit is called an *archiphoneme*. If the phoneme is defined as the sum of the relevant features, the archiphoneme is the sum of the relevant features common to two or more phonemes which alone present them all. Where an archiphoneme is manifested there is said to be neutralization. In Russian, the oppositions /p/–/b/ /t/–/d/, etc., that is in general terms the opposition of voiced and voiceless, are neutralized at the end of a word and more generally at the end of a syllable. The same is true of German, where *Rad* and *Rat* are pronounced identically, and in many other languages. But this is not the case in French and English, where *rate* /rat/ and *rade* /rad/, *cat* and *cad* are kept distinct.

Neutralization may affect more than two phonemes: in Spanish the three nasal phonemes observed, for instance, at the beginning of a syllable in *cama, cana caña* have their oppositions neutralized at the end of a syllable, where the choice of the sounds [m], [n], [ñ] and [ŋ] is dictated by the context and is not subject to the choice of the speaker. Let us consider the word *razón*. Before a pause the final segment will be manifested as [n] or sometimes as [ŋ] without the speakers being aware of the difference. At the end of the form *gran* we have [m] in *gran poeta* [n] in *gran torero* [ñ] in *Gran Chaco* [ŋ] in *gran conquistador*. As the examples show, these assimilations take place even with an intervening potential pause.

3.19 Neutralization and partial complementarity

We may speak of neutralization and of an archiphoneme in certain cases where the units in question do not enter into the proportional system, but where a partial complementarity confirms the indications of affinity suggested by the phonic analysis. We may, in order to oppose Spanish *cerro* and *cero*, speak of a strong trill in the first word and a weak trill in the second. But we could also consider them perfectly different: a trill in the first case and a flap in the second. However, at the beginning of a word we encounter only the strong variety, and the weak variety only at the end of a syllable. If we consider only these two positions we may be induced to see in the strong and weak forms mere variants of one and the same unit, the strong variant in *rico* and the weak variant in *amor*. This unit which splits into two in the intervocalic position is an archiphoneme characterized by apical vibrations, and the phonemes which it embraces are (1) a strong trill /r/ (*cerro*) and (2) a weak trill /r/ (*cero*). In the case of the vocalic system in French it is, again, the partial complementarity of certain distinctive units which enables us to unravel the precise nature of the oppositions of the system. At the end of the word Parisian French distinguishes between four degrees of opening for the front vowels, as is shown by the words *riz, ré, raie* and *rat*. In checked position, that is when the syllable ends with one or more consonants, only three degrees of opening are distinguished: e.g. *bile, belle, bal*. A word beginning with /b/ and ending in /l/ which has a vowel with the timbre of *é* as in *ré* between these consonants not only does not exist but is actually impossible to pronounce for the ordinary Parisian. What enables us to affirm that it is the opposition *ré-raie* which is here neutralized and not the opposition *riz-ré*, is the fact that the timbres of *ré* and of *raie* are in partial complementary distribution, that of *raie* being normal in a closed syllable and that of *ré* tending to be normal in the open syllable elsewhere than in a final position, e.g. in *maison, pêcheur, descendre*, despite the traditions of correct speaking and whatever indications could be derived from the orthography. In this case we should speak of an archiphoneme (noted /E/ or more simply /e/) which splits into two phonemes only at the end of a word, even though some people occasionally try to make a distinction between *pêcher* and *péché*. In discussing the non-nasal vowels of French it is expedient to start with archiphonemes, often denoted by means of capital letters /I E A O U Ü Ö/ which represent, in this part of the system, the sole distinctions common to all French speakers.

3.20 Neutralization revealed by alternation

When we are not engaged in a rigorous analysis into relevant features we generally become aware of the facts of neutralization by observing the modifications undergone by words in the course of inflection. Let us consider the example of the word *repérer*. In the infinitive the [e] placed between /-p-/ and /-r-/ has the same timbre as that of *ré*. In *il repère* the vowel [ɛ] in this position has the quality of that of *grès*. This is what is indicated of course by the acute and the grave accents, which in this example gives

71

trustworthy guidance. There is thus an alternation, but one determined by the phonic environment and not dependent on a choice by the speaker. The average Parisian would find difficulty in pronouncing the *é* of *ré* in *il repère*, but this *é* is the sole pronunciation which comes naturally to him in the second syllable of *repérer*. This alternation, which is determined by the actual phonic environment and reflects a characteristic piece of phonological behaviour in contemporary French, cannot be regarded as on all fours with the alternation of *eu* and *ou* in *il peuvent, nous pouvons*, which reflects a differentiation, the phonic determination of which ceased to exist more than a thousand years ago. Nothing in the phonology of modern French would rule out forms such as **il pouvent* or **nous peuvons*, rhyming with *elles couvent, nous abreuvons*.

3.21 Vowels and consonants

In a language such as French it often happens that consonants and vowels occur in the same context: e.g. in *chaos* /kao/ and *cap* /kap/, in *abbaye* /abei/ and *abeille* /abej/. If we said that the context is not the same because the syllabification is different, we should be forgetting that vocality and syllabicity are here one and the same feature. It is however mostly expedient to distinguish between the systems of consonants and vowels: what is expected of consonants and vowels is not that they should appear in the same contexts, that is they should be in opposition, but that they should follow one another in the chain of speech; in other words, we expect them to be in contrast.

This does not mean that certain sounds cannot, according to this context, function as the syllabic peak, which is normal for a vowel, or as the flanking unit of this peak, which is normal for a consonant. [i] in many languages is a syllabic peak before a consonant and the adjunct of such a peak before a vowel: e.g. French *vite* and *viens*. [l] is a syllabic peak, i.e. a vowel, in the English *battle* or Czech *vlk* 'wolf', but a consonant in English *lake* or Czech *léto* 'year'. In these circumstances there is no point in distinguishing two phonemes, one vocalic and the other consonantal. This holds good also if [i] before a consonant alternates with [j] before a vowel because these two sounds are distinguished in fact only by a slightly greater degree of closure for [j] than for [i], and because this supplementary degree of closure is normal to mark the contrast between [j] and the neighbouring vowel or vowels. If it is necessary, in French, to distinguish a phoneme /j/ from a phoneme /i/, this is because *paye* and *abeille* are not identical with *pays* and *abbaye*. But we must note that the opposition is neutralized everywhere except at the end of a syllable. It is not possible, in French, to distinguish a word *vi-ens* in two syllables from *viens*. Even in the languages which distinguish /i/ from /j/ and /u/ from /w/ it is normal for /j/ and /w/ to be attached rather to the vowel system in virtue of their relevant features.

3.22 Elements without distinctive function

The combined operations described so far will enable us in principle to establish the phonemes, and the archiphonemes, of a language and at the same time to classify each of them according to the relationships which it has with the other phonemes and archiphonemes of the system. Everything is based on the operation called *commutation*, the one which permitted us to oppose the first segment of *lampe* to that of *rampe* and to analyse into two successive elements the initial part of *cruche* by opposing it to *ruche*. We know in theory how to determine the number of successive phonemes comprised in a given significans. In practice we find ourselves faced with situations which may cause embarrassment.

Let us consider, for instance, the French word *devant*. Comparison with *revend* and again with *divan* would appear to indicate that what precedes *-vant* in *devant* is composed of two phonemes—/d/ followed by /ə/. But whereas we had concluded that the initial /k/ of *cruche* was an autonomous phonematic segment because its disappearance results in a different word *ruche*, we cannot apply this criterion to the first vowel of *devant*.

When this disappears, as in *là-devant* or *sens devant derrière*, the word concerned is the same and this seems to indicate that, at least in this position, the vowel does not have a distinctive value. There is no French word [dəvã] distinct from [dvã]. On the other hand, if we note that in French [ə] is necessarily preceded by a consonant, we may be tempted to conclude that [də] is nothing but the variant of the phoneme /d/ when this occurs in the utterance between the two consonants: *là-devant* /ladvã/ with /d/=[d] but *par devant* /pardvã/ with /d/=[də] (notice the same [də] in a name like *Hérold-Paquis* where there is no orthographic indication of the *e*). This interpretation is certainly correct.

But there are some contexts where the presence of [ə] is distinctive: *l'être* /letr/—*le hêtre* /lə etr/, *dors* /dor/—*dehors* /dəor/. We shall say therefore that the opposition between [ə] and zero, which exists in certain special contexts, is neutralized everywhere else: *recevoir* will be transcribed /rsvuar/ because the insertion of an /ə/ between two of the initial consonants is automatically regulated by the context and because the localization (before or after /-s/) does not alter the identity of the word.

3.23 Two succesive sounds as a single phoneme

Let us now consider the English word *chip*, phonetically [tšɪp]. The case of [tš] here is different from that of the Spanish *mucho*. In English [š] does exist without a preceding [t]: side by side with *chip* we have *ship* [šɪp] and *tip* [tɪp]. We might therefore be tempted to analyse the word as /tšɪp/. But in the English system the initial part of *chip* is opposed to that of *gin* [džɪn], the former being the voiceless counterpart of the latter, so that the two ought to be treated alike. Now the [dž] of *gin* is as unanalysable as the [tš] of the Spanish *mucho* and for a similar reason: [ž] never appears in English at the beginning of a word without a preceding [d]. Thus *gin* is composed of three phonemes represented as /ǧɪn/. As a consequence *chip* will also be analysed into three phonemes—/čɪp/. For similar reasons

74

non-homogenous phonic products, such as affricates or diph-
thongs in widely differing languages, are to be interpreted as
single phonemes.

(iii) PROSODY

3.24 The physical nature of prosodic facts

We assign to prosody all the facts of speech which do not
fall within the phonematic framework, in other words those
which for one reason or another elude the second articulation.
Physically, what is involved are physical phenomena which are
of necessity present in all spoken utterances. Whether the energy
used in articulation is great or small, it is always present in
some degree. As soon as voice is perceptible, the vibration of
the glottis must have a certain frequency and this will impart a
certain melodic pitch to the voice as long as it remains perceptible. Another feature capable of prosodic exploitation is
duration, which naturally is an inescapable physical aspect of
speech since utterances take place over a period of time. It will
be understood that these facts cannot have linguistic value
through their presence or absence at a given point, but rather
by their modalities, which may vary from one part of the
utterance to another. Consequently they lend themselves less
well to the characterization of discrete units than others, e.g.
nasality or labial closure, which may figure or not figure in an
utterance. In *allez chercher les livres*, there is neither nasality
nor labial closure, but normally it is not possible to pronounce
this order without introducing, whether consciously or no,
duration on the one hand and melodic pitch and articulatory
energy on the other, which vary from the beginning to the end
of the utterance. We know, however, that tones, which are
prosodic facts because they elude phonematic segmentation,
are discrete units in the same sense as phonemes.

3.25 Intonation

Voice results from vibrations of the vocal cords, and these vibrations imply a tension of these organs. When a cord is tightly stretched it vibrates on a high note. If the tension is less, it vibrates on a lower note. The same is true of the vocal cords. In singing the rise and fall of the voice are made in steps—the notes of the scale. In speech the rise and fall are continuous and this resembles rather the noise of a siren than a tune played on the piano. Since the cords at any moment vibrate at a given pitch, it is possible with any utterance to trace out a curve of the melodic pitches (with some brief interruptions corresponding to the voiceless consonants). This speech melody is thus, in some sense, automatic, that is the speaker does not choose between its presence and absence. Although the range of linguistic exploitation of this is limited, it nevertheless plays some part, the nature and importance of which varies greatly from one language to another. Only some of them use pitch in the form of discrete units: these are tones. Accentual exploitation, however, is by no means rare. What remains of the melodic curve, once we have taken account of tones and facts of accent, may be summed up in the term *intonation.*

As we have seen above (1.16) the movement of the intonational curve is largely governed by the necessity to stretch the vocal cords when beginning an utterance and the economical tendency to relax them when the end of the utterance is in sight. However, speakers may utilize this movement for certain purposes of differentiation according to principles which seem common to all mankind, but under forms that may vary from one community to another. Hence, intonation cannot be denied some sort of linguistic value. But its operation does not fall within the framework of the double articulation, since the sign represented by the rise in pitch at the end does not fit into the succession of monemes, nor does it present a significans which is analysable into a series of phonemes. The variations of the curve of intonation do in fact exercise certain complex functions, difficult to unravel. The function is directly significant in *il pleut* compared with *il pleut?* but most often it is of the type we have called 'expressive'. What must be stressed apropos of speech melody in a language like French is that variations of its curve are not capable of changing the identity of a moneme or word. The *pleut* of *il pleut?* on a rising pitch is not a different word from the *pleut* of the statement *il pleut*, with a falling pitch. Even if the difference between the two curves is manifested only in a single word, it is not the value of the word which is affected but that of a large segment, which may be the whole sentence.

3.26 Tones

In French these facts of intonation exhaust the linguistic usage made of melodic pitch. But in other languages, notably some spoken in Africa, south of the Sahara, and in south-east Asia, this same physical reality is exploited for distinctive purposes in the form of discrete units, like phonemes. These however are not classed among phonematic features because they affect segments of the utterance which do not necessarily coincide with the units of the second articulation. The phenomena in question are what are called *tones*. In a 'tone language' a word or moneme is not perfectly identified until the tones have been established in addition to the phonemes. It would be as inaccurate to state that in Chinese the pear and the chestnut are both called *li* as to assert of French that *le pré* and *le prêt* are perfect homonyms. In fact the Chinese word designating the pear is pronounced with a rising pitch while the word for the chestnut has a falling pitch, and the difference between these two tones is as effective as the difference in vocalic timbre which distinguishes *pré* from *prêt*.

3.27 Punctual tones

A tone comprises a melodic movement of variable duration. The whole of the movement need not however be relevant, if by relevant we understand what enables us to distinguish the tone in question from all other tones employed in the language.

There are languages in which the tones are *punctual*, in that a single point of the melodic curve serves as the mark of identification. This point may be the highest melodic pitch (the most acute) or the lowest (the most grave). The rise in the curve towards the highest point and the succeeding fall, like the corresponding fall and rise on either side of the lowest point are automatic and so lack linguistic value. In a language which distinguishes two punctual tones one of these tones is necessarily high and the other low. Some languages distinguish three punctual tones, high, middle and low. Such a language is said to have three relevant tone levels or three *registers*. In the majority of languages with punctual tones, the tone characterizes the syllable and each syllable has a tone. Let us consider the example of Lonkundo, a language with two registers spoken in the Congo region: the word *lokolo* with a low tone on all three syllables designates the fruit of a palm tree. If however there is a low tone in the first syllable and a high tone in each of the succeeding ones, *lokolo* means 'exorcism'. If we denote the high tone by means of an acute accent and the low by the grave accent, we shall write *lòkòlò* in one case and *lòkóló* in the other. In the same language *àtáòmà* is to be translated 'you have not killed today' whereas *àtáòmá* means 'you did not kill yesterday'. It should be noted that the high and the low tones have the same functional status and that it is not obligatory for a word to have one syllable with a high tone. Since the men, women and children who speak these languages have voices which are naturally more or less deep or high, it follows that a high tone is recognized as such not by its absolute pitch but by its relationship to the tone of the adjoining syllables.

3.28 Melodic tones

Apart from punctual tones there are languages with *melodic tones*; these are not defined by reference to a single point on the curve but by the direction or the changes of the curve. In the simplest case a distinction is made between a rising and a falling tone, but in addition to these we also find a level tone with no appreciable rise or fall. One or more tones characterized by a single direction may be opposed to a complex tone exhibiting a change of direction. In Swedish, for instance, the word *komma* 'comma' exhibits a tone with a single direction, rising or falling, according to dialect. But the word *komma* 'to come' is pronounced with a tone which first falls and then rises. Melodic tones quite often characterize segments which coincide with syllables, so that each syllable has its own tone. But, as we have just seen, from the example of Swedish, there are languages in which the melodic tone characterizes segments longer than a syllable. In fact the distinction between the two tones in this language requires at least two syllables for its manifestation. A monosyllable in Swedish cannot exhibit a complex melodic movement.

The melodic tones of a language may belong to a single register. This does not mean that the start of a rising tone is necessarily of the same pitch as the end of a falling tone, but simply that two tones in such a language are never distinguished solely by the fact of their respective pitch level. However, there are languages which combine melodic tones and registers, e.g. those which distinguish a high rising tone from a low rising tone, each point of the melody of the first being higher than the corresponding point of the second.

The abrupt tension of the vocal cords necessary for a rapid rise of the voice may lead to a momentary closure of the glottis. This is why there are tones which are characterized not so much by a particular form of the melodic movement as by a brief interruption or simply a kind of constriction of the voice. It is such a constriction which constitutes the essential difference between Danish *anden* 'the duck' and *anden* 'other'. In Vietnamese we find six tones distributed in two registers which may be defined as follows: (1) high rising (2) low rising (3) high punctual (4) low punctual (5) high 'constricted' (6) low 'constricted'. From this it will emerge that punctual tones may coexist with melodic tones. Only those languages are said to be 'punctual tone languages' in which *all* the tones can be analysed in terms of punctual tones.

3.29 Morae

In the interests of simplicity of description it is sometimes expedient to consider a melodic tone simply as a succession of two punctual tones: a rising tone is analysed as a low tone followed by a high tone and a falling tone as a high tone followed by a low tone. In this case each of the segments characterized by one of the successive punctual tones is called a mora. Recourse to this type of analysis is particularly expedient in the case of languages where the tones are normally punctual but which at rare intervals exhibit melodic movements within the limits of a single syllable: in a segment -*tata*- with a high tone in the first syllable and a rising tone in the second it will be convenient to analyse the latter as two successive punctual tones (low, high) especially as, which is frequently the case, the rising tone is found to have the same morphological or derivational function as a low tone followed by a high tone in two successive syllables.

3.30 Tones and intonation

The existence of tones in a language does not exclude that of intonation. It is still normal for the vocal cords to be less taut at the beginning of an utterance and the organs will tend to be relaxed in anticipation of the cessation of the utterance. It is even understandable that the speakers of that language should exploit this universal phenomenon in the way already described; the absence of the normal fall of the melodic curve at the end of the utterance requires a complement, e.g. in the shape of a reply. Here we have a situation in which one and the same physical reality, the vibrational frequency of the voice, is exploited in the same language, in the same utterance, for two different linguistic purposes. Naturally we may anticipate some measure of interference: for instance, the requirements of intonation may demand a rise where the tone necessitates a fall, and vice versa. It is observed, in fact, that a high tone at the end of an utterance may, with one and the same speaker, get much lower than a low tone in the middle of an utterance. If the melodic fall is particularly steep, it often comes about that a tone which is linguistically high, is in point of physical fact actually lower than the linguistically low tone which precedes it. All this goes to show that hearers, in order to judge whether a tone is high or low, do not use as their criterion the position of the voice with reference to what could be described as the normal pitch of the speaker: they perceive as high what is more acute, and as low what is more grave, than the pitch which the shape of the curve of intonation would lead one to expect at any given point.

3.31 Accentual prominence

By *accent* we understand the prominence given to a syllable and only one syllable within what, in the given language, constitutes the accentual unit. In the majority of languages the accentual unit is what is usually called the word. In languages like Russian, Polish, Italian and Spanish each word exhibits one syllable, and only one, which is prominent often at the expense of the other syllables of the word. The accented syllable is the first of Russian *gorod*, Polish *ryba*, Italian *donna*, Spanish *mesa*, and the second in Russian *sobaka*, Polish *wysoki*, Italian *mattina*, Spanish *cabeza*. The same holds good in English and German for simple (non-compound) words like *father*, *Vater*, accented on the first syllable and *career*, *Kartoffel* accented on the second syllable. When the word occurs in isolation, the accentual prominence is always manifested. In a context such a prominence is always more or less pronounced, and this is not without its effects on the contents of the message; a kind of hierarchy is established among the different accents of a whole utterance, partly determined by acquired habits, but capable of modification by the speaker to alter the content of the utterance. In English the message is not the same if in the utterance *we did* the prominence of *we* is greater than that of *did* or vice versa.

The phonic features generally utilized for accentual prominence are articulatory energy, melodic pitch, and the duration, actual or perceived, of the accented syllable. In many languages the accented syllable tends to be articulated in a more energetic way, on a higher pitch and with longer duration than the adjoining unaccented syllable in contrast with it; and it is the degree of energy, pitch, and duration which enables us to establish the hierarchy of the accents in the utterance. But the physical nature of the accent varies from one language to another. In a language like Portuguese, duration contributes decisively to the prominence of the accented syllable whereas in Castilian, the vowel of the accented syllable is not longer than that of a following non-accented syllable. Scholars have long regarded the accent of most modern European languages as a stress accent, represented by a peak in the curve of articulatory intensity. But modern observations would appear to indicate that in a language like English the permanent characteristic of every accent is a rapid change in the melodic curve. This feature is however usually accompanied and reinforced by an increase of intensity (stress) and of duration.

3.32 Accents and tones

In accentuation extensive use is thus made of melodic elements, more extensive in fact than has long been believed. This is a physical feature which accents share with tones, and this being the case, we may ask whether one and the same language may exhibit both accent and tones as distinct linguistic entities. In fact it would appear that it is not legitimate to speak of accents in languages where all syllables must show a tone. Where accent and tones coexist in one and the same language, the tones are not opposed as distinct units except in the accented syllable. In other terms, the prominence given to a syllable in each accentual unit is brought about at the expense of the possible tonal distinctions in the other syllables. There are thus tone languages without accent, where each syllable exhibits a distinctive tone; and accentual languages where each word or accentual unit may have only a single distinctive tone confined to the syllable bearing the accent. In the latter case we may be tempted to regard each tone as a type of accent, and to say of a language which distinguishes two tones linked with the accent that it presents two types of accent. Swedish, in which *komma* 'come' is distinguished from *komma* 'comma' by a different melodic pattern, can thus be represented as a language with two types of accent, the simple accent of *komma* 'comma' and the complex accent of *komma* 'come'. It is usually said that the Attic dialect of ancient Greece had two different accents, the acute and the circumflex (the 'grave' accent not being a distinct linguistic unit), which were not in mutual opposition except in the last syllable of those words that contained a long vowel or diphthong. However, in order to draw a clear distinction between the functions, it would be better to say that under the accent Greek distinguished two tones if this syllable contained a long vowel or a diphthong.

3.33 Functions of the accent

The function of tones is essentially distinctive: a tone exists only in opposition to at least one other tone. Thus a language possesses *tones*, never a single *tone*. The function of the accent is essentially contrastive, that is to say it contributes to the individualization of the word or the unit which is characterized in contrast with the other units of the same type represented in the same utterance. Thus a language possesses an *accent* and not *accents*. When, in a given language, the accent is found always on the first or the last syllable of the word, this individualization is perfect, since the word is in this way clearly distinguished from what precedes or follows. Where the position of the accent cannot be predicted but must be learnt for each separate word and so does not mark the beginning or end of the accentual unit, the accent has a function which is called *culminative*: it serves to denote the presence in the utterance of a certain number of important articulations and thus facilitates the analysis of the message. When the position of the accent is not fixed, that is when the succession of phonemes characterizing the unit does not enable us to determine the syllable in which it falls, as is the case in Spanish, where the succession of phonemes /termino/ gives us no indication whether the word is *término* 'term', *termino* /termíno/ 'I terminate', or *terminó*, 'he terminated', we may be tempted to attribute a distinctive value to the accent. But this would be acceptable only if we could conceive of a Spanish word /termino/, the three syllables of which were accented, a third in which /ter/ and /mi/ were accented /-no/ remaining without accent, and so on. What may have distinctive value is the position of the accent. This distinctive role of the position of the accent is generally episodic, but it may acquire some importance, as can be seen in English, where many pairs of words are phonematically homonymous, such as (*an*) *increase*—(*to*) *increase*, or quasi-homonymous, such as (*a*) *permit*—(*to*) *permit*, one of which is a noun and the other a verb, the former having the accent on the first syllable and the latter on the final syllable. This however should not obscure the fundamental function, common to the accent of all languages: it is contrastive and not oppositive.

3.34 The rôle of the accent in the identification of the word

What sometimes tends to obscure the fundamentally contrastive character of the accent is the fact that in languages where the position is not predictable, hearers begin their identification of the word with reference to the peak which constitutes the accent. A Spanish word like *pasé* 'I passed' is first of all identified as belonging to an accentual pattern/– ´/; next, within the framework, it is perceived as distinct from *pasó* 'he passed', which belongs to the same pattern; but there is never any confrontation, conscious or unconscious, with *paso* 'I pass' which is of the accentual pattern /´– –/ and, from this fact alone, eliminated once the pattern /– ´/ of *pasé* has been recognized. This is what is meant when we state that a badly accentuated word is not understood, even if the phonemes of which it is composed are perfectly pronounced. The explanation why the accent is thus perceived as a matter of priority is essentially the fact that the accented syllable is identified by contrast with the adjoining non-accented syllables. This implies that all elements necessary for identification are offered by the speaker, actually present in the utterance, and passively recorded by the hearer. This is not the case with the phonematic constituents. These are identifiable only by an act of memory which confronts them with the units of the system not present at this point of the chain and which stand in opposition with every successive segment of the utterance.

3.35 The hierarchy of accents

To assert, as was done above, that a language has only one accent and not more than one would appear to contradict the accepted view according to which we should distinguish in certain languages between a main and a secondary accent. In an English word like *opposition*, the first and third syllable are accented, but the prominence given to the latter is usually more pronounced. In German *Augenblick* there is a main accent on *Au-* and a secondary accent on *-blick*. The respective position of the two accents is by no means linguistically indifferent since this is what distinguishes *unterhalten* 'hold down' with the main accent on *un-* and the secondary accent on *-hal-* from *unterhalten* 'to entertain' with the reverse distribution of accents. In fact the distinction between a main and a secondary accent does not suffice to give an exhaustive description of the accentual system of the language in question because in theory there are, in a compound word, as many distinctive degrees of accent as there are successive components. German *Wachsfigur* 'wax figure' has a main accent in *Wachs-* and a secondary accent in *-gur*, but the addition of a third component in *Wachsfigurenkabinett* 'room for wax figures' introduces an accent on *-nett* which is intermediate between the main accent of *Wachs-* and the less pronounced accent of *-gu-*.

The situation is clear in a language like German: each element of the compound keeps the accent which characterizes it as an independent word. The second syllable of *Figur* will always be prominent, whether the word is employed as an autonomous member of the utterance or as an element of a compound. The situation is quite different in a language like Russian, where all the elements of a compound except one lose their proper accent: *nos* 'nose' loses the accent and the proper timbre of its vowel in the compound *nosoróg* [nəsɑ'rɔk] 'rhinoceros'. In the German equivalent *Nashorn*, on the other hand, each of the two elements keeps its accent, with that of *horn* simply subordinated to that of *Nas-*. We may sum this up by saying that the *accentual unit* is the word in Russian and the lexeme in German.

The situation in English is complicated by the fact that a great deal of the vocabulary of this language consists of borrowings, first by oral means from mediaeval French, and later from written sources, from Latin and classical Greek. These words are adapted to the accentual patterns of traditional vocabulary. Thus *adduction* and *arisen* both present the pattern – ´ –: *orthodoxy* and *underlying* both have the pattern ´´ – ´ –; *crucifixion* and *understanding* show ´ – ´´ –, etc. What distinguishes, however, the more recent elements from the native Germanic elements, is that the components have a less clear semantic and phonic individuality. No English speaker would have any difficulty in identifying *under-* in *underlying* with the adverb and proposition *under*; but even if *ortho-* is felt as an independent formal unit, few people would be capable of attaching a definite meaning to this element. It is true that this holds good no less of *under-* in *understanding*. Similarly, could any German identify semantically the *unter-* of *untersagen*? It is legitimate, therefore, to group *ortho-*, *-doxy*, *cruci-*, *-fixion* among the accentuated units of English no less than *under-*, *-lying*, and *-standing*.

It is clear that German and English, and Germanic languages in general, differ from the majority in that they preserve within the compound word the hierarchy of accents which is general in the clause or sentence. This hierarchy can be limited to two degrees only if the compound itself comprises two terms, which is not necessarily the case. The addition of a new element to a compound may thus result in the introduction of a supplementary degree of accent in the compound. The complete description of a language will therefore present an analysis of the hierarchy of accents in the units which comprise several accentual units. In the majority of languages these units will be larger than the word; in certain other languages such as the ones mentioned above these units will also include the word.

3.36 Accentual demarcation

The contrastive function, or more specifically, the culminative function (3.33) of the accent may be narrowed down to a demarcational function in circumstances where its position in the word or the accentual unit marks the limits of this word or unit. If the accent is on the first syllable, as in Czech or Hungarian, then this demarcational function is clear. However, the accent is less effective as a mark of delimitation when its position is fixed but determined by the syllabic quantity, as is the case, for instance, in Latin. Here a succession of four short syllables, accented on the first and the fourth, does not provide any certain indication of the limit between the two words. Thus in a syllabic series such as *bónacalígula*, the accents do not enable us to decide whether to segment *bónaca lígula* or, as the meaning requires, *bóna calígula*.

3.37 Other means of demarcation

Among demarcational indicators other than the accent are phonemes or variants of phonemes, or non-distinctive features, or groups of phonemes which examination of the language reveals as appearing only at the beginning or the end of a word or some other significant unit. Thus the /h/ in English is both a phoneme and a sign of demarcation. A borrowed word like *mahogany* is adapted to the scheme of *behaviourist* where *be-* precedes the boundary of a moneme. The glottal stop of German is normally a demarcational non-distinctive sign. In Tamil phonemes designated as /p t k/ are aspirated only at the beginning of the word. In German a combination of phonemes like *-nm-* can only result from the combination of two monemes as

in *un-möglich*. In some languages, notably Finnish, the phenomenon of vowel harmony, within the word, provides indications
as to the limits of the word. Thus certain vowels /a o u/ cannot
occur in the same word as /ä ö y/. Hence the change in an utterance from a syllable containing /a/, /o/ or /u/ to a syllable in /ä/,
/ö/ or /y/ marks the transition from one word to another.

We may speak of negative demarcational signs when a phoneme, a variant of a phoneme, or a group of phonemes appears
solely in the interior of a word or moneme. This is the case for
the phonemes /d/ and /ŋ/ in Finnish. In this language /l/ never
appears in a final position, and it exists at the beginning only
before a vowel. From this it follows that a combination like /lk/
can only appear within a word, that is neither in the initial nor
the final position.

The Franco-Provençal patois of Hauteville gives a good
illustration of the way in which an accent with a non-predictable
position, which alone cannot provide a sure indication of the
limits of the word, may be combined with other features to
guarantee perfect demarcation. In Hauteville the accent may be
on the last syllable of the word as in /pŏ'tă/ 'hollow', /be'rĕ/
'beret', /pe'šo/ 'vine prop', or on the penultimate as in /'fătă/
'pocket' or /'berĕ/ 'to drink', so that it does not indicate where the
word ends. However, if the accent falls on the last syllable, the
vowel (which is always final or followed by /r/) will be of short
duration, even though phonologically speaking it may be non-
short, as in /pe'šo/ or short, as in /pŏ'tă/ or /be'rĕ/. But if the
accent falls on the last syllable but one, the vowel of that syllable
will be considerably lengthened if it is phonologically non-short as
in /'berĕ/ pronounced ['bērə]. If this vowel is phonologically
short, it is the following consonant which is lengthened or even
doubled. Thus, whereas /pŏ'tă/ is pronounced [pɔ'ta] with a short
[t], /'fătă/ is pronounced ['fatta] with a [t] which forms part of
both syllables. This implies that those accents which do not
entail any kind of lengthening mark the last syllable of the word,
while those which are accompanied by a lengthening either of
the vowel or of the following consonant characterize that
syllable as the penultimate.

Phonological Analysis

(v) Utilization of Phonological Units

3.38 Lexical frequency and frequency in speech

We know that the phonological possibilities of a language are never fully exploited—far from it. Let us consider in French two consonantal phonemes taken at random—/š/ and /d/. /š/ may appear before any vowel and /d/ after any vowel. Fourteen vocalic phonemes appear in closed syllables. Thus there are fourteen possible monosyllables of the type /š/ plus vowel plus /d/. Of these fourteen only one is attested in French /šod/, spelt *chaude*, if we exclude the proper name *Chedde* from which the name of the explosive *cheddite* is derived. Another selection, say /s/ and /k/, would have given seven forms actually used of the fourteen possible. The different phonological units of a language are utilized in a very uneven way. Certain phonemes are of frequent use and enter into a large number of words while others are employed more rarely. In French, for example, the phoneme /t/ appears in a large number of words (lexical frequency) and it frequently also figures in utterances (frequency in speech). Of vowels, /i/ is frequent both in the lexicon and in utterances; /l/ which is probably less frequent than /t/ in the lexicon, is more frequent in speech because it appears in the definite article; the phoneme /ñ/ is rare on the whole whether we make our count from the dictionary or from the text; the same is true of the phoneme /œ̃/, even though the frequency in speech is boosted by the use of /œ̃/ as the masculine of the indefinite article.

3.39 Combinations of phonemes

The way in which the phonemes of a language may be grouped to form *significantia* emerges from the comparison of the inventories of distinctive units in different positions. It will however be useful to make matters explicit and in doing so to take account of prosodic features. A method which has proved its worth consists first of drawing up a list of those units which by themselves may constitute an isolable significans and those which, while not attested in this function, may appear in the same inventories as the former. This enables us to determine in many languages what are called vowels. In French /o/ *eau*, /i/ *y*, /ü/ *eu*, *eut* etc. constitute isolable significantia. /ò/ cannot constitute an isolable significans but it appears in the same inventories as /o/, /i/ and /ü/: e.g. in *molle*, *mole*, *mille*, *mule*. We next look for phonemes and their combinations which occur before and after vowels. This gives us the groups of consonants which can figure at the beginning and the end of the significans. It then remains to verify whether the internal groups flanked by two vowels of the same significans are always analysable into a succession evidenced in a final and an initial group. This is what happens in the case of the cluster /kstr/ in French, which is analysed as a final cluster /-ks-/ (cf. *fixe*, *ex*) and an initial cluster /-tr-/ (cf. *très*, *tranche*). But this is not always the case: in Finnish, for instance, the group /-ks-/ appears between vowels, but although /s/ may appear at the beginning before a vowel, /k/ does not exist in a final position. In a case of this kind we must provide a list of internal clusters. We must always bear in mind the possibility of prosodic effects: it frequently happens that combinations of distinctive units are not the same when they appear under the accent, before the accent, and after the accent.

3.40 The canonical form

The examination of phoneme combinations and of prosodic units in the framework of the minimal significans in many languages reveals that the simple lexeme tends to assume a determinate form. In English and in German the simple lexeme comprises for the most part a syllable where the vowel, whether short, long or diphthongized, is either in the initial position or preceded by any phoneme or group of consonantal phonemes permissible in the initial position. If the vowel is short it is bound to be followed by one or more consonants. If it is long or a diphthong it may also appear finally. This syllable, which can be accented, may be followed by a non-accented syllable, the vowel of which (usually [ə]) may be followed by a consonant or, more exceptionally, a group of consonants. If we symbolize by v́ the non-short vowels which may be accented, the accented short vowels by v̆, and the non-accented vowels by v, the consonants or groups of consonants by c, we obtain the formulae (c)v́(cvc) and (c)v̆c(vc), the elements in parentheses being optional. English *I*, German *Ei* are of the type v́, English *ill*, German *all* of the type v̆c, English *fee*, German *roh* of the type cv́, English *fill*, *trill*, *strip*, German *voll*, *tritt*, *streng*, *Takt* of the type cv̆c, English *wonder*, *bottle*, German *Mutter*, *Schatten* of the type cv̆cvc, etc.

The normal form of the lexemes of a language is sometimes called the canonical form. The canonical form in Chinese is the monosyllable, and in the Semitic languages three consonants, either with or without vowels in between. These are languages in which the concept of canonical form has an obvious significance. It is more difficult to determine a canonical form for a language like French. It is worth noting, however, that in current speech long words tend to be reduced to dissyllables of the type *métro*, *vélo*, *télé* or *té-vé*.

3.41 'Morphophonology'

Describers are often tempted to include in their presentation of the phonology of a language a study of the vocalic or consonantal alternations such as those of *eu* and *ou* in *peuvent*, *pouvons*, *meurent*, *mourons*, *preuve*, *prouvons*, etc. or again, the Umlaut phenomena of German exemplified in plurals like *Bücher* or verbal forms like *füllt* or *gibt*. Such a study which is designated by the term morpho(pho)nology, is perfectly justifiable when its purpose is to determine certain automatic processes such as that which induces a German child to form a participle *gebrungen* instead of the correct *gebracht*, from *bringen*, on the model of *singen* : *gesungen*. But that has nothing to do with phonology. What determines the alternation are strictly speaking morphological considerations and it is in no way governed by phonic factors. The term morpho(pho)nology, which suggests a connection with phonology, should therefore be avoided with reference to studies of the use for morphological purposes of the distinctions at the disposal of the speaker.

CHAPTER IV

Significant Units

(i) THE ANALYSIS OF UTTERANCES

4.1 The marginal role of prosodic signs

It would seem natural to identify significant units with the units of the first articulation. But we must not forget that a prosodic feature, like the rise of the melodic curve which turns *il pleut?* into a question, combines a significans, the rise of the curve and a significatum, which we recognize as that of the French moneme *est-ce que*. Thus there are signs which do not enter into the double articulation. Such signs play a by no means unimportant part in human communications. But we may regard them as marginal phenomena because an utterance is properly linguistic in so far as it is doubly articulated. In what follows only the units of the first articulation will be studied although we shall never forget that they may be supplemented by prosodic signs.

4.2 Difficulties of analysis: the amalgam

Just as the first phonological operation consists in analysing the significantia into successive minimal units, the phonemes, in the present study the first operation, consists in analysing the utterances or partial utterances into their successive minimal significant units which we term monemes. It should be pointed out at the outset that the operation may not always be brought to a successful conclusion. The reason for this is that the monemes are units with two facets: a significatum and a significans which forms its manifestation. For the significatum to be manifested it is necessary for the utterance to be phonologically different from what it would be without such a significatum. But it may happen that two significata coexisting in an utterance fuse their significantia in such a way that the resulting product cannot be analysed into successive segments. An example is the French significatum 'à' and the significatum 'le' of the signs /a/ and /l/ respectively, as for instance in *il est à Paris* and *le chapeau*. But when the two signs coexist in the same zone of the spoken chain and are there followed by a consonant, they acquire a unique and unanalysable significans /o/, spelt *au* (*il va à l'hôpital*, but *il va au marché*). Another example is the English significatum 'to cut' and the significatum 'past tense'. The significans of the former is /kʌt/; that of the latter most frequently /d/. But when these signs are brought together in the utterance, they are manifested conjointly in the form /kʌt/, in *he cut* for instance (cf. the corresponding present he cuts /hi kʌts/). In Latin *malorum* 'of the apples', *-orum* serves as the significans for the significata 'genitive' and 'plural' without our being able to say precisely what corresponds to the genitive and what to the plural. In all such cases we shall say that different significantia are *amalgamated*.

The amalgam may be regarded as a special aspect of a more general phenomenon whereby the significatum may be manifested, according to the morphological contexts, in different guises. In French the significatum 'to go' is manifested, according to its contexts, variously as /al/, /va/, /i/ or /aj/; the existence of these variants, identified as such because they are in complementary distribution, shows that one cannot be certain of identifying a moneme by reference to its significans. The concept of an amalgam allows the describer some free play: in a case like German *sang*, the past tense of *singen*, it is of little importance whether he chooses to analyse it as a discontinuous significans /z . . . ŋ/, corresponding to the significatum 'to sing' and a significans /. . . a . . ./, corresponding to the significatum 'past' or whether he prefers the interpretation of /zaŋ/ as an amalgam corresponding to two distinct significata.

4.3 Analysis into monemes

The operation which secures the analysis of utterances into monemes has some analogy with that which leads to the analysis of significantia into phonemes. In both cases the investigator is seeking to determine the segments which have been the object of a particular choice on the part of the speaker. In the case of phonemes he was concerned with segments which he had to choose in such a way as to obtain a given significans. In the case of monemes we have to do with segments which the speaker has selected in view of the meaning to be given to the message. The analysis is carried out by bringing together utterances less and less different in their phonation and of closer and closer semantic approximation. We take by way of example the French /ilkur/, *il court* and /nukuriõ/ *nous courions*. The significantia have the segment /kur/ in common while the significata share the notion 'run'. Both remain broadly distinct. The difference is much less marked in the pair /nukuriõ/ and /nukurõ/ which share /nukur . . . õ/ and the significata 'run' and 'first person plural' (the last two dissociated by the comparison of /nukuriõ/ and /vukurie/, *vous couriez*, /nukurõ/ and /vukure/, *vous courez*. The significantia are distinguished only by the insertion of /. . . . i . . . ./ in the first and the absence of /. . . i . . ./ in the second, while the significata are differentiated by the notion of 'imperfect', which exists in the first and not in the second. We shall thus posit a moneme with a significatum 'imperfect' and a significans /i/ inserted in the complex before a final /õ/. This sign for the imperfect has the same significans /i/ when it coexists with the notion of 'second person plural', but in other contexts it is expressed by means of the significans /-è/ (/ilkurè/). In certain contexts (*que nous courions* /knukuriõ/) this same significans /-i/ corresponds to a quite different significatum called 'subjunctive'. This significatum, when it coexists with the 'persons' which entail for the 'imperfect' the significans /-è/, does not possess (in the case of 'to run') any distinct expression. After *il veut* /ilvö/ we find the subjunctive *que nous courions* /knukuriõ/, and after *il voit* /ilvua/ the indicative *que nous courons*

/knukurɔ̃/. Yet, in combination with the third person singular the form is the same in both cases: /kilkur/ despite the orthographic differences: *qu'il coure* and *qu'il court*. In such a case the significans is often said to be zero.

On the basis of the very limited study just outlined we might assume the existence in French of a significatum 'imperfect' expressed according to the contexts by /-i-/ or by /-è/ and again a significatum 'subjunctive', the significans of which is sometimes /-i-/ and sometimes zero. A more searching examination which would extend to forms such as *il faisait* /ilfzè/, *qu'il fasse* /kilfas/, would show that if our analysis is to cover all the facts relative to the sign 'imperfect'–/-i-/, /-e/, it would need some complementation in the case of 'subjunctive'–/-i-/, zero, since the subjunctive /kilfas/ is not identical with the indicative /kilfè/. This would lead us to add the proviso that in coexistence with the significata 'to do', 'to finish', 'to lie' and many others the significatum 'subjunctive' requires the employment of a particular variant of the corresponding significantia: /fas/, /finis/, /mãt/ instead of /fè/, /fini/, /mã/, which are found in coexistence with the significata 'indicative' and 'singular'.

4.4 Discontinuous significantia

If we now compare /nukurɔ̃/ *nous courons* with /kurɔ̃/ *courons*, we see that the significantia have in common the features 'to run' and 'first person plural', but the feature 'statement' characterizes the first as opposed to the 'imperative' of the second. We may be tempted to say that /nu/ is the significans corresponding to 'statement'. In that case we should have to recognize a variant /vu/ in /vukure/ *vous courez*, which is opposed to /kure/ *courez*. But other contexts such as *il nous l'a dit* or *c'est pour vous* enable us to identify /nu/ *nous* with 'first person plural' and /vu/ with 'second person plural'. We must therefore posit that in /nukurɔ̃/, /nu/ and /ɔ̃/ represent the discontinuous significans of the significatum 'first person plural' and, further, /nu/, but not /ɔ̃/, combines the expression of this significatum with that of 'enunciation' and as such is opposed to the zero significans of 'imperative'.

Significant Units

4.5 Concord

Discontinuous significantia such as /nu . . . . õ/ in /nukurõ/ are often the result of what is called concord. In /lezanimopes/ *les animaux paissent*, as contrasted with /lanimalpè/ *l'animal paît*, the sign 'plural' receives three distinct expressions: /leza . . ./ instead of /la . . ./ /. . . mo. . . / instead of /. . . mal . . ./, and /. . . pes/ instead of /. . . pè/. We might say that the significans of the plural is /-ez-/ accompanied by particular variants of the significantia corresponding to the significata 'animal' and 'browse'. There is, of course, only one plural moneme, the one whose significans is simply /-e/ in /lešamãž/ *les chats mangent*.

In a case of concord such as one of gender in /la ɡrãdmõtañblãš/ *la grande montagne blanche* the 'feminine' characteristic is included in 'montagne' since one can never dissociate 'feminine' from 'montagne'. If French possesses a moneme with a significans of great variability (/-es/ *-esse* for instance) corresponding to 'female sex', there is no such significans corresponding to a 'feminine gender'. What one finds is monemes or combinations of monemes said to be 'of feminine gender', the significans of which is normally discontinuous in the sense that apart from the central expression (in the example under discussion /. . . mõtãñ . . ./) it is manifested at other points of the utterance: /la . . ./, /. . . ãd . . ./, /. . . ãš/, instead of /l . . ./, /. . . ã . . ./, /. . . . ã/, which would make their appearance if we replaced the 'feminine' *montagne* by the 'masculine' *rideau*.

4.6 Varying complexity in the structure of monemes

The illustrations borrowed from French that we have employed hitherto suggest that the analysis of utterances into monemes is a complex operation. It is in fact usually the case. But this complexity varies greatly from one language to another and even, within one and the same language, from one type of moneme to another. There are languages where the invariability and the continuity of significantia is a rule which admits no exceptions. Where a Frenchman with reference to a given significatum will

97

say in different circumstances *je*, *me*, or *moi*, a Vietnamese will use solely *tôi*. In certain cases the significans of the 'first person singular' will have its effect in French on the neighbouring verb: e.g. /žsüi/ *je suis* as opposed to /tüè/ *tu es*, /ilè/ *il est*, /žve/ *je vais* as opposed to /tüva/ *tu vas*, /ilva/ *il va*, etc., whereas the Vietnamese equivalents of the French verbs have an invariable root. Even in French invariability of monemes is by no means rare: 'yellow' is always /žón/ whether employed as an independent word or as an element of derivatives (cf. /žón-is/ *jaunisse*, /žón-è/ *jaunet*). Further, the stem of the great majority of the verbs of the language such as /dòn-/ 'give' /šāt/ 'sing' /mãž/ 'eat' remains identical throughout the conjugation.

4.7 Variants of significantia and variants of significata

We may compare the variants of the significantia of monemes and those of phonemes by speaking in both cases of combinatory or contextual variants. It should be noted, of course, that the context which determines the variations is a phonic context in the case of phonemes and a significant context in the case of monemes: /. . . i . . ./ is employed when 'imperfect' coexists with 'first or second person plural'; /. . . è/ when it coexists with other 'persons'. There are however cases in which the factors governing the use of two moneme variants are expressed in terms of phonic context. The English plural is expressed by /. . . ɪz/ after a sibilant or 'hushing sound', by /. . . z/ after every other phoneme manifested as voiced, and by /. . . s/ after every other phoneme manifested as voiceless. The plural of *sin* /sɪn/ will thus be /sɪnz/. The alternation of /s/ and /z/ is however not *phonologically* determined by the phonic context because *since* /sɪns/ exists as well as /sɪnz/. Its conditioning may be formulated in phonic terms but this only holds good for a precise morphological use.

Apart from combinatory variants of significantia there exist optional variants such as /žpö/ i.e. *je peux* /žpüi/ '*je puis*' with mutual relations similar to those we noted above (3.17) between the 'throaty' and the 'rolled' *r* in the speech of the actor. If it is legitimate to use here the same terminology for the units of the two articulations of language, it should be pointed out that there is a fundamental difference between the variants of significantia and variants of phonemes. This is bound up with the fact that phoneme variants cannot be defined in terms of discrete magnitudes. Every manifestation of a phoneme is a variant since it differs physically, to however slight a degree, from any other manifestation according to the context or the temper of the speaker. On the contrary, variants of significantia are defined in terms of phonemes, i.e. discrete units. /kur/ *cours, coure, courent*, pronounced by a rustic with a rolled *r*, is not a variant of the significans /kur/ but is the significans /kur/, which as such does not have any variant. We have a variant of a significans however when the significatum 'to go' is expressed by /...al.../ in /nuzalõ/ *nous allons* and by /...i.../ in /nuzirõ/, *nous irons*. A significans or a variant of a significans is always identifiable in terms of discrete distinctive units or of zero. It is quite different with the significatum facet of the moneme, the value of which varies according to the context or situations, as widely as the manifestations of a phoneme. We may compare *il court après l'autobus, il court après la fortune, il court le cerf, c'est un coureur* (used on the stadium of a runner or in the drawing-room of a philanderer).

(ii) The Hierarchy of Monemes

4.8 The position of the moneme is not always relevant

To establish the inventory of phonemes we began by picking out the units capable of appearing in a given context. Our purpose was to discover the units between which the speaker has to choose at each point of his utterance to make it adequate for the desired message. If this message includes the word /mal/ *mal* he will have in the first place to choose /m/ from among the consonantal phonemes which can figure in this position, then /a/ from the vocalic phonemes which may appear in a closed (checked) syllable, and lastly /l/ from among the consonants which may occupy the final position. But once we have picked out these three phonemes, /m/, /a/ and /l/, we are not free to put them in any order we please because in that event we might arrive either at an unpronounceable combination, e.g. /aml/, or some other moneme (e.g. /lam/ *lame*). In other words the phoneme is effective in its distinguishing function when it is in a given position.

The significant function of monemes brings about a rather different state of affairs. A sentence like *Pierre bat Paul* changes its meaning if we reverse the positions of *Pierre* and *Paul*. This is similar to the case of *mal* which becomes a different word if we interchange /m/ and /l/. But as against this there are utterances such as *je partirai demain*, the meaning of which does not vary if I change the order of certain monemes and say *demain je partirai*. If in *je partirai demain* I replace *demain* by *en voiture* or by *avec mes valises*, this does not mean that I have to choose between *demain*, *en voiture* and *avec mes valises*, the use of one excluding that of the others just as the change of /m/ at the beginning of *mal* excludes /b/, and the use of *Pierre* in *Pierre bat Paul* excludes *Jean*. I may employ the three segments simultaneously and say, for instance, *je partirai demain en voiture avec mes valises*. Here we see that the linguistic use of 'opposition' is in fact little different from the ordinary use of the term: *demain* is not 'opposed' to the presence in the same utterance of *en voiture* and *avec mes valises*; but it is opposed to that of *hier* or *aujourd'hui* in the same way as /m/ is opposed to the presence of /b/ at the beginning of the word *mal*. As regards phonemes, opposition implies incompatibility at a given point. In *mal* /m/ is opposed to /b/ at the particular point of the chain, but it does not exclude it in a neighbouring position, as we see from the word /emabl/ *aimable*. For monemes or more complex signs opposition may imply incompatibility in a given utterance; it is not possible to say *aujourd'hui, je partirai demain*. For monemes, as well as for phonemes, membership in one and the same system implies opposition, i.e. *exclusive choice*. We shall say, therefore, that *demain*, *aujourd'hui* and *hier* belong to one and the same system, whereas *demain* and *en voiture* belong to different systems. But in the case of monemes it will not be possible to proceed without restrictions to the establishment of systems of units capable of appearing at one and the same point of the chain.

4.9 Syntactic freedom and economy

Both the fixity of phonemes and the relative degree of freedom enjoyed by speakers in arranging the monemes in the utterance are easy to explain. In the case of the phonemes it has the advantage of economy if not only their oppositional features are relevant but also their mutual positions. Let us take the three French phonemes /a/, /p/ and /l/ and suppose that their respective position in the significans were irrelevant; they could together form only one significans which would be pronounced at will [apl], [pal], [lap] etc. It is the fact that their position is not irrelevant which enables them to form the four distinct words /pal/, /pla/, /alp/ and /lap/, i.e. *pal, plat, alpe* and *lape*. The relevance of the respective positions of the monemes (e.g. *Pierre bat Paul*) also involves some measure of economy but there are obvious advantages for the speaker if he enjoys some measure of freedom in the order of the monemes or the more complex signs, since it enables him to analyse the experience to be communicated in an order adapted to the special circumstances in which he is placed. This freedom of construction may be secured in different ways, as the following analysis will show.

4.10 Three ways of indicating the relationships of a moneme

The experience to be transmitted may be considered as a totality, certain aspects of which are selected and emphasized by the language chosen for the communication. *Hier, il y avait fête au village*; I can imagine a language in which the information conveyed by this French utterance could be communicated in the form of three monemes arranged in any order: one which by itself would denote not only the idea of 'festival', but the actual existence of a festival; another which would designate not merely a village but a village where an event occurs; and a third, the exact equivalent of *hier*, which would refer to the day preceding that when the message is transmitted non *per se* but as the period within which the event takes place. To the first of these monemes corresponds in French the group of monemes *il y avait fête*, which comprises in addition a moneme of the 'past' which duplicates *hier* but with less precision, the notion of 'festival' and that of 'effective existence' being here dissociated. To the second moneme of our imaginary language French responds again with a group of monemes *au village* which gives separate expression to the notion of 'village' and that of 'the place where something happens', with further the indication that the village is not simply any village. The third moneme finds its French equivalent in the single moneme *hier*, which by itself establishes a definite relationship between the day which precedes the present one and the event which is being reported. *Hier* may be regarded as combining the sense 'in' with that of 'day preceding the present one'. This does not mean that we would be justified in analysing the significatum of *hier* into two distinct *significantia*. The fact is that these two ideas are always coupled in French and form a single linguistic unit. For a simple moneme to be able to appear without changing the message either here or there, it must belong to the type of those which, like *hier, aujourd'hui, demain*, imply their own relationship to the rest of the utterance. Otherwise, some freedom of position may be secured to it by the addition of particular monemes which indicate its relations with the context, for instance *à, en, avec* in *au village, en voiture, avec mes valises*. A moneme which does not so imply its relations with the context and has no added monemes of relationship, will be bound to indicate its relations with the rest of the utterance by the position it occupies. *Paul* will be marked as the object of the assault by the position after *bat* in *Pierre bat Paul*, but as the one who administers the treatment by its position before *bat* in *Paul bat Pierre*.

Significant Units

4.11 Autonomous monemes

Autonomous monemes such as *hier*, which imply not only a reference to an element of experience but also a definite relationship to the other elements of experience to be communicated, are not solely temporal even in French. *Vite*, for instance is of the same type; it denotes not merely 'rapidity' but also the rapidity with which the process in question takes place. These units, which belong to the traditional class of adverbs, are however not particularly numerous. They are only economical when they are of frequent occurrence and more frequent than the expression of the isolated element of experience; *vite* is more frequent than *rapidité*. As for *hier*, it is so much more frequent than the same idea without the adverbial character, that is the plain reference to a particular fact, that we must have recourse to a designation as complex as '*le jour qui précède celui-ci*' in order to express the latter.

4.12 Functional monemes

In all cases where an element of experience is conceived as capable of entering into different relationships with its context, it is more economical to devise a distinct expression of this element and others again to express each type of relation. Let us suppose we had a language which possesses a moneme with the value 'man' as 'agent of the event' with a significans like /bak/; another meaning 'the man who undergoes the action' with a significans /som/; and finally a third with the sense 'man who benefits from the action' with a significans /tin/. Instead of our single word *man* /mæn/ we should find three perfectly distinct 'words' :/bak/, which would be used in the equivalent of *the man eats*, /som/ in *I saw the man*, and /tin/ in *he gave it to the man*.

If this situation were the same in all equivalents of our nouns, that language would have three times the number of 'nouns' that we find in English, which would be a considerable burden on the memory. This is why no such language has ever been observed. It is evidently preferable to have only one moneme for 'man', another for 'woman' another for 'animal' and so on. To these are added, as the need arises, other monemes with the value 'the agent of the action' or with the sense 'the sufferer of the action' and a third meaning 'the beneficiary of the action'. This is what we encounter in many languages where a moneme exists designating a neighbouring segment as the author of the action, a moneme which fulfils the same function for the sufferer, and a third for the beneficiary. In French the moneme /a/ *à* designates the beneficiary of the action. In *il a donné le livre à Jean*, *à* denotes the function of *Jean*. Function here designates the linguistic fact which corresponds to the relationship between an element of experience and the total experience. We propose to call 'functional monemes' or just 'functionals' those monemes which serve to indicate the function of another moneme.

4.13 The autonomous syntagm

The name syntagm is given to every combination of monemes. An autonomous syntagm is a combination of two or more monemes the function of which does not depend on the position in the utterance. It may be of the type *l'an dernier* where it is the whole group of the monemes in question which indicates its relations with the context. But it is more usually provided with a functional moneme which secures the autonomy of the group. The segments of an utterance *en voiture, avec mes valises* are autonomous syntagms. A moneme like *hier* suffices by itself to express its relations with the context. In *en voiture* it is the first moneme *en* which expresses the relations of the second moneme *voiture* with the context. The same holds good of the minimal autonomous syntagm *avec plaisir* or of the more complex syntagms such as *avec mes valises* or *avec le plus grand plaisir*. In the Finnish *kirkkossa* 'in [the] church' it is the second moneme *-ssa* which expresses the function of the first, *kirkko-*.

Significant Units

4.14 The tendency towards amalgamation in the autonomous syntagm

The autonomy enjoyed by a syntagm endowed with a functional moneme is well illustrated by nominal forms in Latin, each of which is provided with what is called a case ending, which often suffices to indicate its function and offers the user some freedom of construction. This autonomy of the whole group finds its counterpart in a closer union of the component monemes. The autonomous syntagm in most languages tends to constitute an accentual unit within which all the phenomena attendant on a virtual pause may be attenuated or disappear altogether. This tendency to reduce the autonomy of the successive elements of the syntagm is inhibited in so far as the component monemes remain separable, that is if one or more monemes can be inserted between the primary components: *avec plaisir*, *avec grand plaisir, avec le plus grand plaisir*. When this is not the case, phonetic development may rapidly blur the boundaries of the significantia. The final and the initial phonemes of the significantia are now constantly in a definite context and they may be subject to the influence from this context. In a language where /k/ and /g/ are palatalized before /i/ or /e/, a final /k/ of a moneme followed by an initial /i/ of the following moneme may escape this palatalization if there is a pause, even an optional pause, when passing from one moneme to another. But if the boundaries of the moneme are blurred because of the non-separability of the successive elements of the syntagm, /-k i-/ becomes /-ki-/, in which /k/ is palatalized and the group may subsequently become /-či-/. Since, however, in other contexts /-k-/ is preserved without change, this will have the result that the same moneme will sometimes terminate in /-k/ and sometimes in /-č/. In Czech, the root meaning 'hand' has the form *ruk-* when the moneme is combined with that of the nominative and that of the singular (*ruka*), the form *ruc-* (=/ruts/) in *ruce*, the locative singular, and the form *ruč-* in the adjective *ruč-n-i*, 'manual'. The differentiation of these forms of the root goes back to successive palatalizations, in different contexts, of a form with a final /-k/. The action of the contexts is effective in both directions and so may affect the functional moneme as well as the other elements of the syntagm. In Greek an ancestral *-*m*, the significans of the functional monene of the accusative, is normally represented by /-n/ when the preceding significans ends in a vowel, but by /-a/ when it ends in a consonant: *logo-n*, *korak-a*. Phenomena of this kind lie behind most of the variants of significantia. An extreme example of such a tendency is the overlapping of significantia, which may end in a complete amalgam, as in French *au* for *à* and *le*, English *cut* for *cut + ed*. The mutual influence exerted by two significantia in contact is often accompanied by a mutual influence of the corresponding significata. The monemes *arbre* and *commande* have quite a different meaning in *arbre de commande* 'chain of command', in *arbre à pain* 'bread tree', and *commande d'épicerie* 'grocery order'. The formal amalgamation which results in *au* from *à* and *le* has its counterpart in the semantic amalgam *bull's eye* which has nothing in common either with an eye or a bull. But this does not apply to the relationships between a functional moneme and the moneme whose function it indicates, because the necessities of communication require that the semantic individuality of both components should remain intact.

4.15 The 'word'

An autonomous syntagm formed of non-separable monemes is what is commonly called a word. However, this designation is sometimes extended to autonomous monemes such as *vite*, *hier*, as well as to non-autonomous monemes, functionals as in the case of *pour*, *avec*, or non-functional as with *le*, *livre*, *rouge*, the phonological individuality of which is usually well-defined even if their separability is not always certain. The three elements of *le livre rouge* are separable as is shown by *le petit livre noir et rouge*. But *pour le*, *avec le* are only in exceptional cases dissociated by an inserted element (*pour tout le*), while the blend *du* for *de le*, and the amalgam *au* for *à le* witness to the close cohesion of syntagms formed of prepositions and articles.

Significant Units

It would be a vain endeavour to seek to define more closely the concept of 'word' in general linguistics. We might be tempted to do so within the framework of a given language. But even in this case the application of rigorous criteria often leads to analyses which do not accord with the current use of the term. Satisfactory results may, however, be attained with a language like Latin where the word usually coincides with the accentual unit and the significantia of the component monemes are often inextricably interwoven. Take the example of *dominus*; we disregard the complications raised by the analysis of gender, which in principle will not differ from that attempted above (4.5) for French. We posit three monemes, the significata of which are 'master', 'nominative', and 'singular'. We may not say that the significans of the first is *domin-*. This is certainly the 'root' in classical Latin, since it is the element which does not change in the course of declension, but *domin-* means 'master' only in combination with a particular series of inflexions. The situation is clear when we consider *clavus, clavis* and *clava*, three words with the same root, but clearly distinct because of the circumstance that they exhibit each its own set of endings, that is significantia of monemes which indicate the various functions. The significans corresponding to the significatum 'master' is thus *domin-* in combination with a series of special endings. The significans corresponding to 'nominative' is *-us*, but in combination with *domin-*, *-us* is also, at the same time, the significans of the moneme 'singular'. It is clear that analysis into distinct significantia could only complicate the exposition without bringing any real advantage. This is why in Latin it is certainly preferable to follow the traditional method of expounding the facts according to which *dominus* is a word of the 'second declension'. The existence of enclitics such as *-que* does not prevent our identifying the word thus delineated with the word as an accentual unit, for the group *word* plus *enclitic* does not behave accentually as the word alone does, e.g. with three shorts, *bonáque*, as opposed to *pópulus*.

4.16 Difficulties in delimiting the 'word'

It is much less easy to grasp a unit of the same type in languages like English or German. It is known that the accentual unit of these languages does not coincide with what might be called the word, and this is linked with the difficulty experienced in deciding the number of words contained in utterances or segments like *I'll go out* or *um nachzusehen*. English presents the additional difficulty of the notorious 'genitives' of the type *the King of England's*. In French it is likewise difficult to decide in all cases whether two or three words are concerned: *bonne d'enfant* /bóndãfã/ behaves just like its German counterpart *Kindermädchen*, and it is usually considered as a compound. But if we use formal criteria and not semantic ones, as we should if arbitrary decisions are to be avoided, and base ourselves on forms of the plural in deciding whether there are two or more words, we should be tempted to consider *sac á main* as a single word since the plural is /sakamē/ and not /sakzamē/. But *cheval à bascule* should be regarded as consisting of three words since its plural is *chevaux à bascule*. We should be in a quandary over *cartes à jouer*, since some people say /kartažué/ and others /kartzažué/.

4.17 The autonomous syntagm is to be preferred to the 'word'

The general tendency not to separate in the utterance monemes felt as closely connected by their sense is so natural that traces of it are to be expected in all languages. Hence we should be tempted to operate in general with a larger significant unit than the moneme, which would be called the 'word'. There is nothing against this if we bear in mind that the term 'word' necessarily embraces particular types of syntagmatic relations in each separate language and if a clear distinction is drawn, among the facts which suggest this unit, between phonic features, either demarcational or culminative, on the one hand, formal features such as separability and amalgamation on the other, and finally the indications provided by the semantic side. In point of fact we find an infinite number of possible degrees between complete inseparability and amalgamation at one end of the scale and complete independence at the other. In so far as *j'ai vu* in spoken French is the normal past tense of *je vois*, *ai vu* does not comprise two distinct significantia but is rather the amalgam of two monemes with the significata 'see' and 'past'. Formally, however, *ai* and *vu* are separable (*j'ai souvent vu*) although the adverb *hier* cannot be inserted at this point nor a complement like *avec mes lunettes*. A complex such as *je le donne* is easily analysed into successive signs, but it comprises variants of the monemes of the first and third person /ž/ and /l/, which for the corresponding significata appear only in contexts of this type (elsewhere /mua/, /lüi/). The component elements are certainly not inseparable since we find *je te le donne, je le lui donne*, but the choice of these inserted elements is very limited, and some linguists have been inclined to regard *je te le donne* as a single word /ž-t-l-dòn/ on a par with the Basque *da-kar-t* 'I carry it.' What, however, is important to stress in this connexion is that the Latin form *homini* and its modern equivalents *for the man, pour l'homme, para el hombre*, are all autonomous syntagms, and this is more important than the diagnosis of the former as a 'word'. This word status is merely the culmination of a gradual anchylosis, which makes a formal analysis hazardous and problematical, although it does not rule out an analysis into distinct significata, that is it does not absolve the speaker from the necessity to choose between several possible functions for the moneme 'man'. In order to understand the foundations of linguistic structure, attention should be concentrated on the autonomous syntagm rather than on the particular type of autonomous syntagm characterized by the inseparability of its elements and classed under the rubric 'word' with the monemes which do not enter into such syntagms.

4.18 Dependent, governed and determinant monemes

Monemes which do not contain an indication of their function (as autonomous monemes do) may be called dependent monemes. In autonomous syntagms such as *avec toi* or *avec les grosses valises*, all the monemes except the functional *avec* are dependent in the sense that they depend for the indication of their relationship to the rest of the utterance either on a functional moneme or on their position relatively to the other elements of an utterance.

Among linguistic functions we must distinguish between *primary functions* corresponding to the constitutive relations of the sentence, e.g. those established between the five members of the utterance (1) *hier*, (2) *le directeur de la banque*, (3) *a dicté*, (4) *une lettre de quatre pages*, (5) *au secrétaire particulier qu'il avait fait venir*. The primary functions are those of elements that are directly connected with the utterance as a whole, not with a particular segment of that utterance. In the preceding illustration the function of *la banque* and that of *quatre pages* marked by the functional *de*, that of *particulier* denoted by its meaning and position, that of *qu'il a fait venir* indicated by *que*, the amalgam of a pronoun and a functional moneme, are non-primary functions.

Among dependent monemes there are some which have a primary function. Such is the case with *toi* and /valiz/ *valises* in *avec toi*, and *avec les grosses valises*; both have the function denoted by *avec*. They may be called governed monemes. Others have no relationship with the rest of the utterance except via those already discussed. Such is the case with the monemes 'definite' (/l/), 'plural' (/e/) and /grós/ in *avec grosses valises*. These may be called determinants.

4.19 Lexemes and morphemes; modifiers

A further distinction will be made between grammatical monemes (morphemes) and lexical monemes (lexemes). To make the distinction inventories are drawn up of units capable of appearing at a given point in the framework of the autonomous syntagm. Lexical monemes are those which belong to unlimited inventories. Grammatical monemes are those which alternate in the said positions with a comparatively small number of other monemes. The average frequency of grammatical monemes such as French *de, pour, avec* or Latin 'genitive' 'dative', 'ablative' is far superior to that of lexical monemes like *homme, riche, mange.* If we take any text and count all the prepositions and all the substantives encountered therein and we divide the numbers for each category by the number of distinct prepositions for the one set and by the number of different substantives for the other, the quotient will be much higher for the prepositions than for the substantives.

Functional monemes are grammatical monemes. Dependent monemes may be either grammatical or not. Of these the governed monemes may belong to different inventories. Some are unlimited, such as could be drawn up for the context *avec un(e)*. . . . Others are limited, such as that which includes the monemes which may appear immediately after *avec* but never after *avec* plus one or more determinants. We shall say that *valise*, which belongs to the former, is a lexical moneme and that *toi*, which belongs to the second, is grammatical. Determinants, too, may be either lexical (*grosse*) or grammatical ('definite', 'plural'). Grammatical determinants will hereafter be called modifiers.

4.20 Modifiers and functional monemes

Modifiers like the articles and monemes of number in French have long been more or less confused with functional monemes. But the difference between the two types is fundamental. If, in the autonomous syntagm *avec le sourire*, the governed moneme *sourire* is regarded as the centre of the syntagm, the grammatical determinant *le* is a centripetal element, the functional moneme *avec* is a centrifugal element, this corresponding to the schema $\leftarrow avec\ le \rightarrow sourire$. In a language like French, where the amalgamation of the two types is exceptional (*au, du*), we observe that whereas the presence of an indicator of function like *avec* confers syntactic autonomy on the complex *avec mes valises*, the use of the modifier *le* in *le chasseur tue la bête* does not give any autonomy to *chasseur*, which always owes to its position in the sentence its identification as the subject. In general terms, the possibility of the use of this or that functional moneme is determined by elements external to the autonomous syntagm of which it forms a part. One type of proposition may comprise a complement in the dative, but another may not. Doubtless a speaker may often have some freedom to use or not to use a certain autonomous syntagm which is legitimate in the scheme of the utterance he has chosen. Thus after *distribuer* one may always indicate a beneficiary but equally well refrain from doing so. We may say *il distribue des prospectus aux passants* or *il distribue des prospectus*. This is still clearer in the case of autonomous syntagms introduced by *avec*. But it is still true to say that the necessities of communication influence the choice of the functional moneme in so far as the initial choice of a particular scheme for the utterance constitutes a bias in favour of one rather than another.

The case is quite different with modifiers, since here the choice of a particular one at a point of the chain is directly a function of the needs of communication or, more precisely, of the experience to be communicated. In this respect modifiers do not differ from other non-functional monemes. I choose between *le cerf* or *un cerf* in order to say what I want to, just as I choose between *cerf* and *biche*. The difference is that in the case of the modifiers my choice is narrowly limited: it is either 'definite' or 'indefinite' whereas the number of animals among which I may choose to complete an utterance such as *le chasseur tue* ... is practically unlimited. It will be noted that if one modifier is replaced by another, a singular by a plural, a definite article by an indefinite, the general scheme of the utterance is not changed. This is, of course, bound up with the fact that in a Latin or French sentence every substantive may, at the discretion of the speaker, be either singular or plural. On the other hand a sentence of a certain type in Latin implies one functional moneme of the dative and only one, even if it is expressed twice by means of two co-ordinated words: *urbi et orbi*.

112

4.21 A confusion caused by amalgamation and concord

A number of facts conspire to obscure the fundamental difference between functional monemes and modifiers. In the first place, when they are adjacent in the autonomous syntagm, they will tend in the course of time to overlap and to amalgamate their significantia. Further, both may participate in phenomena of concord: the discontinuous significantia which are the result of this exist both for functional monemes and for modifiers. This may be corroborated in a language like Latin where their significantia are largely amalgamated. In *prudentibus hominibus* the functional 'dative' and the modifier 'plural' have a single significans which here exhibits the discontinuous variant ...*ibus* ...*ibus*. In *pueri ludunt* the functional moneme 'nominative' is represented only in the significans -*i*, but the modifier 'plural' is signified successively in -*i* and in -*nt*. In French, where we have seen (4.5) that the modifier 'plural' is signified three times in succession in *les animaux paissent*, the functional monemes are for the most part separable, that is their significans is not indissolubly linked with another, as -*ibus* is to *prudent-* and to *homin-* in *prudentibus hominibus*. There are however discontinuous significantia in *à mon père et à ma mère* as contrasted with the English *to my father and mother* and the French syntagm *avec mon père et ma mère*, where the functional moneme *avec*, of greater phonic 'weight' than *à*, is not repeated.

The preceding examples might convey the impression that, whereas in the case of modifiers the field of concord is a wide one, it can be established, in so far as functional monemes are concerned, only within an autonomous syntagm. The only items marked as datives would be what are commonly called attributive complements and the adjectives which qualify them. But that would be to limit unduly the range of linguistic possibilities. In Basque *gizonari eman-diot*, 'I have given it to the man', the functional moneme 'dative' is marked not only by the -*i* of the attributive complement *gizonari*, but also in the verb by the -*io*- of *eman-diot* which combines the expression of the 'dative' with that of 'third person singular'.

4.22 Examples of entanglement

Concord is often conceived as a means, a somewhat uneconomical means, of marking the relationships in the utterance. The agreement of the verb with the subject 'serves' to indicate which two words of the utterance are in the relation of subject and predicate. In many cases of concord of this type the function of the two elements in question is clearly indicated without the help of concord. In *pater pueros amat* it is not the agreement of the verb as regards the singular 'number' which enables us to identify *pater* as the subject. However, there are cases where, either by chance or otherwise, concord serves to indicate the function of certain elements. In Latin *venatores animal occidunt* neither *venatores* nor *animal* has a formal feature which indicates which is subject and which is object. However, *occidunt*, which agrees in number with *venatores*, shows that the latter is the subject and, hence, that animal is the object. The concord would of course be superfluous if the subject were *viri*; it would be of no avail if the object were also in the plural (e.g. *venatores animalia occidunt*). But in the context here considered we might suppose that it is the significans of the modifier 'plural' which serves to indicate the function 'subject' of *venator* and that the distinction between functional moneme and modifier is blurred here. It should be realized in fact that the significans of 'nominative', when combined with a radical of the third declension and the moneme of the 'plural', is manifested in the shape of a discontinuous amalgam /... -es ... nt/ whereas the accusative in the same instance simply has the form /... es/; the segment /... nt/, which is a part of the discontinuous significans of the 'plural' alone when the subject has a non-ambiguous form like *viri*, here forms part of the significans of the 'nominative', a functional moneme. It is evidently the often inextricable entanglement of their significantia in certain languages which has obscured and delayed the recognition of the fundamental distinction between the functional moneme and modifiers.

4.23 The question of 'gender'

The phenomena of concord may extend to other monemes than modifiers and the indicators of function since, in languages like French, we have concord of gender; this is simply the name given to the discontinuous significans of a moneme corresponding to what is called a substantive. Since the elements of this significans, when detached from their central nucleus (/. . . a . . . d . . . š/ detached from /mõtañ/ in *la grande montagne blanche*), exhibit a formal behaviour which recalls that of modifiers, we may be tempted to posit for French a 'feminine' modifier which is opposed to a corresponding 'masculine'. The fact that the difference between *grande* and *grand* may function by itself (*la cour des grands, la cour des grandes*) might appear to justify such a step until it is remembered that the choice between *grands* and *grandes* is normally dictated, not by the sex of the persons in question, but by the genders of the words *garçons* and *filles* which are here represented by the two adjectives: in other words the choice is dictated by an aspect of the meaning of *garçon* and an aspect of the meaning of *fille*. The use of *grande* instead of *grand* does not imply a choice distinct from that of *fille* (which here is latent) instead of *garçon*. It should be noted, however, that the use of the pronoun *elle* is sometimes determined not by the gender of the word but by the sex of the person in question: *le docteur . . . elle. . . .*

4.24 The predicative syntagm

We now return to the message which served as our starting point above: *Hier, il y avait fête au village.* This French utterance comprises an autonomous moneme *hier* and an autonomous syntagm *au village*. The autonomy of these two segments is secured by the meaning of the moneme in one case and by the use of a functional moneme in the other. Both may be eliminated without the utterance ceasing to be a normal sentence: *il y avait fête*; *hier* and *au village* simply complete this utterance, and this is what is meant by the traditional terminology which speaks of them as 'complements'. Since the segment '*il y avait fête*' can constitute the message by itself, it is not called upon to indicate its relations with possible additions, and the complements are identified as such precisely because they correspond to elements of experience whose relationships to the total experience the speaker deems it necessary to mark, such a relationship corresponding, on the linguistic plane, to function. The syntagm *il y avait*, from this point of view, is not autonomous but independent. We shall call it a *predicative syntagm*.

4.25 Actualization

Above we envisaged the possibility of expressing by means of a single moneme the idea of 'festival' and the effective existence of a festival. This is not possible in French where the two ideas must be conveyed by distinct expressions. In many languages the fact that a moneme is employed in a well defined situation by a given speaker under such and such circumstances does not suffice to pick out which of the semantic possibilities offered by a word is meant in the circumstances, in other words to make the utterance into one which is linguistically adequate. Thus *fête* is not by itself a linguistic message; for it to become one it must be anchored in reality by indicating its effective existence (*il y avait fête*), its possible existence (*il y aurait fête*) or its non-existence (*il n'y a pas fête*). It is necessary to actualize the moneme. For this a context is required, that is at least two monemes one of which is more specifically the bearer of the message while the other may be regarded as the actualizer. French is a language of this type. In French the situation alone rarely suffices to actualize a single moneme: examples are orders, insults and greetings: *va! cours! vole! vite! ici! traître! salut!* In replies such as *oui, non Jean, demain*, the foregoing question provides the necessary context for actualization. In other examples utterances consisting of a single moneme are abbreviated forms of larger utterances of identical meaning: *défendu!* for *c'est défendu*. These are mutilated utterances which the speaker can always reconstitute if it proves necessary, rather like the

German who says [naˑmt] for *Guten Abend* but can furnish the complete form [guˑtn ʔaˑbnt] if invited to repeat it.

4.26 The subject

Where actualization is obligatory, it may be achieved by the creation of any given context. To attain this end it may suffice to add a grammatical moneme to the central moneme of the utterance. Thus in French the moneme *tue* /tü/ can be actualized by the addition of the morphemes *je* /ž/ or *on* /ő/. A lexeme, of course, whether accompanied or not by determinants may also serve as the actualizing context: *l'alcool tue* /lalkòl tü/. This means that the minimal utterance must consist of two terms, one of which normally designates a state of affairs or an event to which attention is drawn, this being called the *predicate* while the other, called the *subject*, refers to a participant, whose role, whether active or passive, is in principle emphasized by its choice as the subject. The subject may be a morpheme in *il marche* /il marš/ or it may comprise a lexeme in *l'homme marche* /lòm marš/, or again combine lexeme and morpheme as in popular French *l'homme il marche* or Latin *vir ambulat*. Semantically, the subject may designate the sufferer or the beneficiary of the action as well as the agent: *he* designates the sufferer in *he suffered, he was killed* and the beneficiary in *he was given a book*. According to the language concerned, the subject may or may not form an autonomous syntagm: in Latin the subject is either a modifier of the predicate, e.g. *occidunt*, or an autonomous syntagm (accompanied by a modifier of the verb) in *viri occidunt*, *viri* comprising an indicator of function. In French the subject is not autonomous, the function being marked by the position with respect to the predicate.

Formally, therefore, the subject is always characterized, either by a functional moneme or by the position. But what enables us to identify it as such and to distinguish it from complements is its obligatory presence in a certain type of utterance. In *les chiens mangent la soupe* or *ils mangent la soupe*, it is not possible to suppress *les chiens* or *ils* any more than the predicative nucleus *mangent*; *la soupe*, on the other hand, may be eliminated without mutilating the utterance or modifying the economy of what remains. It is thus with good reason that such a segment in the traditional terminology is called a 'complement'. Of the two obligatory elements, subject and predicate, that moneme will be the subject which is most likely also to appear among the complements: *les Chinois mangent les chiens* where *chiens*, our former subject, has the function of a complement.

4.27 Nominal predicates in languages which express the subject

In a language like French, where the combination subject-predicate is obligatory apart from the few cases where the situation suffices for actualization, certain regular constructions have been practically reduced to the function of actualizers of the real predicate. Such is the case with *il y a*, in which there seems to be a subject *il* and a predicative moneme *a*. This analysis is synchronically correct in *il y a son argent*, 'he has his money there', where the pronunciation in the most colloquial form of speech is always /il i (j)a/. But in *il y a des gens sur la place*, *il y a* merely introduces the real predicate *gens* and here it is pronounced normally /ja/. In the same way *voici*, *voilà* (from *vois ci*, *vois là*) are no more than actualizers of a following predicate.

4.28 Languages without a subject

Although the type of organization subject-predicate is quite common, it would be wrong to believe that it is universal. There are languages in which a perfectly normal utterance, neither imperative nor elliptical, may comprise a single moneme which could be translated 'rain' instead of 'it is raining', 'fox' instead of 'there is a fox', and so on. Moreover, such utterances figure not only in marginal cases like commands and elliptical expressions but also in properly enunciated messages. Since, of course, an utterance consisting of a single moneme exhibits the same intonational curve as larger utterances of the same type (affirmative, interrogatory, etc.), it would be tempting to speak in such a case of an actualizing moneme with an intonational significans. But in the interest of clear exposition we should perhaps speak of actualization only in the case where the moneme in question is a unit of the first articulation, that is a segmental moneme.

4.29 The predicative moneme and the 'voices'

The predicate comprises a predicative moneme, accompanied or not by modifiers. The predicative moneme is the element around which the sentence is organized, the other constituent elements marking their function by reference to it. It should be noted however that in certain languages, notably in French, speakers are free to orientate the predicate with respect to the participants in the action. To take the example of the action of 'opening', with a 'patient', the garden gate, and an agent, the gardener, if we use the form of the predicate called the 'active voice', we shall say *le jardinier ouvre le portail du jardin*; if, however, the 'passive voice' is used, the utterance will assume the form *le portail du jardin est ouvert par le jardinier*. In the first case the predicate (*ouvre*), is orientated with respect to the gardener; in the second case the predicate (*est ouvert*) is orientated with respect to the gate. In a language like Malagasy it is also possible to orientate the predicate with respect to what in French would be a circumstantial complement. On the other hand, other languages, like Basque, lack this possibility of orientating the predicate; once the action, the participants and the circumstances are known, the structure of the utterance is totally determined.

(iii) EXPANSION

4.30 Expansion: everything which is not indispensable

Expansion is the name given to every element added to an utterance which does not modify the mutual relationships and the function of the pre-existing elements. If the utterance consists of an isolated predicative moneme, every addition of other monemes which does not modify the predicative character of the original moneme represents an expansion of the primary predication. These monemes may be of widely different types. If we start with the French utterance *va!* expansion will yield *va vite!* with an autonomous moneme, *va le chercher* with a governed moneme (*le*) and a governed lexeme accompanied by a modifier (*cherch-er*), *va chez la voisine!* with an autonomous syntagm, *va le chercher chez la voisine*, with these three elements combined. In a certain sense, then, it is true to say that everything in an utterance can be considered as an expansion of the predicative moneme, apart from the elements indispensable for its actualization, such as the subject where it exists. In *les chiens mangent la soupe*, *la soupe* is an expansion of the predicate, but *les chiens* is not. But expansion is not limited to elements which may at will be joined to the predicative moneme. It comprises additions not only to the central nucleus of the utterance but to any of the types of segment examined hitherto. Its importance in the constitution of messages should thus be clear.

4.31 Coordination

We first distinguish between two types of expansion: expansion by coordination and expansion by subordination. There is said to be expansion by coordination when the function of the added element is identical with that of an element already present in the same framework, such that the structure of the original utterance would remain unchanged if the pre-existing element were suppressed (together with the mark of coordination where this is present) and the added element left in its stead. An example will make this clear: in the utterance *il vend des meubles* there will be expansion by coordination if we add after *vend* the word *achète* preceded by a particular moneme (*et*) which marks a certain type of coordination. This will result in the utterance *il vend et achète des meubles*, where *achète* has exactly the same role as *vend*, viz. predicative, and is in the same framework, i.e. in the same relationships with the other elements of the utterance. If we now suppress the original predicate *vend* (and the mark of the coordination *et*), we get *il achète des meubles*, which has a different sense but the same structure as the original utterance.

Expansion by coordination may affect any of the units examined hitherto: an autonomous moneme in *aujourd'hui et demain*, a functional moneme in *avec et sans ses valises*, a modifier in *with his and her bags*, a lexeme in *rouge et noir*, *homme et femme*, a predicative syntagm in *il dessine et il peint avec talent*. It will be noted that elements may be coordinated which are mutually exclusive as autonomous elements in one and the same utterance; e.g. *aujourd'hui* and *demain*, in *le beau temps se maintiendra aujourd'hui et demain*.

4.32 Subordination

Expansion by *subordination* is characterized by the fact that the function of the added element is not to be found in a pre-existent element in the same framework. This function is indicated either by the position of the new element with respect to the unit alongside which this element fulfils the function, or by a functional moneme. The expansion represented by *la soupe* in *les chiens mangent la soupe* has its function indicated by the position after the predicative nucleus formed by the predicative moneme accompanied by its modifiers. The expansion of the type *de la route*, in *poussière de la route*, has its function marked by the functional moneme *de*. This expansion shows that it is possible to complete non-predicative elements of the utterance in the same way that the predicate is completed, although different linguistic means may be used. In French the function of direct object is distinct from that of 'complement of the noun' in that the one is marked by position and the other by the functional moneme *de*. However, nothing prevents the function from being the same in both cases, for instance in a language where the complete utterance used above would have a form like *il y a manger de la soupe par les chiens*, where *la soupe* would stand linguistically in the same relation to *manger* as *la route* does to *poussière*.

The subordinated element may characterize (or in traditional terms 'depend on') almost any element of the first articulation, a simple moneme or a syntagm, including modifiers (*plus grand*>*bien plus grand*) and even indicators of function (*sans argent*> *absolument sans argent*, where however it can be argued that *absolument* bears upon the whole following syntagm). It is found giving precision to the value of an autonomous moneme (*vite*>*très vite*) or of a governed lexeme (*la robe*>*la robe rouge, la robe de bal, la robe qui est rouge, le pinceau de l'artiste*). This element may also itself be an expansion by subordination to another lexeme (*il va vite*>*il va très vite, la belle robe*>*la très belle robe*). The subordinate element may characterize a predicative moneme: *il dit* >*il le lui dit, il dit un mot, il dit qu'il viendra; il part* >*il part demain, il part quand elle arrive.*

The subordinate element may take the form of a single moneme, either autonomous (*il court*>*il court vite*) or non-autonomous (*grand*>*très grand*). This moneme may be lexical (*la robe*>*la belle robe*) or grammatical (*grand*>*plus grand*). It may be also a syntagm of predicative form, normally made autonomous by the addition of a functional moneme, called a 'subordinating conjunction', but it can also be indicated as an expansion simply by the position it occupies in the utterance: *il part*>*il part quand elle arrive, la robe*>*la robe qu'elle porte* and, without a functional moneme, *the face was black*>*the face he saw was black.*

4.33 The sentence

The subordinate elements of predicative form (the nucleus of 'subordinate clauses') cannot be considered real predicates since they lack the character of non-marginality and independence which we have considered as the characteristic feature of the predicate. This allows us to define the sentence as an utterance, all the elements of which are attached to a single predicate or to several coordinated predicates, and in this way we can dispense with the criterion of intonation in the definition, which is a real gain in view of the marginally linguistic nature of this phenomenon.

(iv) COMPOSITION AND DERIVATION

4.34 Composition and derivation are not expansion

The procedures which go under the names of 'composition' and 'derivation' may, in certain cases, be considered as particular forms of expansion. But often they result in syntagms which cannot be described as the result of the addition to an utterance of an element 'which does not modify the mutual relations and the functions of pre-existing elements'. If we replace *route* by *autoroute* in *il est venu par la route*, this abides by the conditions characteristic of expansion, since the addition of a supplementary specification did not change the order of the utterance nor the nature of the mutual relations of its elements (the change of /la/ of *la route* to /l/ in *l'autoroute* does not change the identity of the moneme). The same is true if I replace *maison* by *maisonnette* in *il a pénétré dans la maison*. In both examples the subtraction of the added monemes *auto-, -ette* will cause no difficulty. The situation is quite different if I attempt to suppress a moneme of the compound *vide-poche* or the derivative *lavage* in the utterance *je l'ai mis dans le vide-poche* or *elle procède au lavage*. In *vide-poche* and *lavage*, from *vide* and *poche* and *lav-* /lav-/ and *-age* /až/ there certainly is no expansion, i.e., syntagmatic addition to an existing utterance, but the paradigmatic creation, out of context, of a new unit. In reality the use of compounds like *autoroute* or derivatives like *maisonnette* does not fall under the heading of expansion, for as a rule we choose between *route* and *autoroute* just as we choose between *route* and *chemin*, between *maisonnette* and *maison* just as between *maison* and *villa*. But there is a difference between the last mentioned cases and *vide-poche* and *lavage*, for there is nothing against their genesis in the form of expansions, *autoroute* being first thought of as *route*, but a *route* of a particular kind which is denoted by the addition of *auto-*. There are certain cases where *petite maison* represents a choice as unique as *maisonnette*, and here the interpretation of *petite* as an expansion of *maison* is inescapable. Thus there are instances of composition and derivation which undeniably may go back to cases of expansion; but this eventuality is excluded as formally impossible in other cases. For the former type we could speak of endocentric composition and derivation, which would serve as a reminder that the mutual action of the elements concerned does not affect the relations of the whole compound or derivative to what is external to it. Replacing the segment *maison* by *maisonnette* results in a change of the segment itself but not in the relations to what lies outside this segment. For syntagms of the type *vide-poche, lavage* we shall speak of exocentric composition and derivation. The joining together of these two elements serves to create new relations with what is external to the compound or derivative.

4.35 Common features of composition and derivation

What is common to all compounds and all derivatives is in the first place the semantic unity of the syntagm, which is indicated by the fact that each normally corresponds to a single choice. But this feature is too difficult to establish, even by introspection, for it to serve to identify these syntagms and to oppose them to looser syntagms. The sole characteristic we should pick on is that they behave in their relations with the rest of the utterance exactly as single monemes appearing in the same context as they, which implies, for instance, that they can be accompanied by the same modifiers and that these modifiers could never affect only one element of the compositional or the derivational syntagm. A *chaise-longue* of unusual dimensions is not a *chaise-plus-longue* but a longer *chaise-longue* (French *chaise-longue plus longue*) than others of the kind.

We should also expect the monemes brought together by composition and derivation to be formally indissociable and that they should not be in the mutual relationship examined above under the name 'concord'. This would in fact tend to introduce between them a fragment of a discontinuous significans, as happens between *petite* and *église* when we pass from the singular *la petite église* /laptit-egliz/ to the plural /leptit-z-egliz/. But we saw above when discussing the concept of the 'word' how unreliable such a criterion is. We should hardly hesitate to say that *bonhomme* is a compound. It is clear that we could not, for instance, combine the first of its components with a modifier of the comparative and say *un moins bonhomme* or *un meilleur homme* without destroying *bonhomme*. This does not prevent these two components from being dissociated in the plural: *bonshommes* /bõ-z-òm/. The substandard plural *bonhommes* /bònòm/ underlines both the anomaly of this internal concord and its perfectly natural character with a wide range of speakers.

It will thus not always be easy to distinguish between compounds and derivatives on the one hand and looser syntagms on the other. From a diachronic point of view, composition and derivation may at times appear as intermediate stages between the juxtaposition of monemes brought into contact by the needs of communication, and amalgamation in a single moneme. The compound Latin *collocare* is the half-way stage between *con locare* and French *coucher*.

4.36 Differences between composition and derivation

The difference between composition and derivation may be summed up thus: the monemes which form a compound exist elsewhere than in compounds; whereas one of those which form a derivative exists solely in derivatives, this being what in traditional terminology is called an affix. The passage of a moneme from the status of an element of a compound to that of an affix is completed once this moneme ceases to be employed otherwise than in composition. This appears to be a contradiction in terms, but it is a good illustration of the close affinity of the two procedures. Today the moneme *-hood* of *boyhood* and the moneme *-heit* of the German *Freiheit* are affixes because they do not occur outside indissociable syntagms like *boyhood* and *Freiheit*. But they remained elements of compounds as long as the Old English *hád* and Old High German *heit* occurred in contexts analogous to those in which *boyhood* and *Freiheit* were encountered.

The preceding discussion does not account for the case where two associated monemes do not exist outside combinations of this type. This applies specially to so-called 'learned' elements which originally formed part of words borrowed from a 'classical' language and are recognized as forming significant units only by those who originally introduced them. However, when words of this type become common and numerous, the sense of their components may be recognized. All users of the language know that *thermostat* is formed of two elements *thermo* and *stat* which are represented in many other combinations of the same kind, their meaning being sufficiently clear for a speaker, without being an expert, to venture to coin other words in *thermo-* and *-stat*. The fairly high semantic specificity of the two elements, sometimes supported by a knowledge of etymology, may lead to the interpretation of such syntagms as compounds. But an element like *tele-*, which has been especially favoured by the discoveries of the last few centuries and which today combines freely with monemes and syntagms that exist outside the combinations in question (cf. *television* and *vision*, *telecast* and *cast*), behaves in fact like an affix. Here we have a special linguistic situation which is identifiable neither with composition in the real sense nor in a general way with derivation, which implies the combination of elements of different status. Perhaps in the case where a new syntagm is formed we might speak of 'recomposition' from elements which are extracted by analysis.

4.37 The criterion of productivity

In synchronic linguistics there is some advantage in speaking of composition and derivation only in the case of productive processes. It is of course sometimes difficult to make a pronouncement on the productivity of this or that suffix. Should we be justified in deciding that *-ceté* is a suffix if a child on the model of *méchanceté* coins *cochonceté* from *cochon*? Do we still hear words being coined by means of the suffix *-aison*? What must at all events be avoided is to carry analysis beyond the limits set by the meaning: it would be absurd to regard *avalanche* as a derivative of *avaler* since only the etymologists can now see any semantic connection between the two words. It would be wrong to set up a moneme *-cevoir* extracted from *recevoir, percevoir, décevoir* since the average speaker is never influenced by the feeling that there is anything more than a formal resemblance between these words, and it requires a significans and a significatum to make a moneme.

It sometimes happens that of two elements of a compound, one loses its autonomy and survives in the language only in this one compound. Such is the case, for instance, of *cran-* in *cranberry*. Here we should not be justified in speaking of an affix, since an affix is an instrument of derivation and derivation is a process that is productive of new syntagms.

4.38 The affix: modifier or lexeme?

Hesitation might be felt about classing affixes among lexemes on the grounds that no articles are devoted to them in the dictionaries. But this would be to attribute too much importance to a tradition which is not everywhere respected, and it would be better to examine the linguistic realities which in the last resort determine the practice of the lexicographers. The question to be decided is in fact whether affixes should or should not be classed as modifiers. The criterion used above (4.19) to distinguish between lexemes and morphemes was the limited character of the inventory in the case of the latter, and it will be of interest to see whether it applies here. The point at issue is not whether we can enumerate exactly the monemes capable of appearing in a given context, but rather to see either if the moneme belongs to an open series, which may at the moment comprise only a limited number of units but may be increased at any moment, or whether it belongs to a closed series such that the number of elements which it comprises cannot vary without entailing a structural reorganization. There would be little point in making a count to establish how many suffixes French possesses of the type -*age* or -*is* (in *cordage*, *lattis*) capable of forming substantives from other substantives, because they form a system so loose that another suffix of the same type could appear at any moment which would not affect their value and use. It is quite different with a system such as that of number or articles in French, where two opposed units cover the whole field in such a way that where the question arises we must necessarily choose between singular and plural, definite and indefinite. In a case of this kind every new unit must carve out for itself some territory at the expense of the traditional units. This implies that, given the conditions which determine the use of a certain type of modifiers, the speaker must necessarily choose from among a limited number of monemes. In French we can speak of a *coin de rue* with no article before *rue*. But if in the message we wish to emphasize the notion of *rue*, we are bound to use *la rue* or *une rue*. There would thus seem to be some advantage in regarding affixes as a special type of lexemes.

4.39 The affix may govern the choice of modifiers

The admittedly vague criterion of the non-limitation of inventories is the only one which applies to derivation as a whole. We might be tempted to say that an affix is identified as that which forms with a non-derivative lexeme a syntagm capable of functioning exactly like a simple lexeme and combining with the same modifiers: *maisonnette* functions exactly like *maison* and is combined with the same modifiers. But we could conceive of a language in which the substantive accompanied by an article would behave in all respects like the same substantive without an article, and yet we should not be inclined to regard the syntagm article plus substantive as a derivative with the the article as an affix, because the fact that the article belongs to a limited inventory gives it a general and abstract character which is, at bottom, the striking characteristic of modifiers.

However, there are cases where examination of the possibilities of combination enables us to draw a clear distinction between affixes and modifiers. If we consider *tisse* /tis/ and *tissage* /tis+až/, we see that the first combines with a whole series of modifiers, personal, temporal and so on, in other words, those which may be called 'verbal', whereas the second is not compatible with any of them, admitting only modifiers of a quite different type, such as the article, possession, number. As we shall see, it is the permissible combinations within autonomous syntagms which enable us to determine the identity of lexemes (simple or complex). This means that the identity of *tisse* and that of *tissage* are as different as it is possible for them to be, and the moneme *-age* which has the power of transforming a 'verb' into a 'noun', is quite different from a modifier, the presence of which can only confirm the verbal or nominal character of the lexeme; it cannot change its character. Semantically, this can be summed up by saying that affixes have a more central character, less marginal than the modifiers, and this carries the corollary, on the formal plane, that in the group formed by lexeme, affixes and modifiers, the affixes are generally more central, i.e., in contact with the lexeme, and the modifiers more peripheral, i.e., separated from the lexemes by the affixes. To sum up, we may say that the difficulty experienced in general linguistics in distinguishing between affixes and modifiers results from the fact that lexemes and morphemes represent two poles which do not exclude the existence of intermediate elements of a greater specificity than modifiers or functional monemes but less than that of the average lexeme.

(v) THE CLASSIFICATION OF MONEMES

4.40 Compounds and derivatives treated as monemes

At the outset it should be emphasized that what will be said hereafter about the classification of monemes applies equally well to combinations of monemes which are in the same relationships as the simple monemes to the rest of the utterance. In other terms, compounds and derivatives will be taken into account: what is said of the autonomous moneme *vite* will hold good of the derivative *vivement*, and what is said of the simple lexeme *route* will be true of the compounds *autoroute*, *vide-poche* or *chemin de fer*. What prevents us here from speaking of 'words' is the fact that this term includes the combinations, not only of lexical elements in the proper sense and affixes, but also of these elements and the modifiers and functional monemes in the form of inflections. 'Word', then, may designate a syntagm which includes what we propose to treat as context even though the significantia in question may exhibit a high degree of entanglement. In traditional terminology, we shall operate in the case of lexemes with 'radicals' or 'stems'.

4.41 One and the same moneme in different classes

The hierarchy of monemes established above is founded on the degree of syntactic autonomy possessed by the significant segment, considered in a given context. A given segment in a given context is a moneme or an autonomous syntagm. In another context it can quite well be a moneme or a dependent syntagm. *Le dimanche* is autonomous in *les enfants s'ennuient le dimanche* but dependent in *le dimanche s'écoule tristement*. It is true that we have been induced to state that French *pour* is a functional moneme, i.e., to posit that such is its function in all the contexts in which it appears. But what is probably true of this French unit is not necessarily true of its equivalents elsewhere. In many languages the moneme which indicates the beneficiary of the action is the same as that which in a different environment may have a predicative function and corresponds to the verb *give*. What in fact characterizes each language is the way in which the classes of monemes capable of assuming the same functions are established.

4.42 Overlapping, transference, difficult cases

These classes are rarely exactly delimited. In languages where the equivalent of *give* serves both as an indicator of function ('to', 'for') and as a predicate, a large number of monemes are usually employed as indicators of function without ever being used as predicates, and vice versa. French has a class of 'adjectives' characterized by uses which are quasi-predicative (when accompanied by a 'copula' or a verb expressing a state); but this class is also used as lexical determinants ('attributes'). The monemes of this class may be employed as 'governed' monemes with all the functions of the class of 'substantives'. There is thus overlapping. Further, we must distinguish here the uses resulting from ellipse still felt as such (e.g. *la cour des grands* (*garçons*), where the missing element may be restored without hesitation, from the cases where there is really transference from one category to another (*les grands de ce monde, un grand d'Espagne*). It is not always easy to draw a clear distinction between the two following linguistic situations. On the one hand, a verb and a substantive may have the same root without our being able to say that it is the contexts alone, where they appear, which are responsible for the semantic difference. In English, *fish* is pronounced alike in *a fish* and *to fish*. The meanings evidently have some affinity, but it is clear that if *fish* represented in both cases the same unit, *I fish* would mean '*I am a fish*', or '*I behave like a fish*'. On the other hand, one and the same moneme may be employed either in a predicative function or as an expansion of the predicate. The semantic differences noted between the two uses result directly and synchronically from the influence of the different contexts and respective functions. This is the case in languages where, for instance, the leg is designated by means of a form which will be understood elsewhere as '*he walks*'. Another example is that of Kalipsel, an Amerindian language of the State of Washington, where a tree is designated as *es-šit*, which will be translated in a context where it has predicative function as '*he keeps erect*'. In these cases we have one and the same linguistic unit because in these languages, unlike what is the rule in French, a given linguistic element may, without changing its identity, function as a predicate or as an expansion of the predicate.

4.43 'Nouns' and 'verbs'

As regards lexemes, we first distinguish, if possible, between those capable of predicative use and the rest. This distinction does not necessarily coincide with the traditional distinction between nouns and verbs. In Latin *Paulus bonus* 'Paul is good' and Russian *dom nov* 'the house is new', *bonus* and *nov* are predicative without being verbs. Languages which lack this distinction, i.e., where all lexemes may be used as predicates, are by no means exceptions. This does not mean, of course, that in such languages we shall refrain from establishing different classes of lexemes founded on their possible modes of combinations with different morphemes. Thus certain units which may combine with the modifiers of time and aspect will be called 'verbs'. Others, which combine with the modifiers of number and possession will be called 'nouns'. But the use of these terms has the drawback that they evoke linguistic realities peculiar to the languages of the scholars who established the traditional grammatical terminology. It would be better to abandon in all cases the terms 'nouns' and 'verbs' when describing a language where all lexemes can be combined with the modifiers of person and mood, but only some, which we might be tempted to call 'verbs', admit the modifiers of aspect, that is those which present the object or the event in its duration, independent of its duration, or as a result of something else. In Kalipsel monemes like *tumʔ* 'mother' or *cítxᵘ* 'house' are combined with modifiers corresponding (1) to our personal pronouns (*čin-túmʔ* 'I [am] the mother'), (2) to our possessive adjectives (*an-cítxᵘ* 'it [is] your house'), (3) to our subjunctive (*q-cítxᵘ* 'let this be the house'). Other monemes like *moqᵘ* 'mountain' or *kup* 'push' are combined with the same modifiers but add others, notably those of aspect, e.g., the continuative aspect, whereby the thing or event is considered in its duration. This aspect is denoted by *es(ə)-* or *es-* . . . *-i* as in *esə-móqᵘ* '[it is] a mountain' and *es-kúp-i* 'he is pushing [something])'. It is clear that the lexemes of this language which combine with aspects, and those which do not, cannot be regarded as forming two diametrically opposed classes like our nouns and verbs. They are rather two subdivisions of one and the same class of units which are all capable of assuming predicative and non-predicative functions. It is natural enough that monemes which designate actions and those that designate objects should tend to combine with different modifiers. But the foregoing example shows that the sign designating the object 'mountain' may be 'inflected' like the sign denoting the action of pushing and not like that which designates another object, the house.

4.44 'Adjectives'

Monemes designating states or qualities are eminently suited for use as predicates. They may be of the type of the Russian *dom nov* 'the house is new', or of the type of the Latin *caelum albet* 'the sky is white' or again of the French type with the transference of the predicative function to a 'copula', *la maison est neuve*. But these monemes are frequently used also as attributes, i.e., as an expansion of non-predicative lexemes. In Russian an indicator of function is used in this instance (*dom nov-yi* . . . 'the new house'). This is combined formally with an indication of case, number and gender, which must have been the equivalent of a relative 'the house which [is] new'. This explains the existence in many languages of a particular class of 'adjectives', which from language to language are more or less clearly distinct from verbs and nouns.

4.45 'Adverbs'

What are traditionally called 'adverbs' comprise units belonging to quite different classes. Among them we find notably autonomous monemes like *hier* and *vite* and derived lexemes of similar behaviour like *vivement*, *doucement*. These are expansions of the predicate. When the predicate corresponds to an action, the adverb is naturally a complement of this action: *il allait tristement*. If it corresponds to a state, the adverb will be a determinant of this state, even if the predicate is no longer the moneme designating this state but a 'copula'; in *il est tristement célèbre, tristement* refers not to *est* but to *célèbre*. The division will be *il est . . . tristement célèbre* and not *il est tristement . . . célèbre.* This entails the transference of the adverb to adjectival constructions: *l'individu tristement célèbre*; but this does not imply, of course, a fusion of the two classes of determinants of the verb and determinants of the adjective. Thus *très* belongs solely to the second class and *beaucoup* solely to the first.

4.46 'Prepositions' and 'conjunctions'

What is called a 'preposition' belongs directly to the class of indicators of function, without however exhausting that class, since it includes with equal right monemes with a desinential (or inflectional) significans, conjunctions of subordination and even relative pronouns. Monemes usually termed coordinating conjunctions are not all of the same linguistic status: *car*, for instance, does not appear in all the contexts where we find *et* or *ou*. Monemes properly called 'coordinating' like the last two form a special class, which though certainly to be ranked with morphemes, cannot be identified either with modifiers or with indicators of function.

4.47 'Pronouns'

What pronouns have in common with lexemes is use in a primary function, that is as governed monemes. But their membership of limited inventories ranks them with morphemes. It frequently happens that one and the same pronoun assumes different guises in contexts where it alternates with lexemes ('substantives') and where it is closely integrated with a predicative syntagm. In French, for instance, *te* and *Jean* do not appear in the same context (*Je te vois, je vois Jean*) whereas *toi* and *Jean* may alternate (*je vais avec toi, je vais avec Jean*). In a case of this kind we might regard *te* and *toi* as variants of the significans of one and the same moneme; alternatively, we can identify *toi* as a governed moneme and *te* as a modifier of the predicate. In the same way the possessives *ton* and *tien* can be regarded as combinatory variants or the former as a modifier of a lexeme (*avec ton livre*), the latter as a governed moneme (*avec le tien*), itself accompanied by various modifiers ('definite', 'singular'). The fact that *I* or *you* refers, according to the circumstances, to different real persons, has not more linguistic significance than that *today* refers to different actual days according as it is used, say, on December 10th, 1958 or May 5th, 1959.

CHAPTER V

The Variety of Languages and Linguistic Usage

5.1 The heterogeneity of socio-linguistic structure

We have hitherto assumed that everybody belongs to one linguistic community and one only. We have mentioned in passing that not every member of such a community speaks in an identical fashion and that these divergences may at some point concern even the structure of the language. But we deliberately disregarded these differences so as not to complicate our exposition: the analysis of a supposedly uniform language is such a delicate task that one needs to simplify the data as much as possible. However, now that this analysis is accomplished we must necessarily introduce into our examination all the facts which we provisionally set aside.

5.2 The linguistic community and the body politic

We must first of all attempt to define the notion of a linguistic community, if such a thing is possible. Today the world is divided into political units, each of which, as a general rule, uses one special official language. There is a tendency therefore to believe that all the members of one and the same nation form a linguistic community which is homogeneous and closed. Many French people find it difficult to believe that citizens of the United States are English-speaking, and some of them are convinced that once their own northern frontier is passed, people speak 'Belgian'. The official languages are usually presented in a written form mostly fixed in every detail, which is the form with which the foreigner gets acquainted first. Within the frontier of his own country the citizen is generally very sensitive to the prestige of the written form. Because this written form, fixed in all details, is the same for everyone he readily believes that this applies to the official language itself. Linguists themselves have long concentrated their attention on the great literary languages, which they study *qua* 'philologists', i.e. students of literary texts. Only very recently have they come to realize the importance of the investigation of the illiterate idioms which coexist with the official languages. It took even longer for them to take note of the often considerable differences which exist between the official and literary languages, on the one hand, and the colloquial language even of those prestige figures whose behaviour generally appears most worthy of imitation.

The general use of the word 'language' in a restricted sense is founded on the same simple identification of the national body politic and the linguistic community. A form of speech deserves the title 'language' only in so far as it is the instrument of an organized state. Even educated people hesitate to regard Catalan as a language, in spite of the literature of which it can boast. Moreover, to talk of a Basque or a Breton language may lay oneself open to the charge of autonomist intrigue. This same restriction is mirrored in the use of the term 'bilingual'. In ordinary usage, to be bilingual means to be able to use with equal ease two *national* languages. Thus a peasant of the Basque country or of Finistère is not bilingual in this sense, although he rings the changes between French and his local form of speech according to his audience.

5.3 Mutual intelligibility as a criterion

The linguist, of course, cannot be satisfied with the use of terms founded on so summary a view of the facts. If we keep to the definition which we have given above of a language, we may say that a language exists if communications are established within the framework of a double articulation of a vocal type and that we have to do with one and the same language if communication is effectively assured. This covers the usual application of the term. French is, in fact, the instrument which is successfully used for mutual communication by a number of human beings. But we cannot deny the label 'language' to the local idiom of our Basque or Breton peasant, seeing that it is undeniably an instrument of communication for the rural populations of a certain region; further, it is an instrument different from French since it does not allow communication with an ordinary French speaker.

Unfortunately, the criterion of mutual intelligibility is not always decisive. There are, for instance, regions in which the population of each valley or each canton understands its immediate neighbours without difficulty. Consequently we shall say that they speak the same language even though, from district to district, we find differences affecting the vocabulary, the grammar or even the phonological system. However, if we confront the inhabitants of the opposite extremes of such a territory, it is quite possible that they will no longer understand one another. Generally speaking, there are all possible shades between full understanding and absolute incomprehensibility. On the other hand, communication may be easily established on certain topics, although this may be impossible with others. Thus a Frenchman, as a general rule, will understand the people of Quebec province in Canada; but if he cannot have recourse to English, he may at times find difficulty in communicating say, with the garage man, or with waitresses in restaurants. It frequently happens that there is initial failure to understand, but this is replaced by practical normal linguistic intercourse once the first unfamiliarity has been overcome and certain systematic correspondences have been recognized. Thus a Dane and a Norwegian, who recognized that one says /sk/ where the other says /š/ are already on the way to mutual understanding.

However, there are necessarily borderline cases; it may happen that the linguist allows extrinsic considerations to intervene and so will speak of languages instead of dialects if the two varieties in question become the official idioms of two separate political bodies. On the other hand, the linguist may find it advisable to group together and classify different linguistic varieties according to the nature of their employment or their geographical and social distribution, disregarding the degree of intelligibility between the people who speak the varieties in question. The dialects of one and the same language are regarded as forming one whole without this necessarily implying overall general intelligibility.

5.4 Bilingualism and 'diglossia'

The idea that bilingualism implies two languages of equal status is so widespread and so well established that linguists have proposed the term 'diglossia' to designate a situation where a community uses, according to circumstances, both a more colloquial idiom of less prestige and another of more learned and refined status. This implies that 'bilingualism' is found only with individuals, whereas 'diglossia' is a phenomenon of whole communities. However, there are so many possibilities of symbiosis between two idioms that we may prefer to retain the term bilingualism to cover them all, rather than to attempt a classification on the basis of a rudimentary dichotomy. French and English are two national languages of great prestige, but in Canada one cannot say that they are really on an equal footing. In these circumstances should we speak rather of 'diglossia' in Quebec province?

5.5 The complexity of linguistic situations

Before attempting to illustrate the variety of languages and linguistic usages it will be useful to recall a certain number of facts: (1) No linguistic community must be considered as composed of individuals all speaking a language which is in every way identical. (2) There are millions of human beings who belong to two or more linguistic communities, that is to say they use one or the other language according to the person addressed.

(3) It is not uncommon for a person who only speaks one language to understand several, both in the spoken and the written form. (4) The majority of people are capable of using very different forms of one and the same language according to the situation. (5) Those who do not actively make use of different forms of this type as a general rule understand them without difficulty, provided that they have occasion to hear them often enough.

5.6 Unnoticed differences

The linguistic ideal would doubtless be the situation in which speakers always used precisely the same phonic, morphological and lexical distinctions, in other words, if they all used the same linguistic structure. In reality absolute identity of systems seems to be the exception rather than the rule in intercourse between members of the same community. Of 66 Parisians between the ages of 20–60, mainly of middle-class background, assembled at random in 1941, no two were found to give identical replies to 50 questions designed to elicit the vowel system of each informant. What is remarkable, in this connection, is that the linguistic differences illustrated by these divergent answers do not affect intelligibility and are neither noticed nor pointed out. Each person believes that he talks like everybody else, since they all 'speak the same language'. This identity of language, which the needs of the community require us to postulate, imposes itself on the minds of the speakers, makes them deaf to differences and inclines them to regard as a personal idiosyncrasy any special linguistic feature, such as lisping or stuttering, which happens to attract the attention of the hearer.

This automatic tolerance is acquired at the same time as the speech habits themselves, that is to say in early infancy. The child who learns 'its' language does so by imitation of its environment. To the extent to which this environment is not wholly homogeneous linguistically, the child will have to choose, to syncretize, to compromise. He will finally acquire a system of distinctive oppositions which he himself will use actively; but no linguistic trait to which he was exposed during his apprenticeship will appear to him abnormal, whether or no it forms part of his personal system. Moreover, a trait may appear to him unpleasant, vulgar and gross or refined, sensitive and fascinating, according to the feelings he entertained for the persons of his environment who exhibited it. Thus a number of linguistic habits will appear to him, even if he does not himself use them, so normal and so usual that he will not feel them as differences. In other words, every person has his active linguistic norm, governing the use he makes of his language and also a passive norm which is much more lax and tolerant. The Frenchman who distinguishes front /a/ from back /â/ is conditioned to understand a form of French where *patte* and *pâte*, *tache* and *tâche* are pronounced identically and he does not even 'hear' when some of his fellow citizens pronounce *âge* or *sable* with a front *a*, where he would employ a back *a*. As for the person who does not distinguish at all between the two *a*'s, he will not pay any attention to the distinction made by his contemporaries, as long as their variations in producing the two phonemes do not go beyond the limits to which he is accustomed. As for vocabulary, the limit of tolerance is still wider. It is often, but not necessarily, more conscious: the same object may be called *pain* or *miche*; for mixing the salad I myself use the word *brasser* while others employ *remuer*; again, one person will speak of *citrouille* where another says *courge*. As far as grammatical 'facts' are concerned, the French norm has largely been standardized by hundreds of years of deliberate intervention. To this extent the state of affairs in French constitutes an exception rather than the rule. However, even in French there remains some latitude. It is still possible to say either *il s'assied* or *il s'assoit*, either *je puis* or *je peux*.

5.7 Social differences

It sometimes happens, that a whole complex of divergencies appears with especial frequency and great coherence among people who, like domestic servants, are part of the environment but have a special social status. A complex of the same type may be the property of nearly all persons but only become manifest under certain circumstances. In all these cases the child identifies these various linguistic traits not only with realities to which it feels they correspond, but also with the personality of those who exhibit them and with the circumstances where they are manifested. Adults are often astonished to hear young children use terms with an exact sense of their appropriateness, that is of the circumstances in which society expects them to be used. However, this is easily understandable if one considers the conditions under which children learn their language.

5.8 Complexity of a unilingual situation

The number of varieties of language which a child can be brought to identify depends on the community in which he lives and the social status which his family enjoys. Thirty years ago, a child belonging to the Parisian middle classes quickly learned to distinguish from the speech form which he himself employed in everyday life, a lower-class type of speech, remarkable especially for its syntax and prosody (the automatic accent on the penultimate syllable), a literary form characterized by facts of vocabulary and syntax plus some specific tenses like the 'passé simple', as well as a poetical form which adds to the traits of the literary language metrical exigencies and special phonological features (the mute *e* in the syllabic count). To this one might add the slang, often coarse, used in the school playgrounds but generally avoided at home. Other linguistic experiences, such as Latin in church and in school, or the various modern languages, do not concern us here since they did not represent a part of 'his' language for the child. This separation between 'mother tongue' and foreign languages is doubtless justified in the case which we have just examined; the different forms of French which we have enumerated have in common the essence of their phonological, morphological, syntactical and lexicological systems and are in their entirety opposed to what one may call 'Latin' or 'English'. But it is not always possible to draw such clear boundaries.

5.9 Patois

In large parts of the French countryside in the nineteenth century and in some rural communities today the child is exposed before its tenth year to linguistic forms so different in phonology, morphology, syntax and vocabulary as to suggest to the linguistic observer that two different languages exist concurrently rather than two varieties of the same language. In such a case the linguistic form which is learned first is normally that employed within the family circle and is called a patois. Along with the patois the child identifies and frequently uses a form of speech which one would not hesitate to recognize as French, even if it differs in a good many points from the kind of French spoken in Paris or the provincial towns. As soon as he goes to school, the child becomes familiar with the literary and poetical forms of the language, just like the young Parisian. It is of very little consequence whether the dialect is Romance, that is derived from Latin like French and consequently fairly close to it, or more remotely related, as is the case in the villages of Flanders or lower Brittany, or again, a language whose relationship to other families of languages is debatable, as in the Basque country. The distinctive traits of the patois situation are the following: on the one hand the two systems are sufficiently different for the speaker of a patois to regard his vernacular speech and the local form of the general language as two different categories. On the other hand, the local speech is considered as an imperfect linguistic form which stands to gain from any form of borrowing from the national language. From this it follows that the patois will survive only so long as there are people who in some situations find it easier to use than the national language. Thus the patois are, one might almost say by definition, doomed to disappear. They may disappear by a progressive fusion with the local form of the standard language: there are regions of France where the local speech is

143

more or less tinged with patois elements according to the circumstances and the persons addressed. A patois may also disappear simply by being abandoned, as when parents decide that they will no longer use patois when talking to their children. The patois situation may also be eliminated if the local speech or a neighbouring form acquires in the eyes of speakers a measure of prestige sufficient to reverse the current tendency to deprive it of its autonomy in favour of the general language. A Flemish dialect of northern France remains a patois so long as it is maintained only by the inertia of those who speak it. But it becomes a variety of Dutch in the eyes of those who deliberately regard it as such. This difference of esteem will rapidly bring about appreciable differences in the linguistic behaviour of speakers who will avoid certain words and forms and favour others.

5.10 Decline of the patois

The term 'patois' has no equivalents outside French, and this suggests that the situation which obtains in France has no exact parallel elsewhere. It is a country where the national language has for a long time enjoyed considerable prestige and has won widespread acceptance, so that the inhabitants of a given province living in villages some distance apart use it by preference for communication with one another rather than a local dialect which varies from canton to canton and even from parish to parish. Since a language is learned by practice, the national language, everyday French, becomes better and better known. On the other hand people lose the opportunity of comparing their vernaculars, and the differences between them to which they might have become accustomed and which might finally have been eliminated will become formidable obstacles to communication. This leads ultimately to restriction in the use of the patois to people from the same village or neighbouring localities. The patois speakers who also speak the national language with almost equal fluency become convinced that the patois has no practical value and even if they continue, out of inertia, to employ it with their contemporaries, they get into the habit of speaking French to their children and to all the young people of the village.

5.11 Dialects

In countries where the official language has acquired its status only in recent times and especially where there is a long-standing tradition of resistance to the central power, local speech continues to be used over fairly wide areas and often in all circumstances of life apart from communication with the national authorities. It is spoken in the town as well as in the country, among the well-to-do as well as other classes. Often it may also be written. Within these regions, which often coincide with a province, there are frequently considerable differences in speech, but the people are used to them and know how to discount them, so that it is likely that in the long run they will be eliminated if the situation here described becomes stabilized. In such cases we speak of a *dialect*, disregarding the differences of local speech. Dialects of this type are those which have been traditionally recognized in countries like Germany and Italy: there is a Swabian dialect, a Bavarian dialect, a Piedmontese dialect, a Sicilian dialect etc. It is clear, however, that a dialect situation such as this may quickly degenerate into a patois situation analogous to the one described for France as soon as the progress of national unity reinforces the position of the official language. Naturally, there is no precise dividing line between dialect and patois. The process of disintegration which culminates in the elimination of local speech begins in fact as soon as an external linguistic form is imposed at the expense of the local forms. It is not certain that the situation in Gascony and Piedmont is as different as the clear-cut opposition made above between France and Italy might lead one to expect.

5.12 'Dialect' and 'language'

What should be noted is that when applied to Italy, Germany and other countries the term 'dialect' in current use implies a judgement of value. Certainly this judgement is not as severe as that implied in the word 'patois'. But whatever sentiments a German or Italian may entertain for his dialect, he would not think of putting it on the same footing as the national language. Bavarian is certainly German and Piedmontese is certainly Italian, but there is a form of German as there is a form of Italian which is not 'dialect' but 'language'. In this sense there are Germans and Italians who do not speak any 'dialect' but only the national language. However, it sometimes happens that the official and common language is not identical with any vernacular, and it is not spoken as a first language by any member of a community. Its usage is limited to certain occasions for which the vernacular would be inadmissible. It may be that this language is primarily a traditional literary or sacred language which is badly adapted to the more varied need of the community, like classical Arabic in Moslem countries. This creates conditions under which a second common language makes its appearance which is better adapted to daily needs. Where a common language of restricted use and certain vernaculars are closely related, speakers are generally more conscious of the similarities than of the differences and so tend to consider the common language and their vernacular rather as two styles of the same language than two distinct languages.

5.13 Dialects as varieties of a language

The word 'dialect' has another quite different use, as for instance in the United States, where the term denotes every local form of English but without any suggestion that a more acceptable form of the language exists distinct from the dialects. Every American speaks a dialect, the Boston, the New York, the Chicago dialect etc.; or, if he has travelled about a good deal, he may speak a hybrid dialect. Yet he never has the feeling that he speaks anything but American English in a form which is perfectly acceptable in all circumstances of life. This situation recalls what happens in Paris and in the urban centres in France, apart from the south, where there exist many varieties of French which, on the lips of educated people, seem so acceptable that the peculiarities generally pass unnoticed. The American dialects correspond fairly closely to what is called local French and not to the patois of France, or again, to the dialects of Germany or Italy. The latter, as we have said, are too different from one another to be intelligible throughout the national territory. This use of the word corresponds to the meaning given to it when we speak of the ancient Greek dialects before the koine was established in post-classical times. This language was founded on the speech of Athens, which reduced the other Greek dialects to the status of mere vernaculars with the result that they were all eliminated except one (Laconian, a variety of which survives under the name of Tsakonian). In the sixth century B.C. the speech of Athens was not 'Greek' but the Attic dialect; similarly the Thebans spoke a Boeotian dialect, the Lacedaemonians a Laconian dialect, and so on. But the differences were not great and probably did not prevent mutual intelligibility at least in the centre of the Greek world.

5.14 Divergence and convergence

The above considerations allow us to map out a process which must have been repeated thousands of times in human history: a group of people, aggressive or prolific, extend their domain to such an extent that contacts between the several constituent tribes lose their frequency and intimacy. This brings about a process of linguistic differentiation which gains impetus as contacts between the tribes become weakened and new contacts are made with tribes of other groups. The initial language becomes dialectalized and this fragmentation may result, as between one region and another, in total incomprehensibility. But one tribe which is more aggressive, more prolific, more inventive, or more civilized than its neighbours may one day impose upon the others a political or cultural hegemony. Its dialect will become the official language or the literary language over the range of its hegemony and as such will tend to oust the local dialects. This may take place by a process of convergence leading to complete fusion if they are not much differentiated; otherwise there will be simple replacement. This does not mean that the limits of the said hegemony will coincide with the original expansion of the group. It may surpass it at certain points and the new language may find acceptance in regions which had a local speech of quite different origin. At yet other points it may even contract and certain dialects of our hypothetical group may be integrated in another nation, or another sphere of cultural expansion in which they may finally be swallowed up. Dialectalization is not an inescapable consequence of geographical expansion. It is not the remoteness itself which produces the linguistic differentiation but the loosening of contacts. If the increase in distance is accompanied by improved communications, linguistic habits remain identical. As long as it took weeks to cross the Atlantic, the English of England and America tended to diverge. Thus railway vocabulary is by and large different in Great Britain and the United States. But conditions have changed in an epoch when it only takes a few hours to get to London from New York and the voice crosses the Atlantic almost instantaneously. Today we observe convergence rather than divergence. If one day the Soviet Union were to establish an observer station on the moon, there would be little likelihood of a distinct Russian dialect developing there so long as communications with the earth continued uninterrupted.

5.15 The definition of 'dialect'

The linguist has a means of removing the ambiguity of the term 'dialect'. This consists in stating precisely in each case of which common language the variety of speech in question is a divergent product. In this way we can distinguish in Spain between the Spanish dialect of Andalusia, which in the last analysis is only a provincial form of Castilian, and on the other hand a Romance dialect of Spain like Asturian, which represents basically a local differentiation of the Latin which was imported into the peninsula in ancient times. To turn to Greece, Tsakonian is a proto-Greek dialect unlike most modern Greek dialects which are differentiations of the koine. As for the local forms of speech spoken in Greece by the educated middle classes, they must be labelled 'dialects of modern Greek'. There are unfortunately many cases where it is difficult to reconstruct the process of differentiation. Thus all we can say of Swabian and Bavarian is that they are German dialects, although this does not imply that they are varieties of 'standard' modern German.

5.16 Creoles

The languages called Creoles are spoken by the descendants of slaves brought from Africa to the New World and to the islands of the Indian Ocean. They must be the result of special processes the stages of which are a matter of speculation. But their relations today to the cultural language of which they seem a deformed and mutilated version are reminiscent of the relationships of dialects and patois. The situation of a French creole, like that of Dominica, which is the vernacular of people whose official language is English, finds its counterpart in France, where Dutch patois are the everyday speech of people who use French as a national language.

5.17 Social dialects

The term 'dialect' is used most frequently with reference to linguistic varieties with a given geographical localization. But nothing prevents its use also for the forms of speech used by certain social classes. Here, too, there has been a diminution in the frequency and intimacy of contact between two sections of the population. This has resulted in a process of linguistic differentiation which is curbed only by the minimum amount of cooperation which coexistence in the same town necessitates.

5.18 Spoken and written language

Belief in the unity and homogeneity of each national language has the result that not only do people forget the variety of linguistic forms within the frontiers of each state but also that they are convinced, quite wrongly, of a necessary identity between the spoken and written languages. When a linguistic community, hitherto illiterate, becomes acquainted with writing, it is with a form of writing used for another language. In such a case to dissociate script and language demands analytical powers which may at first be wanting, and it is most likely that people who first attempt to write will do so in a foreign language. It may happen that this situation becomes stabilized so that educated people, who continue to speak in the vernacular to the exclusion of any other idiom, can write only in the foreign language. In many cases the language adopted in the written form is that of a 'classical' literature or liturgical texts, like Latin in Europe until early modern times, and, again, down to the present day in the case of Sanskrit in India and the Arabic of the Koran in Moslem countries. This of course does not rule out attempts to write in the vernacular. In the Middle Ages French, English and German were all written concurrently with Latin when the aim was to reach a wider public than the clerks.

5.19 Another language or another style?

There are grounds for distinguishing the case of a written language which is 'a different language' from the vernacular from those where the written and spoken languages are simply different styles of the same language. But a clear-cut decision is not always possible. When the written language is recognizable as an earlier stage of everyday speech, it is difficult to define precisely the degree of differentiation which permits us to speak of two languages instead of two styles. Are we entitled to say that the Romance-speaking clerks of the eighteenth century in their written documents (in Latin, but what kind of Latin!) used an archaic style of their own language or that they used, according to circumstances, variously a local Romance language and another language, Latin? Or, to take a present-day example, how are we to classify the relationships in Egypt of spoken Arabic, the language of the newspapers, and the language of the Koran? It is clear, that the existence of a common label ('romane loqui, Arabic') is an indication that the unity lying behind the differences is always felt, and it contributes largely to the conviction that the differences are stylistic rather than fundamental. We might say that unity persists as long as the different linguistic forms are felt to be complementary, so that each social situation requires a certain form to the exclusion of all others with the result that a speaker is never faced with a choice. The existence of various styles of the spoken and written language presenting a broad linguistic continuum, a kind of spectrum with imperceptible gradations, serves to reinforce this impression of unity. This is precisely the case in contemporary France, and it contributes to the obscuring of the considerable differences between the literary language and everyday speech. Between a written form which uses the simple past as the tense of narration, which uses the inversion of the subject as a means of interrogation, which knows only *nous* as the unstressed pronoun of the first person plural and, on the other hand, informal colloquial speech, where a story is told in the present tense, where questions are marked by a rise in intonation or by the use of *est-ce-que*, where *nous partons* becomes *on se trotte*, there are intermediate styles which reject the simple past but recognize the interrogative inversion (*veux-tu . . .?*) as a variant and preserve unstressed *nous* to the exclusion of *on* for the first person plural or as an alternative to it.

5.20 Spoken and written forms of the same language

It should not be forgotten that the opposition between a traditional literary language and everyday speech is not to be confused with the much more clear-cut opposition that exists between the primary spoken form and the secondary written form; the spoken form *est-ce-que* has a written form as well as

151

a spoken form and the simple past *ils dévorèrent* can be pronounced as well as written. But it sometimes happens that one
hesitates over the orthography of a colloquial word like /pagaj/
(*pagaye, pagaïe* or *pagaille?*) or over the pronunciation of a
literary word like *pusillanime*, or *transi*. It often happens in
English that people do not know how to pronounce a word
which they know in the written form. Thus in the course of the
discussion on a thesis about Chinese writing, the members of
an American board of examiners showed that they agreed
neither on the position of the accent in *ideogram* nor on the
quality of the first two vowels of the word.

5.21 Spoken and written French

In French, the differences between the written and the spoken
forms are of such a nature that it may be said without exaggeration that the structure of the written language cannot be identified with that of the spoken language. In the one, the plural of
substantives is regularly indicated by an -*s* and also secondarily
by phenomena of grammatical concord; in the other the plural is
expressed primarily by formal modifications to the determinants
of the substantives (/le(z)/ instead of /l/, /la/; /de(z)/ instead of
/œ̃/, /ün/). These divergencies are even more striking if we take
into account the different inventories of forms in the colloquial
language and the literary language (absence of the simple past
definite and the imperfect subjunctive from the former). A
French grammar based entirely on spoken French in its phonic
form would show a structure differing profoundly from that of
the classical grammars which concentrate almost exclusively
on the traditional language in its written form. In our colloquial
grammar there would be no mention, for instance, of different
conjugations, but a distinction would be made between verbs
with an unchanging stem (e.g. /dòn/ 'donner') and the verbs with
variable stems (e.g. /fini- finis-/: /fini fini-ra/ but /finis-õ, finis-iõ/;
/sè sav so-/: /il se nu sav-õ, il so-ra/). In fact, the notion of a
unity underlying the various divergent forms of French can be
maintained in the consciousness of the speaker only by means

of a long training which enables the child to identify the syntagm /izem/, which it has pronounced ever since it could speak, with the written form *ils aiment*, which is believed to render fairly accurately the succession of phonemes and monemes used a thousand or so years ago.

5.22 Special conditioning of literary usage

We may deplore a state of affairs which forces young French speakers to devote to this training long hours of study which might be better employed in the acquisition of more useful attainments. It is true that French orthography, which allows the foreigner to determine with comparative ease the pronunciation of a word which he knows only in the written form, presents particular difficulties to those who have learned to pronounce the language before learning to read or write it. But we must be clear in our minds that it is quite normal for differences between spoken and written usage to occur. It is often pointed out that since the written form gives little indication of the melodic elements of speech, it is not surprising that there should be some compensation in the way of additional details. The orthographical distinction between homonyms, so frequent in French spelling, finds its justification here. But this is only one aspect of the fundamental situational differences which condition speech and literary activity. In everyday life more often than not speech merely comments on a situation and many elliptical terms are allowed: *'par ici!'* in the passages of the underground accompanied by a gesture; *'quel tête!'*, *'là -bas!'* etc. Speech is the domain of the pronoun of the first and second person and words or syntagms which, like *ici*, *hier* and *demain*, have no concrete meaning except with reference to the situation in which they are uttered. It is of course not unusual for speakers to depart from the situation in which they are placed. Slander, which is not necessarily to be regarded as a literary activity, usually entails a form of linguistic behaviour not anchored in the particular situation in which the conversation takes place. We might say indeed that the use of language independently of circumstances of any kind is the ideal, since only in this way is communication established by strictly linguistic means. But whereas speech rarely escapes altogether from contingencies of a given situation, an author faced with a blank page is virtually compelled to practise this ideal since he cannot foresee the conditions under which his message will be delivered. Letters are of course in a different class, because as a general rule they do not share in the desire for generality and permanence which is necessarily attributable to an author. In this connection we may recall that oral literature preceded the written literature with which we are familiar and that increase in recording apparatus may stimulate a renaissance of oral composition and its transmission by phonic means. But in so far as such an oral literature remains strictly 'linguistic', not being accompanied by noises or pictures designed to reconstitute a situation, it will present our linguistic ideal of communication established solely by means of arbitrary signs. However, this ideal, represented by the graphic notation solely of the relevant features of utterance, may be impaired by the possible intrusion of non-linguistic elements such as the quality of a speaker's voice and the part played by emphasis and the non-discrete elements of the melodic curve.

5.23 Sabirs and 'pidgins'

Up till now we have tried to illustrate the variety of situations of a socio-linguistic nature only within a territory where the existence of a common language implies a certain unity. The situation which we shall now consider is one where an individual or a group of individuals tries to establish contacts outside the domain of the given common language. If, as is probable, such an individual (or group) desires to establish linguistic communications, he must either learn the language of this new people or persuade them to learn his language. It is not impossible however that the desire for communication is felt by both parties and that each of the two groups in contact makes an effort to identify what the other has said and to imitate it to the best of their ability. The result will be a mixture of languages, which each of the groups in contact will be tempted to identify more or less with the language of the other group, but which is in reality a half-way house. This idiom will be for all users an auxiliary language, of an ill-defined structure and a vocabulary limited to the needs which brought it into existence and which permit it to survive. These somewhat sketchy tools of communication are often called *sabirs* after the language which long flourished in the Mediterranean ports and is also known as the *lingua franca*. Sabirs are not necessarily limited to members of two ethnic groups but, like the lingua franca itself, they may be used by all the peoples living in a given geographical area. The popular expression *macache bono*, which is taken from the North African sabir, is a good illustration of the composite character of this idiom. *Macache* is a distorted form of the Arabic *ma kān ši* 'it isn't' and *bono* is a sort of common denominator of the Romance forms of the word for 'good'. Among mixed languages of this type we may also mention the Chinook jargon used in the nineteenth century by Indians of the North Pacific coast of America for communication among the Indian nations and with the French and English trappers. Nearer to ourselves in space and time is *Russenorsk*, the product of contacts between Russian and Norwegian fishermen on the shores of the Arctic Ocean, which had an ephemeral existence but has been adequately described. It is an excellent example of a mixed language to which two well-known languages have contributed in almost equal proportions.

There is no precise delimitation between sabirs and what are called '*pidgins*', except that the latter have a vocabulary borrowed in the main from a single language, English. In fact pidgin proper and its congeners have played and continue to play the same role in the Pacific as the lingua franca in the Mediterranean basin. But nearly all pidgins show at least some traces of the influence of other languages besides English. Everywhere we find the word *savvy* 'know', which is obviously of Romance origin (cf. *sabir*) and is automatically used by a monoglot English speaker who tries to make himself understood by a foreigner. '*Petit nègre*' is the nearest equivalent in French to pidgin, and it serves likewise as an auxiliary language in contacts between peoples speaking different languages.

5.24 The difference between sabirs and creoles

The creole languages represent synchronically an altogether different phenomenon, since they are spoken to the exclusion of any other form of speech and in all circumstances of life by compact groups of speakers. We may, of course, assume that, like pidgin or petit nègre, they started as auxiliary languages but that they finally replaced the African languages in all circumstances in those regions where, as in the West Indies, the slave trade brought together slaves from various regions speaking different languages. Since these creoles must have arisen as a result of intercourse between people of African origin, and since Europeans have always thought fit to use them in addressing negroes, it is not surprising to find in the structure of different creoles, whether they are of English, French, Spanish, Dutch or Portuguese vocabulary, a number of common features which are more reminiscent of Africa than of Europe. Nothing in its linguistic structure disqualifies creole in principle from reaching the status of a cultural language. But in so far as a creole language is felt and identified as a bastard form of a major civilized language, its status differs little from that of a metropolitan patois.

5.25 The individual living abroad

The individual or the group which goes abroad and becomes expatriate generally finds it advantageous to learn as quickly as possible and as perfectly as possible the language of the host country, because there are no prospects of forcing its own language on the inhabitants of that country. The persons in question may escape this obligation only if they find in the foreign country large groups of their own compatriots to which they become attached. One often encounters in the large towns of the United States old women who have lived there for a long period of years but know no word of English. According to the age at which he arrives in the country, his state of education, his intelligence and the milieu in which he lives, the immigrant will make himself barely understood or he may end up by speaking the new language like a native to the general satisfaction. He may even completely forget his first language, or, if he continues to use it, do so with less assurance than his second language. Yet another immigrant may retain his first language as the only one in which he really feels at ease.

If the individual or the little group uses either as his first language or one acquired later a language of great prestige, and if his means allow him to pay for the services of people able to speak this language, he will be able to dispense with learning any vernacular, however far from home he may venture. An Englishman may pass his life in the hotels of the Riviera without knowing a word of French. The case where a group invades a new country and establishes itself by right of conquest may initially produce a socio-linguistic situation which differs only in degree from that which we have just considered. In the long run, however, after several generations, it is normal for communication to be established between conqueror and conquered, and when linguistic unity is created, the factors of culture and numbers will weigh more heavily than any initial military superiority. The Roman conquest of Gaul resulted in the linguistic Romanization of the country, whereas the Frankish conquest succeeded in Germanizing only the northern and eastern fringes.

5.26 Learning a foreign language

Among linguistic contacts we must not forget those which come about indirectly through the medium of literature. Here, contact may be made after a long lapse of time, if the literature which is studied survives the linguistic community in which it flourished. In certain cases the learning of a foreign language, living or dead, may be institutionalized and its acquisition is regarded as a necessary accomplishment for all the young people of a certain class. In the modern world cultured people and specialists of every kind are induced to learn to read, if not to speak, several languages. It is easy to see how a foreign language which is learned and used by the most influential classes of a nation may cease to be a foreign language and become a common language which gradually eliminates the ancient national language, the process being one of dialectalization and fragmentation. This is what must have happened in Gaul when Latin replaced Celtic, starting in the first century B.C.

5.27 'Mother tongue', monoglots and bilinguals

All the contingencies envisaged hitherto have resulted in situations in which speakers are either bilingual or multilingual. Careful examination of these different cases suggests that we should abandon the naive conception of a well-defined state of affairs called 'bilingualism' which obtains when one and the same individual uses two languages with equal perfection, such a situation having nothing in common with the case of an individual who speaks, often with great ease, a number of languages in addition to the one learned first, the so-called 'mother tongue'. It would be well to remind ourselves at this point of some well established facts which may help us to discard some prejudices which nineteenth-century romanticism foisted on the monoglot middle classes of the leading European nations. The first language learned by a child is not necessarily that of the mother but quite often that of the servants or other persons who are in constant contact with the child. This first language is not necessarily the same as the one which the individual will speak in later life with the greatest ease. A child of five is capable of learning a second language within four months and in the process cease to be able to say anything in the first language or even to understand a word of it. Millions of adolescents the world over learn to use a new language with greater assurance and precision than the one which they used exclusively in infancy, whether that language was a patois, a dialect or a national language. It is clear that this first language will run smaller risks of obliteration and deterioration the more it retains its utility and prestige for the individual in question, and it would then appear that the acquisition of a second language proceeds with less speed and precision the better the first language is preserved. When the two languages remain in competition, each is normally employed preferentially and with greater ease in certain given situations. It is conceivable that a musically minded doctor might be practically incapable of conducting a conversation on music in the only language in which he is capable of practising his profession. As for 'bilingual' people in the ordinary sense, that is people who from early infancy have used concurrently two languages, it needs a quite exceptional conjuncture of circumstances for the two idioms to be retained on a footing of real equality, and what is observed in practice almost of necessity is the preferential use referred to above.

The criterion of perfection has in fact little practical value in determining cases of bilingualism. In all linguistic communities, even monoglot speakers may use forms which are considered generally as incorrect. A monoglot speaker does not speak his language to perfection but merely to the satisfaction of his immediate entourage which recognizes him as a member of the group. Here we have a criterion which it is not possible to apply to all the languages spoken by a multilingual person, at least not simultaneously, because it needs a certain length of time before he can be regarded as integrated in a given social group. There are in point of fact, on the one hand, people who in all their linguistic communications never bring into play more than one set of habits, who always use the same phonological structure, the same morphology, the same syntax and even the same vocabulary. These are the true monoglots. The monoglot person has a certain range and freedom of choice offered by the structure of his language: he may employ different styles. In French, according to the person addressed, he may say either *Monsieur votre père vient-il?* or *Il vient, ton père?* On the other hand, there are those who are able, with varying success, to change their code completely, to employ a different phonology and a different syntax. These are the bilingual speakers, or if they possess more than two codes, the multilinguals, whatever degree of perfection they may achieve in handling each of the said languages.

5.28 Interference

The problem which faces the linguist is to know how far the bilingual speaker succeeds in keeping separate in every detail the two linguistic structures on which he rings the changes. In principle the signs of each language form a structure *sui generis*, that is to say they are opposed to each other in such a fashion that there is no exact semantic one-to-one correspondence between the two languages. However, the bilingual person who speaks French and English is quite aware that in the majority of cases when he says *chien* in one language, he says *dog* in the other. This may lead him to identify *chien* with *dog*, so that all experiences which evoke *dog* in one register evoke *chien* in the other. This may lead to his using *chien chaud* on the model of *hot dog* to describe a Frankfurt sausage in a sandwich. The result is a unit with a single significatum and two significantia. On the level of the second articulation it often happens that the bilingual person identifies a phoneme of one language with a phoneme of the other and articulates them in an identical way. Many Anglo-Spanish bilinguals in the United States identify /h/ in English and *jota* of Spanish, the pronunciation of which wavers between [h] and [x], so that their rendering of English *have* varies between [hæv] and [xæv]. Doubtless these semantic and phonic identifications are not automatic, and educated bilinguals succeed in avoiding them. But they represent such an economy and therefore are so natural that it is only by constant vigilance that they can keep both structures apart, and exclude these identifications from their linguistic behaviour. There are in fact only a few linguistic virtuosi who are capable of manipulating two or more languages without ever being guilty of the phenomenon called linguistic interference. Interference may be manifested on all levels of languages in contact and in all gradations. In the sphere of the vocabulary it will determine, apart from extensions of meaning or use (e.g. the extension of the use of *chien*), borrowing pure and simple (e.g. *living-room, film, gag, star, western* in French), the 'calque', that is the combination of two existing signs on a foreign model (e.g. *fin de semaine* on the model of *week-end, autoroute* and German *Autobahn* on the model of Italian *autostrada*), the 'quasi-calque' (for instance *gratte-ciel* for *sky-scraper* and the Canadian French *vivoir*, which comes from the English *living-room*), and the suggested equivalent (e.g. the recent French word (*salle de*) *séjour* as the equivalent to *living-room*). In all these cases the interferences are almost fixtures in the debtor language, that is to say they are part of the usage of monoglots and are no longer manifestations of individual linguistic behaviour, as for instance the use of *solver* for *résoudre* by a Franco-English bilingual. But the use by French monoglots of *il est supposé* (*sortir*) instead of *il semble qu'* (*il sortira*), a calque of English *he is supposed* (*to go out*), is a good illustration of the process which leads from 'interference' in the bilingual speaker to adoption by the community as a whole.

As regards sounds, an interference, as we have seen, may have the result of increasing the range of phoneme variation (English /h/ with variations extending from [h] to [x]). But it may equally well affect the system when two different phonemes of one language are confused on the model of another. Certain Anglo-Spanish bilinguals, with whom the phoneme /y/ in Spanish varies from [j] to [dj] and [dž] (*yo* 'I' being pronounced according to circumstances [jo], [djo], [džo]), confuse the phonemes /y/ and /ǧ/ (pronounced /dž/) of English and so pronounce the common words *yet* and *jet* indifferently as [jet], [djet], or [džet]. As regards syntax, interferences are particularly common where languages with a fixed word order, that is languages where the function of the syntagm is very frequently marked by its position in the utterance, act on languages where the word order is free, that is those in which the different determinants of the predicate are characterized by means of specific functional monemes. Nothing deters the Franco-Russian bilingual from placing his Russian accusatives automatically in the position required for the direct object in French, since the identification of their functions is not thereby affected. But Russian treated in this manner acquires an unusual stiffness. It should be noted that the same bilingual speaker could not avail himself in French of the syntactical liberties of Russian because this would result in a confusion of functions. In the expression of function interference will be apparent not so much through the transfer of monemes from one language to another, although this may happen (French *à* has been adopted by several European languages in syntagms of the type *livre à dix francs*), but through the appearance of calques (e.g. the use in English of *at*, ordinarily equivalent to French *à*, to indicate the price: *books at a dollar each*). To say, as is often done, that morphological structures are not borrowed, or at any rate very infrequently, is merely to say that the bilingual speaker finds it as difficult as the monoglot to analyse an amalgam and that he transfers from one language to another only formally well delimited monemes.

5.29 'Interference' as the generic term for borrowing

Any attempt to distinguish between 'popular' and 'learned' borrowing would result in a distortion of the facts if 'popular' borrowings from one contemporary linguistic community by another were alone considered as resulting from interference, and 'learned' borrowings regarded as stray items culled from the lexicons of ancient languages. The history of French words as different as *haïr, ange, sucre, causer, fraction, théorie, abeille, redingote, rail* implies bilingualism and interference or, more exactly, bilingual situations and periods of interference distinct from those which we must suppose existed at the birth of the language, when peoples of Gaulish speech in the centre of the northern half of the hexagon formed by present-day France for a period lasting several centuries learned to speak Latin concurrently with their Celtic vernacular. This underlines the importance of linguistic contact phenomena in accounting for the way in which languages change in the course of history.

CHAPTER VI

The Evolution of Languages

(i) SOCIAL CHANGE AND LINGUISTIC CHANGE

6.1 All languages change constantly

In French, it suffices to scan the *Chanson de Roland* or, not to go as far back, to read Rabelais or Montaigne in the original to realize that languages change in the course of time. No person, however, gets the impression that the language which he himself speaks changes during his own lifetime or that the different generations living together do not express themselves in a uniform manner. Everything conspires to convince people of the immobility and homogeneity of the speech which they use: the stability of the written form, the conservatism of the official and literary language, and their own inability to remember how they talked 10 or 20 years back. Apart from this, there are advantages in not noticing what might delay the understanding of a message and in ignoring all differences which do not hinder such comprehension. I pronounce *âge* with an [a]; the person I am addressing may pronounce it [ɑ]; if he asks me *quel âge avez vous?* I shall immediately perceive the sense of the question and I shall never have the time to notice that he pronounces *âge* differently from myself.

It is a fact, however, that every language is at every moment in the process of evolution. Examination of the details of its functioning will reveal the diverse processes which may in the long run make it unrecognizable. Everything may change in a language: the form and meaning of the monemes, that is the

163

morphology and vocabulary; the order of monemes in the utterance, in other words syntax; finally, the nature and conditions of use of the distinctive units, that is phonology. New phonemes, new words, new constructions make their appearance while old units and old turns of phrase lose their frequency and fall into oblivion. All this happens without the speakers ever having the feeling that the language which they speak and which is spoken round them is no longer the same.

To simplify our analysis, we shall assume that the language in process of evolution is that of a strictly monoglot community, perfectly homogeneous in the sense that observable differences represent successive stages of the same usage and not concurrent usages. This, of course, does not correspond to the facts observed, for instance, in the case of French as it is spoken in Paris, where all sorts of influences overlap and where usages of social and geographical origin exist side by side. However, we must here disregard these variations as we did above in the case of descriptive linguistics, and we shall assume a homogeneity which will be manifested only in very exceptional circumstances.

6.2 Lexicological and syntactical innovations

In the first place we shall posit that the evolution of a language depends on changes in the needs of communication of the group which uses it. The evolution of these needs is of course directly dependent on the intellectual, social, and economic evolution of the group. This is evident in so far as the development of vocabulary is concerned: the appearance of a new article of consumption necessitates new designations; the increasing division of labour creates new terms corresponding to new functions and new techniques. This goes hand in hand with the loss of terms for abandoned techniques and objects.

It is only very occasionally that the designations of new objects or new techniques result in the appearance of new monemes, unless of course these terms are directly borrowed from another language, a possibility which we disregard for the moment. The more usual procedure is to specify an already existing moneme or group of monemes by means of one or more monemes like-wise belonging to the inherited stock: *way, railway, metropolitan railway*. This is evidently only a particular aspect of the fundamental linguistic phenomenon of the first articulation, according to which a specific experience is articulated into a linear succession of less specific, polyvalent elements. This implies that the need to designate new objects or new experiences will bring about not only an enlargement of vocabulary but essentially an increase in the complexity of utterance. On seeing the ship that Denis Papin launched on the Fulda in 1707 one could have said 'this ship is steam driven', thus combining pre-existing monemes according to a traditional pattern. But once such a machine has become common, it must be possible not only to affirm the conjunction of steam and locomotion on water but also to indicate the relationships established between the new machine and other observable realities. We ought therefore to be able to say 'the ship, which is steam driven, . . .' or 'the steam ship . . .' and in the end simply 'the steamer . . .'. Syntactical refinements represented by the relative clause or the attributive use of the adjective are, of course, much older than the steam engine, but the foregoing illustration indicates how they could have arisen in response to technical needs. The comparison of Indo-European languages shows that the relative clause is a comparatively recent acquisition, and synchronic observation indicates that the type of expansion represented by subordinate clauses has been imposed in some communities only as a result of pressure of new needs introduced by western culture.

6.3 The appearance of new functions

A growth in the complexity of human relations necessarily results in a more acute perception of the variety of relations between the different elements of experience. This will result in the devising of new linguistic means whereby these relations will be indicated. In other words, new functions will appear. The new functionals (prepositions, conjunctions, and prepositional or conjunctional phrases) are previously autonomous elements. These may be autonomous monemes (English *up* as in *he went up, up he went*, which is used as a functional moneme in *up the hill*) or autonomous syntagms (French *sans égard* [*pour*]). In languages where the functional monemes are amalgamated with modifiers and inseparable from the elements whose function they denote (inflecting languages), the new functionals (often fully independent adverbs of ancient date) introduce new modes of formal behaviour. Certain functions may, it is true, be indicated by the combination of a free functional and an amalgamated functional (*in urbem, in urbe, in die Stadt, in der Stadt*); but a tendency will manifest itself in the course of time to eliminate the amalgamated functional and to transfer the distinction to the predicate (*il entre dans la ville, il erre dans la ville*), or to the free functional (*into the city, in the city*).

6.4 Only internal causality concerns the linguist

What has just been said of the expressions of functions may also be used to illustrate the repercussions which changes of social structure have in the long run on linguistic structure. It is important to note that the appearance and extension of new functional monemes with a special formal behaviour are the source of a disequilibrium which may be resolved by the total elimination of a central feature of the traditional structure. But this elimination takes centuries or even millennia to be completed. This means that the linguistic consequences of a social change make their appearance only after a lapse of time and that they come into conflict with innovations brought about in new evolutionary stages with which they necessarily establish a modus vivendi. This modus vivendi is the very structure of the language at each instant of its evolution. This is tantamount to saying that it is extremely difficult to diagnose exactly the causality of linguistic changes by linking them with re-organizations of social structure and the modifications in communicative needs which result from these changes. Linguists, once they have recognized the decisive influence of social structure on linguistic structure, will have some prospects of rigorous proof only if they limit their study to a fairly limited period in the evolution of a given language and rest content with discerning in the language itself traces of external influence and with noting the chain reactions which such influences may have caused without attempting to determine the pre-linguistic links in the chain of causality. Certain features of the language under examination will necessarily have to be considered as empirical facts, whose existence one cannot account for except by means of unverifiable hypotheses. The real object of linguistic research will thus be the study of the conflicts which exist within a particular language in the setting of the permanent needs of human beings who use language for purposes of communication.

(ii) LANGUAGE ECONOMY

6.5 Least effort

Linguistic evolution may be regarded as governed by the permanent conflict between man's communicative needs and his tendency to reduce to a minimum his mental and physical activity. Here, as elsewhere, human behaviour is subject to the law of least effort, according to which man gives of himself only so much as is necessary to attain the end he has in view. It could be objected that human activity in general and linguistic activity in particular may be an end in itself, a game. Thus chatting is often a pointless activity which has no real communicative purpose but is rather a kind of communion, a very different thing. But this does not imply that linguistic evolution is not governed by the law of least effort. The game is in fact satisfying to the player in so far as he respects its rules, and for language the rules are those which are laid down by the communicative uses of the linguistic tool.

At each stage of the evolution an equilibrium is established between the needs of communication, which demand more numerous and more specific units, each of which appears with less frequency in utterances, and on the other hand, man's inertia, which impels him to make do with a restricted number of units of more general meaning and more frequent use.

6.6 Syntagmatic and paradigmatic economy

To remedy the lack of specificity of a term we can use a device other than its simple replacement: we can specify a term of general meaning by conjoining it with another term likewise of general purport. *Machine* and *laver* are both terms with a wide range of application; but a *machine à laver* is a well-defined object. To secure satisfaction of their communicative needs men will thus have a choice between increasing the number of the units of the system (the housewife may, for instance, speak of her *Bendix*) or increasing the number of units used in the spoken chain of utterance (in that case the housewife will say 'ma machine à laver'). In the first case there will be syntagmatic economy, one moneme instead of three, the two syllables and six phonemes of /bĕdiks/ instead of the five syllables and ten phonemes of /mašinalave/. In the second place there will be paradigmatic economy, since we shall avoid a new item in the list of substances which the speaker must memorize and among which he must choose when he speaks. In principle what will determine the final choice between one solution or the other will be frequency of use. If the object in question is mentioned frequently, it will be more economical to adopt a brief designation even if this involves an increased burden on the memory. If, on the other hand, there are only a few occasions when the object has to be named, it will be more economical not to burden the memory but to preserve the longer syntagm. Other factors, of course, come into play.

In our example *Bendix* is handicapped with respect to its competitor by the fact that it designates only machines of a certain make, so that another housewife will speak of her *Hoover* or her *Servis*. In many cases, the brief designation consisting of a single moneme is an abbreviated form without regard for the etymology of the underlying long form: *ciné* for *cinéma* for *cinématograph*, *métro* for *chemin de fer métropolitain* and this fact suffices to inhibit its general adoption by a conservative community.

What one may call the economy of a language is this permanent search for equilibrium between the contradictory needs which it must satisfy: communicative needs on the one hand and articulatory and mental inertia on the other, the two latter in permanent conflict. The play of these factors is limited by various taboos which tend to fix a language through avoidance of any innovation which is too obvious.

6.7 Communication alone shapes language

To understand how and why languages change we must be aware that every utterance and every fragment of an utterance requires on the part of the speaker some expenditure of mental and physical energy. The expenditure may seem insignificant to anyone who carries out observations on his own person in the ordinary circumstances of life when the wish to communicate or to express oneself exactly balances this expenditure. But a state of great fatigue reveals even to the most loquacious person that the choice of the right word and the appropriate phoneme or even the simple exercise of the organs of speech increases in an appreciable way the impression of fatigue. There are moments when 'one cannot find the right word' and others when we are affected by a real physical fatigue and our speech becomes blurred because of the inadequate differentiation of successive phonemes.

The individual gladly undertakes this expenditure of energy for the satisfaction of his needs. The needs satisfied by his use of language are of course manifold, but all imply an employment of the language the modalities of which are determined by the use made of it for communicative purposes. A language is a tool fashioned in the course of ages to achieve these ends, and it is its use for such ends that guarantees the perpetuation of its functioning. It is therefore the communicative uses of language which must engage our attention if we wish to discover the causation of linguistic changes. What we shall establish and be able to formulate will not necessarily hold good for those linguistic utterances which do not serve the purpose of communication. But we shall be disposed to disregard these since they are modelled on communicative utterances and so offer nothing which will not be found in these. In other words, the traits we shall find in non-communicative utterances are those which we shall encounter in messages in the real sense. But whereas the latter are constantly and narrowly determined and controlled by the necessity to get the message across, they have, in the more or less camouflaged forms of soliloquy, no other guarantees of their integrity than the desire to enact as best they can the comedy of communication.

This said, we may posit that the energy expended for linguistic purposes will tend to be proportional to the mass of information transmitted. In more simple and direct terms, we shall say that when we speak to make ourselves understood we exert ourselves only so much as will ensure that what we say gets across.

6.8 Redundancy

Taken *au pied de la lettre* these assertions seem to imply that nothing will be retained in a language which does not make a precise contribution to communication and that each element of the utterance requires an effort of production strictly proportional to the function it fulfils. In fact, all this, though justified as a general principle, is not compatible with the circumstances in which communicative activity takes place. Linguistic exchanges take place almost invariably in conditions which are far from being ideal. It is quite exceptional for them to take place in absolute silence. Normally words are exchanged against a background of diverse noises, confused din, backfiring motorcars, the surge of the sea, the howling of the wind and so on. It also happens that the attention of the hearer is divided between the message we are trying to transmit to him and his personal preoccupations. This is why the normal linguistic message cannot be 'telegraphic' or minimal. Words are rarely as short as they could be if each phoneme exerted its distinctive function with certainty and in all circumstances. Even out of context, the word *dictionnaire* has no need of its final part *-nnaire* in order for it to be distinct from all other words of the language. Strict economy would seem to require that we should not use words of three or more phonemes until we had exhausted all the possible combinations of two phonemes. Now in French, where incidentally words of two phonemes are particularly numerous, of the 18 possible combinations of consonant plus /œ̃/ only a single one is utilized: *jeun* /žœ̃/. Thus the practical necessities of language require of the linguistic form that it should be constantly and on all planes largely *redundant*.

This redundancy, indispensable for the practice of language, is likewise indispensable when the child is acquiring the language from its environment. The infant is of course conditioned to associate certain sounds with certain items of experience: e.g. the sound [hɔ:s] with the perception of the animal horse, and it is certainly in this way that it learns the elements of its language; but it is no rarity for a child to acquire words by identifying them in a series of contexts which delimit for him the meaning of the term. It hears an elder brother say 'Mummy, I'm hungry; give me some bread and butter.' Again it will hear from its father 'I'm hungry; when are we going to eat?' Apropos of the family cat it will hear 'She's hungry; give her some meat.' All these utterances are redundant in so far as they signal in two ways the wish of the subject to partake of food, and it is this redundancy which permits the young observer to identify the word 'hungry'. This is also true of the adult when he encounters a new word either in a foreign language or his own. The dictionary article which is his final resource in such cases is after all nothing more than systematic redundancy: 'Ruderary ... growing among rubbish.'

The fundamental necessity to maintain this redundancy is one of the factors which must be kept constantly in mind when we examine the conditions of linguistic evolution. It remains to say that the maintenance of a certain equilibrium between the energy expended and the information transmitted determines to a great extent the direction and detail of this evolution.

6.9 Information theory and the linguist

Telecommunication engineers have found a means of numerically quantifying information transmitted, once the number of the units in the system and the probable occurrence of each one have been determined. In their efforts to reduce the cost of transmitting messages they have measured the cost of information as a function of the system of symbols employed: the morse alphabet and the normal alphabet (26 units), digits (10 units), binary system (2 units). The constants which they have thus succeeded in eliciting have direct interest for the linguist. But it rarely happens that a linguist can simply apply the formulae set up by engineers for the solution of the problems posed by linguistic evolution. Communication engineers in fact achieve rigour by simplifying the data in the light of their own needs. Thus the cost of a word is calculated in terms of the number of letters comprised by its written form or of the number of phonemes of which it is composed. In other words, each of the minimal units, whether letters or phonemes, is considered to have the same cost as any other. This comes fairly close to the actual conditions of some transmissions, but it does not hold good for the ordinary conditions of the use of languages in the graphic and phonic forms. If, as is legitimate, we identify cost and energy, we could not claim that in cursive writing e and f have the same cost. As regards phonemes, which interest us directly, how could we measure and compare the average energy required for the pronunciation of [a] and [f]? We could at best suppose that the pronunciation of /main/ requires on an average more energy than that of /mai/, that is, other things being equal, an extra phoneme requires an extra amount of energy.

In these circumstances the features of information theory which are of use to the linguist are in the main those which result from common sense. What must be determined and exemplified is how and in what sense the variation of certain factors may entail the variation of other elements. These variables are the number of the units between which the speaker has to choose at any point of the utterance; the probability of units measured in terms of their frequency; the cost of each unit, which includes, apart from the energy necessary for its production, what might be called the expense of storing it in the memory; and finally the information conveyed by each unit.

6.10 Information

Everything is deemed to possess information which has the effect of reducing uncertainty and of eliminating certain possibilities. If I hear /hiːhæz p . . ./, /p/ has no meaning by itself, but it possesses information in the sense that it excludes all kinds of possible utterances such as *he has given, he has seen.* If /r/ is added to the utterance (/hiːhæz pr . . ./), uncertainty is further reduced since it excludes *he has paid, he has pushed* etc. and this shows that /r/ also possesses information. Information is therefore not an attribute of meaning, since non-significant units such as /p/ and /r/ participate in it.

The unit of information is defined as the quantity furnished by a unit of a system which comprises two units of the same probability. If in a context only *yes* and *no* may figure, the use of *yes* or *no* gives a quantity of information equivalent to one unit. Here we do not attribute any informational value to the successive phonemes of *yes* or *no* since we have posited that only *yes* or *no* are possible, so that the /. . . es/ of *yes* and the /. . . ou/ of *no* add nothing to the message which was not implied by the /y . . ./ and by the /n . . ./. It may be that the information conveyed was in this case vital, that is of a high quality, but quantitatively it is equal to one. What is measured is the quantity not the quality of information.

It is clear that if the situation and context have persuaded the hearer in advance that the reply will be *yes*, then the information conveyed by *yes* will be nil, since he knew (or thought he knew) that it was *yes* he was going to hear. If he calculated from the

173

outset that *yes* was more likely to emerge than *no*, the information conveyed by *yes* will not be nil but it would be less than would have been provided by *yes* if he had calculated that the chances of *yes* and *no* were even, that is it would be less than a unit of information. In other words, the more a certain reaction is expected, the less informative this reaction will be. In a narration where every sentence begins with 'and then' this segment has no informational value.

If we now suppose that instead of two possible replies, *yes* and *no*, we have four, all equally probable, the hearing of one of them will convey more information than if the choice of the speaker had been limited to two as in our last example. Let us suppose that instead of *yes* and *no* the two units in question had been *right* and *left* and that the four we are now considering are *north, east, south, west*. It will be clear that if the expected reply is meant to direct our search, a reply like *south* is more informative than *left*, since it circumscribes a quarter of the horizon, whereas *left* will limit our search only to one half. A reply comprising a choice between eight units, such as *north, north-east, east* etc. will further reduce the uncertainty of the searcher, since it will reduce the sector from 90 degrees to 45 degrees and so will provide double the information available on the previous hypothesis. To sum up we can say, the greater the number of the units in the system the greater the quantity of information conveyed by each of its units. It is of course easier to memorize and to use a restricted system like *yes-no, right-left* than a more populous system of the type *north-northeast* etc. According to the different needs of communities or groups preference will be given to restricted systems, poor in information, but 'cheap' or to more populous systems, richly informative, but entailing great cost in use and storage. It will be noted that the informational richness of a system is a function of two linked features: the high number of units and the value of each unit, which increases with the number.

6.11 Probability and frequency

It is in fact quite exceptional for the different units of a system to be all equally probable in a given situation and a given point of the utterance. In a particular situation, *no* would be expected rather than *yes*; in a certain locality, with reference to the direction of the wind, *west* will be expected rather than *east*, *south* or *north*. This is quite evident if we think of contexts which permit a wider choice: after *he planted a(n)* . . .: in our climate *apple-tree* is more probable than *baobab*. After so unspecific a beginning as *I've met a* . . ., *friend* is more likely to occur than *dinosaur*. The words *apple-tree* and *friend*, being so much more probable convey a much smaller amount of information.

It would be difficult in practice and of little profit to seek to determine the probabilities of linguistic units in a given context and a given situation. This is why we confine ourselves to determining the probability of each unit in the sum total of all the contexts where it appears, that is we calculate its relative frequency in the language or linguistic usage under examination. If in a corpus of texts chosen as fully representative we find the word friend a thousand times, and *dinosaur* once, it will follow that *friend* is a thousand times more frequent than *dinosaur*. We shall conclude that the greater the frequency of a unit (word, moneme, phoneme), the less informative it is.

6.12 Frequency and cost

If it is probably impossible to determine with absolute precision the absolute amount of energy necessary to produce a given linguistic unit, it is still worth while attempting to find out in what sense and with what rhythm the expenditure of energy varies when information varies. In the first place we may regard a unit of the first articulation, such as a word like *dinosaur*, as an unanalysable whole. Seen from this angle it appears as a luxury article which the memory must store no less than a frequent word like *friend*, but with an infinitely smaller employment. If we suppose that the effort of memory is the same for the two words and that the ratio of their frequencies is 1 : 1000, each use of *dinosaur* will require the same effort as a thousand uses of *friend*. It need hardly be said that these are not exact numbers but rough approximations. This disproportion is automatically compensated, as we have seen, by the great amount of information conveyed by *dinosaur*, which is in direct ratio with its rarity.

If we now consider the word as a significans formed of successive phonemes, we may admit that its cost is a function of the number of phonemes it comprises: /dɑinəsɔ:ə/ with eight phonemes is more costly than /frend/ with five. This being so, we should expect frequent words to be on an average shorter than rare words, and this is in fact statistically verifiable. The relationship of the eight phonemes of *dinosaur* to the five of *friend* is a good illustration of the relationship between the frequency of a word to its formal mass. The ratio of *eight* to *five* is of a quite different order from that of a thousand to one, which we arbitrarily posited as representing the comparative frequency of the two words. These relationships would be of the same order only if the language possessed a single phoneme which was in opposition solely with its absence, that is zero. In that case we should find a single word made of a single phoneme /a/, another word of two phonemes /aa/ and so on. In fact, any normal language disposes of a few dozen phonemes from which the speaker chooses the first phoneme of the word, then the second and so on.

Let us suppose, to simplify matters, that the 36 phonemes of a language may all appear in any position, i.e. that all the inventories of distinctive units are identical. In this language there could be 36 words of one phoneme, $36 \times 36 = 1296$ of two phonemes, $36 \times 36 \times 36 (36^3) = 46,656$ words of three phonemes, $36^4 = 1,679,616$ words of four phonemes, in fact enough to satisfy the most exacting requirements. But linguistic reality is different: at each point of the chain choice is made not between the 36 phonemes of the language but only from a portion of this figure, e.g. from among the vocalic phonemes to the exclusion of the consonantal phonemes and so on. On the other hand we must take into account the necessary redundancy of all messages, which implies that a language will possess words of four phonemes and more without using up all the possible combinations of three phonemes. Yet we understand why a frequency of 8 to 5 in the number of successive phonemes may correspond to a disproportion of one to a thousand in the frequency of the respective words, since nothing in the phonological structure of English would prevent the language from presenting forms of less than 6 phonemes for words of smaller frequency than that of *dinosaur*.

6.13 The looseness of the relationship between frequency and cost

What is relevant to the understanding of linguistic dynamics of the preceding discussion may be summed up in the following propositions: there is a constant and inverse relationship between the frequency of a unit and the information which it conveys, i.e. in a certain sense its efficiency. A constant and inverse relationship tends to develop between the frequency of a unit and its cost, i.e. the amount of energy used each time this unit is produced. A corollary of these two propositions is that any modification in the frequency of a unit causes a variation of its efficiency and foreshadows a modification of its form. This change may take place only after a long lapse of time, for the practical circumstances in which languages function tend to slow down their evolution.

6.14 Frequency and form in the lexicon

The frequency of a linguistic unit may increase as a direct consequence of the needs of society. This is especially true of the so-called lexical units, but it may apply equally to grammatical monemes. In French, broadcast transmissions make great use of the functional moneme *depuis* ('on nous communique depuis Londres'), which must have modified the frequency of this unit in general speech. In other cases the increase in the frequency of a unit is in relationship with the evolution of the structure which, as we know, often reflects an internal determinism only remotely connected with social phenomena.

When the frequency of a unit increases, its form tends to be reduced. This holds good both for a minimal unit and for one of greater size, for a distinctive unit as well as for a significant unit, since it is not necessary for a unit to participate in meaning for it to convey information.

The abbreviation of lexical forms, the frequency of which increases, is well attested. When excavations had to be made in Paris for the underground railway, there was talk of the creation of a 'chemin de fer métropolitain', a designation comprising four monemes and 18 successive phonemes. Today, when this means of transport is utilized twice daily by millions of Parisians, it is designated almost universally by means of the single moneme of five phonemes *métro*. This example illustrates two procedures of abbreviation which must be distinguished. First, an abbreviation by eliminating non-specific elements (here *chemin de fer*) which gives us *métropolitain*. Different is the second abbreviation which leaves us with only one section, the *métro* which was previously non-significant. Only the first procedure is well attested in traditional etymology: an Armenian word like *kogi* 'butter', literally 'of cow', is very likely to be the specific residue of a syntagm meaning 'cow-fat'. The second procedure is the sole resource in civilized languages today when new inventions are designated by means of long learned terms. These words are descriptive and analysable by reference to the classical languages from which their elements are borrowed; but they are monolithic and unanalysable for the average speaker, who can balance frequency and cost only by pruning them regardless of the etymology of which, of course, he has no notion. Abbreviation by such amputation or by using initials (BBC), both condemned by purists, is the consequence of the fact that in modern Europe lexical expansion quite often takes place by means of non-native elements. Such abbreviations result from the inescapable necessity to reduce the form to dimensions corresponding to its frequency, that is to its informational content.

Frequency and cost may also be brought into balance by

replacing a long word with a short one, e.g. *foreman* or *manager* by *boss*. A person burdened with a name of more than two syllables is very likely to be dubbed with a nickname. Other factors of course than the need for informational equilibrium intervene in this process but these are not necessarily the essence of the matter.

6.15 Frequency and form in grammar

The history of the -*s* of the nominative singular in the Indo-European languages and what we may gather of its prehistory is a good illustration of the same implications in the case of an element not exposed to the direct pressure of the needs of society. We may suppose that this inflection was proper to all nouns designating entities capable of being conceived as agents, those which at a later stage are represented by masculines and feminines. This ending, which there was no occasion to use with nouns designating objects conceived of and represented as patients, was necessarily the morpheme of an 'ergative' case, designating the agent of the action. This was not 'nominative', that is essentially a case without a grammatical context like the vocative, a case used 'to name someone' to introduce him or to designate him as the 'subject' of what is going to be said. An ergative case is an indicator of function. A nominative case is scarcely that since the utterance is arranged, to some extent, with reference to the noun thus characterized. An evolution in the structure of Indo-European had the result of making the former ergative undertake the function of a nominative. But this case was represented almost of necessity in each clause. The nominative was also employed out of grammatical contexts, concurrently with the vocative, which became largely identified with it. It thus had an extraordinary frequency which was linked with its lack of functional specificity. A form like Latin *orator*, where the nominative is identical with the stem, represented an ideal which in one way or another was adopted almost everywhere. But it needed millennia before the different languages which have eliminated the -*s* of the nominative found themselves, each in its turn, in a situation where speakers could choose between two regular forms, one with *s* and the other without, and gave their preference to the second. In French it was necessary to wait for the elimination of the noun declension, which brought victory to the oblique case without *-s* in the singular.

6.16 Frequency and form in phonology

The slow rate of change in linguistic equilibrium in the case of grammatical forms and, as we shall see, of phonological units, is explained by the very fact of their great frequency. The child learning its language has soon finished acquiring the habits which such a language represents, and it is only as a consequence of particular conjunctions of circumstances that the tendency to balance frequency and cost has its effects in all these cases. There is a fairly wide-spread phonic feature which may find its frequency greatly increased. This is the doubling of consonants (consonantal gemination), a phonic feature which distinguishes for instance *là-dedans* /laddã/ from *la dent* /ladã/. In the framework of a certain type of linguistic structure speakers tend to replace in certain words the simple by the double consonant: Italian *tutto* 'all' has /tt/ as opposed to the single /t/ of Latin *totus*. English and German *all* with the same meaning come from a form with /-ll/, parallel to one with /l/ as attested in *almighty*. In a language which lacks this phenomenon the double consonants are merely consonantal clusters like others: the geminated /-tt-/ of *netteté* /netté/ does not have a different status from the cluster /-kt-/ in *becqueter* /bekté/ and its frequency is of the same order. This frequency is low enough for /-tt-/ and /-kt-/ to possess information much superior to the simple /-t-/. If I hear /il at . . ./ I should have to guess from among some 40 French verbs; if I hear /il akt . . ./, my uncertainty in every-day life would be limited to two forms *act . . . ive* and *act . . . ualise*. The extra energy required for the addition of /-k-/ to /-t-/ certainly pays and this is true also for the extra energy required by /-tt-/ instead of /-t-/. But in a language where the geminates tend to be as frequent as the corresponding simple consonants, the information conveyed by /-tt-/ tends to be identical with that conveyed by /-t-/, and speakers will be tempted more and more to reduce the energy necessary for the articulation of /-tt-/ to make it correspond with its informational capacity. Since however the identifications of /-tt-/ with /-t-/ would lead to intolerable confusions, their mutual opposition is maintained; but /-t-/ gives way to /-tt-/ (which tends to become simple) and may become, according to the pattern of the systems, either /-d-/ (cf. Latins *scutum* >Spanish *escudo*) or /-θ-/ (O. Irish *bráthir* 'brother', with *-t-* passing to *-th-* between vowels whereas the initial *t* is preserved, e.g. *trí*, 'three'). Where the system offers no avenues of escape the opposition may be maintained for centuries in its original form: in Spanish -rr-, whose frequency is of the same order as that of -r-, maintains a much more energetic pronunciation.

6.17 Effectiveness in a given context

The speaker has little concern for the general frequency of the units which he uses, but he is certainly interested in their effectiveness (and hence their frequency) in a given context and a particular situation. Now it quite often happens that the term which normally designates one element of the experience to be communicated is of extraordinary frequency in a certain context and a certain situation. The speaker, guided by his own experience as a hearer, knows that his audience will receive little or no information from the use of this term. If he wishes this element not to pass unnoticed, he will have to find some means of stimulating the attention of his listeners. We hear so often of an 'économiste distingué' that in this context the word 'distingué' is virtually devoid of meaning. There are, however, various ways of giving greater specificity, that is informational value, to the segment of the utterance in question. We can add a determinant or several successive determinants: the economist in that case will be *très distingué* or *tout particulièrement distingué*. Alternatively, the form with low informational content may be replaced by another with a similar meaning, but unexpected in this context: we may speak then of *un économiste de classe*. Finally, the term of weak information may be pronounced in a special way to attract the attention of the hearer, by separating the syllables, for instance: *un économiste dis-tin-gué*, or by putting a special emphasis on this term or one of the determinants: *un économiste* très *distingué*. These different procedures may be employed concurrently, and this is all the more usual because each of the separate procedures rapidly loses its effectiveness. It often happens that an epithet or an emphasis thus added becomes so common that its absence is more unexpected than its presence and so engages the attention more effectively: in many cases to say simply 'a success' will be more convincing than to speak of 'an amazing success'. The process of reinforcement is extremely simple: a happy invention, a new word, an unexpected turn of phrase, owe their effectiveness to their very novelty. This will be imitated but the greater the use made of it the less successful it will be in arousing the attention of the hearers. So it will be necessary to find something else, another word, another turn of phrase, which in the long run will likewise be dislodged by yet another innovation. The social institution we know as 'fashion' would appear to be governed by similar factors; in the last analysis fashion is nothing but a means of attracting the attention of the opposite sex by novelties of attire, these achieving their purpose only as long as they remain novelties.

6.18 Information and literary style

The linguistic behaviour of the writer and above all the poet is comparable with that of the lexical innovator, although it is less subject to change due to the fact that it is less easily imitated and so less prone to devaluation. The author, too, requires to retain the attention of the reader and this will be achieved by providing a sufficient dose of information. An author may be satisfied with presenting, in the most direct terms, events, real or imaginary, so exceptional that the informational density of the story rivets the attention of the reader. He may also by an original choice of linguistic units be able to raise the informational content of his text and to administer it in exact doses. This will relieve him of the necessity of seeking after the unexpected in the subject-matter itself. In this case it is important not to exceed a certain density of information, which naturally will depend on the intelligence and the culture of the public whose favour he is seeking. The main point is not to reduce the natural and indispensable redundancy, beyond a point where understanding of the text demands an appreciable effort on the part of the reader. The tendency to conciseness, that is to increase the informational density, is frequent in poetry, but less marked of course with the author of long epics than the writer of sonnets. In the one we have the 'homeric epithet', which may serve as a type example for the redundant use of language; in the other the unexpected collocation of two words each of which conveys the whole of its message since the first gives us no hint of the second. The reef on which this device may founder is incoherence. As opposed to *blue sea*, quasi redundant, we might have *intellectual sea*, where the epithet is so unexpected that the first reaction is to doubt whether the message is a real one. An excess of information in a limited utterance leads to obscurity. The economically ideal language would be one in which all the words and all the phonemes could enter into combination with all the others so that each combination would produce a particular message. Our everyday language is far from this. The language of the 'hermetic' poet tends towards this ideal.

6.19 'Affective language'

The processes of renewal of linguistic devices have often been regarded as operating on the margin of normal linguistic functioning. Some scholars have gone so far as to see in such processes manifestations of affective (emotional) language as distinct from grammatical language. In fact such phenomena are sometimes the reactions of individual speakers, but even so they do not depart from what can be expected within the framework of the structure of the language. The frequency of a unit, which determines its informational content, that is its utility to the user in such and such circumstances, is one of the features of this structure. But it is the point at which its instability is perhaps most manifest, the one where the temperament and the different needs of each speaker may to some extent influence the evolution of language. It should not be forgotten however that an innovation, to find acceptance, must conform to, or be integrated in, the totality of linguistic habits which we call the structure.

6.20 Fusion

It may happen that the frequency of a syntagm increases without it being possible to adapt its form to its new probability by abbreviation or truncation. The reason often is that the component elements are of such weak specificity that nothing can be cut from the whole syntagm. In *chemin de fer métropolitain, chemin de fer* can be dropped because *métropolitain* is sufficiently specific. But in *bonhomme* we could not suppress *-homme* without depriving the concept of 'bonhomme' of all identifiable formal support. But if the increase in frequency does not then lead to a reduction of cost, it entails no less inescapably a diminution of the specificity, which becomes equal to that of simple monemes of identical frequency. This will lead speakers to treat the syntagm formally as though it were an indissociable moneme: in French *bon marché* is almost equivalent to the single monemes English *cheap*, German *billig*, Spanish *barato*. There will be therefore a tendency to fuse the syntagm and to say *plus bon-marché* for 'cheaper' instead of *meilleur marché*. An excellent example of such fusion in French is the expression *a l'air*, 'looks'. The frequency of *ça a l'air, il a l'air, elle a l'air, tu as l'air* results in the fusion of the syntagm /a l er/. As a consequence the following adjective no longer agrees with *air* but with the subject: *elle a l'air gentille*, and children are often heard to say *ça m'alairait bon* instead of *ça m'avait l'air bon*.

This phenomenon on the semantic plane is parallel to that which on the phonetic plane resulted in the weakening and simplification of the double consonants when they become as frequent as the corresponding simple consonants. We may sum up the general principle by saying that what has the frequency, and consequently the specificity, of a single moneme will tend to be treated as a single moneme.

Fusion plays an important part in linguistic evolution. The future tense of the western Romance languages is the result of the fusion of a syntagm formed by the infinitive and conjugation forms of the verb *habere*. The Scandinavian passive forms (Danish *at sige* 'to say', *at siges* 'to be said') come from a fusion of the verb and the reflexive pronoun *sik* ($>$-*s*). In colloquial French the pronoun subject tends to fuse with the verb: *mon père il a dit*.

6.21 Frequency and analogical changes

When the frequency of a unit decreases, the informational content automatically increases, but its form does not necessarily change. Nowadays we have far fewer occasions to speak of *rouets* 'spinning wheels' than two hundred years ago, but the word still has three phonemes /ruè/, that is a cost better adapted to its former frequency. It would require a homonymic clash, that is the appearance of another word /rué/ to prompt the appearance of more circumstantial designation like *rouet à filer*.

The decrease in frequency does nevertheless exert a considerable influence on the form and fate of significant units. A child who begins to speak learns to manipulate segments of utterances, and even whole utterances before it is capable of using in other contexts the different monemes of which they are composed. In other words, it remains for it to discover all the resources of the first articulation by comparing, consciously or otherwise, utterances which differ only in a single moneme. A child will thus use a formula like *il faut qu'il fasse* . . . before discovering that *fasse* stands in the same relationship to *fait* as *soit* to *est* and that that relationship is repeated in the *il mange* of *il faut qu'il mange* and that of *je vois qu'il mange*. Only when he has perceived this parallelism of relationship will he be able to oppose the two categories of indicative and subjunctive. Then he can be said to know his language, which implies that like adults he will be able to form the subjunctive of a verb he has heard only in the indicative. This possibility of proceeding by analogy will have the result that the child will no longer be the slave of tradition and he will be less inclined to imitate the so-called irregular forms, which are essentially those forms of variants which the context does not permit us to predict. It would appear that a child normally reaches this stage at about the age of five or six. In a society where the child does not go to school, the linguistic apprenticeship is by then practically finished, the lexical elements acquired thereafter being integrated in pre-existing classes. If a variable significans of the types *il va-nous allons, il fait-il fasse* is of such frequency that the child had the time, before the age of five, to learn to manipulate it sufficiently well to avoid the temptation to 'regularize' it, the traditional forms will be perpetuated. But if the frequency of these forms decreases, they will be liable to regularization by generalization of one of the variants.

The importance of analogical changes of this type in the evolution of languages has long been recognized. Linguists of the nineteenth century saw in 'analogy' the counterpart of pho-netic change and the sole resource of languages against the ceaseless process of degeneration. In linguistic communities as bound by tradition as French, the reduction of variants to one is hardly tolerated. The sole resource for those who hesitate about the form to be given to the different stems of a traditional verb like *résoudre* is to create an equivalent with an invariable radical like *solutionner*. But in so doing they will also be the target for the thunderbolts of the purists. We might say that a language is difficult in proportion to the years of schooling necessary for the native to learn its manipulation to general satisfaction. In this sense French is perhaps the most difficult language in the world.

6.22 The consequences of certain phonetic developments

The disproportion between form and frequency may be the result of phonetic developments which tend to reduce the length of the word and the number of the distinctive features. These developments may produce a number of homonyms, but they also bring about above all a reduction in the indispensable redundancy. This has the effect that traditional forms, now curtailed, give way to synonyms of greater body. The four phonemes of the radical of Latin *auri-s* 'ear' correspond to the four of the French equivalent *oreille* /ɔ̀rej/, but the latter goes back to a synonym *auricula* which was better able to endure phonetic attrition.

(iv) Quality of Units

6.23 Pressure in the utterance and pressure in the system

There are considerable advantages in reducing linguistic facts to quantitative data, as has been done in the preceding section. But it should not be forgotten that the quality of the units in question is an essential element determining the course of evolution. An equal frequency of double and simple consonants is only one of the factors which may result in a simplification of the geminates. For such a simplification actually to take place it must not result in confusions, and this depends essentially on the phonic nature of the units of the system. To understand the direction of evolution in linguistics, we must not forget that each unit of an utterance, whether distinctive or significant, phoneme or moneme, finds the phonic manifestation or its semantic content subject to a twofold pressure: on the one hand, the pressure of the neighbouring units in the spoken chain and on the other, that of the units which form a system with it, that is those units which might have figured in the same position and which had to be avoided in order to say what was meant. These pressures are phonic in one case and semantic in the other, but they are arranged according to similar schemata. Let us consider the word *caught*. Each time a speaker pronounces it, a whole set of attractions and differentiating pressures is brought to bear on each of the three phonemes in question /kɔːt/; the articulation of /k/ tends to adapt itself to that of the following /ɔː/; the tongue is farther back than if the consonant was followed by an /i/ or an /e/; the articulation of /ɔː/ similarly tends to adapt itself to that of its neighbours, and so on. Attractions are symbolized by the horizontal arrow in the following diagrams. Apart from this, the articulation of /k/ is controlled by that of the other phonemes of the system, from which it must be kept distinct for the identification of the monemes to be assured. It must be clearly voiceless so as not to be confused with the corresponding voiced sound /g/; it must not be taken for the apical /t/. Similarly, /ɔː/ must have a monophthongal articulation to avoid confusion with /oᵘ/, and so on. These are the differentiation pressures symbolized by the opposed arrows, vertical or oblique, in the following diagrams.

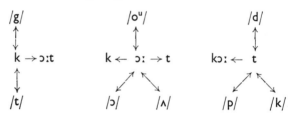

Let us now consider the utterance *the child takes a pen*. To simplify the analysis, we shall suppose that *the child* and *a pen* each represents a single unit. The actual meaning of *the child* is delimited by that of the context, which provides the detail that the child is of an age to use a pen; *takes* in the environment designates an action very different from that referred to by the same word in *he takes a bus* or *he takes a medicine*; there is a mutual semantic attraction between the monemes of a given utterance, and this is what is implied by the horizontal arrows in the diagram. Further, the meaning of *child* is controlled by the existence in English of other words which limit the range of its application and which it was necessary, whether consciously or otherwise, to avoid in order to say what had to be said. The same is true of *takes* and *pen*. This control is indicated by the opposed arrows in the following diagrams.

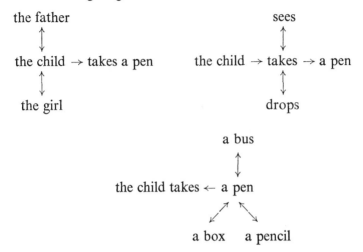

6.24 Equilibrium between the two types of pressure

We might sum up the preceding section by saying that every unit tends to be assimilated to its context in the chain and to be differentiated from its neighbours in the system. It is the necessity to preserve the identity of monemes and phonemes with reference to those from among which they are chosen in making an utterance which essentially limits the range of the variations provoked by the adjacent units in speech. A /t/, pronounced without vibrations of the vocal cords, might tend to be voiced when it comes between two vowels, which are produced by means of such vibrations. This tendency however is inhibited by the presence in the system of a /d/, which is distinguished from /t/ precisely by its glottal vibrations: /ata/ must be kept distinct from /ada/. But if the language makes no distinction between voiced and voiceless consonants and hence does not possess a phoneme /d/, nothing will prevent /t/ from being voiced to /d/ under the influence of two neighbouring vowels since [ada] will always be identified as /ata/. It should however be borne in mind that the necessity to maintain contrasts in the chain likewise limits the field of assimilations to the context. In a language where /t/ is voiced to [d] between vowels, this will take place in fact only within a moneme or word, whereas a succession /. . . a ta . . ./ is pronounced [. . . a ta . . .] and not [. . . a da . . .].

Thus at every point of the spoken chain we may observe the interplay of various tensions which keep in balance. The structure would hence be immobilized but for the fact that changing needs of communication constantly modify the pressures within the system. There will never be a final state of equilibrium established once and for all; the very functioning of language will ensure its incessant evolution.

(v) DYNAMICS OF PHONOLOGICAL SYSTEMS

6.25 Sources of instability in phonological systems

Since in the final analysis the elements of disequilibrium result from the changing needs of the speakers of a language, it is easy to understand how systems of significant units can be affected. New units constantly make their appearance and the very fact of their presence modifies the tensions within the system in which they figure. But it is less easy to see how innovations are introduced into phonematic systems which necessitate the search for new states of equilibrium. Above we saw that the requirements of information may result in an increase in the frequency of geminates which provokes fundamental reorganizations in the phoneme systems. But it is probably through the agency of prosodic facts, like the accent, that needs of communication have their most direct repercussions on phonological systems. Finally, we should never forget the influences languages may exert on one another and the possible borrowing of phonemes or of prosodic features. However, what merits more detailed study is not so much the various ways by which alien agents of disequilibrium infiltrate into phonological systems as what happens within such systems once disequilibrium has been brought about.

6.26 Maximal differentiation

What can be expected above all of the distinctive elements of the language is that they should not be confused with one another. We may suppose therefore that they will tend to be as different from one another as is permitted by the organs of speech which are concerned in their production. If a language has three vowels, we should expect them to be manifested in isolation as [i], [u], and [a] respectively, that is as vowels with the greatest difference that the organs can naturally produce. Similarly, on the syntagmatic plane, all languages favour optimum contrasts, i.e. successions of stops plus vowel. If by accident a given phoneme is not as much differentiated from its neighbours in the system as the organs could achieve, one might expect the articulation of the phoneme in question to be modified until such maximal differentiation is obtained. As a general rule phonemes which are produced in the same articulatory zone will tend to be equally differentiated. To use a spatial metaphor, we shall say that a system will tend to evolve until equidistance between its component phonemes is achieved. Even if we disregard fluctuations determined by the context in the chain, a phoneme is subject to constant accidental variations which depart, however slightly, from what may be regarded as the norm at a given period. These variations will be inhibited and brought to a halt if they approach dangerously close to what is the norm of another phoneme. This will be tolerated if these variations never expose the speaker to the danger of being misunderstood. In the long run the norm of the phoneme will be shifted in the direction where variations are tolerated and away from the zone where they are inhibited. If we imagine a language in which the front vowels are /i/ and a closed /e/, that is fairly close to /i/, and another vowel /a/, every variation of /e/ in the direction of /i/ will entail the risk of unintelligibility. On the other hand, a variation of /e/ in the direction of /a/, an [ɛ] for instance, would not cause any difficulty. The frequency of these variations would increase and the norm of the phoneme /e/ would soon be shifted to a point equidistant between /i/ and

/a/. This is in fact the situation observed in Spanish, which has only one phoneme intermediate between /i/ and /a/.

6.27 Phonological confusion and economy

We must operate with the principle that when two phonemes merge, in all positions of occurrence or only in certain positions, the energy necessary to maintain the distinction has been found more useful elsewhere. This of course is not true if the merging of the two phonemes is due to imitation of another language of greater prestige. Let us consider the French phonemes usually spelt *in* and *un*. They are in process of being merged through neglect of the lip movement which serves to distinguish them: the lips are retracted for *in* and rounded for *un*. On the other hand, the phonemes spelt *an* and *on*, which are differentiated in much the same way, remain clearly distinguished. Now this latter opposition is of great utility: there are hundreds of pairs of words like *temps-ton*, *lent-long*, *blanc-blond*, *semence-semonce*, *penser-poncer*, where the distinction is effected solely by the opposition /ã/ and /õ/. This contrasts with what is observed in the case of the opposition *in-un*, for which we have to search long to find quasi homonyms like *brin* and *brun*, *empreinte* and *emprunte*. Besides, it would be difficult to find these words in identical contexts so that the distinctions are secured only by the difference in lip action. Thus the opposition *in-un* may disappear without risk of producing misunderstanding and with a double economy of articulation and of memory.

The conditions which bring about phonological mergers may be much more complex than our deliberately simplified account of the phonemes *in-un* suggests. Thus French traditionally opposes two phonemes, both rendered as *a* in spelling: thus it distinguishes between *tàche* and *tâche*, *patte* and *pâte*, *lace* and *lasse* and many others. This distinction, which has in the past been of some linguistic use, now seems to be in process of elimination. To understand this phenomenon a number of facts must be noted. The southern French, who in their Provençal or Gascon dialects have only one phoneme *a*, have never learned to distinguish *tache* and *tâche*, *patte* and *pâte* etc. They must have found it easier to avoid clashes by using other words e.g., by replacing *tâche* by *travail*, rather than to reproduce the phonological distinction. Other provincial speakers, in accordance with their local habits, made a kind of distinction of length, which was for long the salient feature of the opposition *tache-tâche*. Parisian, on the other hand, as with other types of vowel, has tended to eliminate the difference of length in favour of the distinction of vowel quality. Since in Paris, the creative centre of the language, the population contains more provincials than Parisians, some kind of modus vivendi has had to be established. Those who pronounced *tache* as [taš] and *tâche* as [tɑš] could hardly manage to distinguish the two words when they were pronounced as [taš] and [tāš]. To be understood, speakers, both provincial and Parisian, have had to improvise in order to avoid word clashes: to speak of their *travail* or their *ouvrage* instead of their *tâche* and to say that they feel *fatigué* instead of *las*. Hence nothing now prevents the merging of the two sounds. In fact, the distinction between the 'back' and the 'front' *a*, being widespread in substandard Parisian, lacks prestige and so is tending to disappear. As for differences of length, they are being eliminated as useless and without parallel in the language today.

6.28 Transference of relevant features

From observation of cases like that of French *in* and *un* the conclusion may be drawn that the fate of a phoneme opposition depends on its functional yield or load, that is on the part it plays in distinguishing signs. What has just been said of the two French *a*-phonemes is however sufficient indication that this functional yield is not the only factor to be considered, but that we should be wrong in minimizing its importance. Even in cases where at first sight an opposition has been removed by the merging of two phonemes despite a considerable functional yield, a more profound examination shows either that the real yield was in fact low, or that the distinction has not after all been abolished but simply transferred to neighbouring segments.

In French during the course of the Middle Ages the affricate /ts/, written as *c* in *cent* and *face* was reduced to [s], without however becoming identical with the sibilant of *sent* and *basse*, which at that time was an apico-alveolar [ś]. Later these two sibilants were merged in a single phoneme, the /s/ of modern French. The present spelling still testifies to the one-time frequency of these two phonemes, one being spelt *c*, *ç* or *z* and the other *s* or *ss*. Now the elimination of this important opposition might have been expected to produce numerous homonymic clashes. In fact, the difference between the pre-dorsal, spelt *c*, and the apical, represented by *s*, has in many cases been transferred to the preceding vowel. The apical pronunciation of [s] brought about a 'deeper' pronunciation of a preceding /a/, in other words a back /ɑ/. This feature became relevant when [ś] was changed to [s], and to this day many speakers make a distinction between the /â/ of *lasse* and the /a/ of *lace*.

6.29 The break-down of phonemes into distinctive features

In principle there is no reason why each phoneme of a language should not be distinguishable from all other phonemes by an articulation *sui generis*. But in fact no language is known where all phonemes show this degree of specificity. Normally more than 80 per cent of phonemes result from the combination of articulatory features which appear in a distinctive role in more than one phoneme. Accordingly each phoneme is distinguished from all the others because it alone presents a certain combination of these features. In French /b/ is 'voiced' like /d/, 'nonnasal' like /p/, and 'bi-labial' like /m/; but it is the only phoneme which has all these features simultaneously: it is 'voiced', 'nonnasal' and 'bi-labial'. In the same language /l/ is the sole phoneme to have a lateral articulation and /r/ is the sole one to be trill or post-velar, according to the speaker. All the other phonemes are phonologically complex. The advantages of phonemes being bundles of distinctive features are evident. Let us consider the case of a language which possesses twelve consonantal phonemes. If each of them had a specific articulation, speakers would have to keep 12 articulations distinct. But if 6 articulations can be combined with one of two different actions of the same organ, the 12 phonemes will now require only 8 articulations to be kept distinct, each of the first 6 always combining with one of the other two. This is the case in French, where by combining 'bilabial', 'labio-dental', 'apical', 'hiss', 'hush' and 'dorsal' at one time with 'voice' and at another with 'voicelessness' one procures the 12 phonemes /p b f v t d s z š ž k g/. The existence of a correlation of sonority (voiced : voiceless) results in an economy of the order of 8:12. Let us now suppose that we have a language where each of the four articulations 'labial', 'apical', 'palatal' and 'velar' is combined with one of four different actions of the glottis, e.g. 'voicelessness', 'voice', 'aspiration' and 'glottal stop'. In this way we shall get $4 \times 4 = 16$ phonemes, for $4 + 4$ different articulations. Here the economy will be of the order of 8:16. In a language where each consonant would result from the combination of three distinct articulations, where each of them was not only 'voiceless', 'voiced' or 'aspirated', and 'lateral', 'apical' or 'dorsal', but also 'palatalized', 'labiovelarized' or '*a*-coloured', we should theoretically get a system of $3 \times 3 \times 3 = 27$ phonemes for $3 + 3 + 3 = 9$ articulations. In such a language the economy would be of the order of 9:27. In a language where each vowel could be 'front' or 'back', 'rounded' or 'retracted', 'nasal' or 'non-nasal', 'long' or 'short', of degree of aperture 1 ([i]), 2 ([e]), 3 ([ɛ]) or 4 ([ɑ]), we should have $2 + 2 + 2 + 2 + 4 = 12$ articulatory types for $2 \times 2 \times 2 \times 2 \times 4 = 64$ vocalic phonemes.

6.30 Phonological integration

In so far as such combinations are easy for the speaker to produce and the hearer to identify, they should represent a real advantage for the system: a given number of phonemes will thus require fewer articulations to be kept distinct. These articulations, being less numerous, will be better distinguished from one another; each of them being more frequent in speech, the users of the language will have more opportunities of perceiving and reproducing them and they will become more quickly established in the speech of children. A phoneme integrated into one of these bundles of oppositions represented by the correlations will be in principle more stable than a non-integrated phoneme. In fact, a non-integrated phoneme which is in opposition to all others in virtue of a specific and unique characteristic will have to rely on its own resources if its existence is at stake as a consequence of the insignificance of its distinctive function. In the most common Parisian usage /ɛ̄/ has long been the sole long phoneme of the system and since the opposition /ɛ/–/ɛ̄/, as manifested in *faite-fête* had an extremely poor yield, it is at present in process of elimination. On the other hand, the two English phonemes /θ/ and /ð/, attested for example as the first sounds of *thin* and *this*, have maintained their opposition for centuries, despite the fact that the output is virtually nil, simply because they are perfectly integrated in the strong correlation of sonority. A 'gap' in a correlation, that is an unused combinatory variant, will tend to be filled; this may come about by borrowing, the corresponding foreign phoneme being reproduced without too much difficulty since it represents a combination of familiar articulations. There may also be attraction and integration of a non-integrated phoneme with an approximate articulation, such as happens when a uvular /r/, in Judeo-German for instance, has its articulation modified to become the voiced partner of a phoneme /x/.

6.31 The asymmetry of the organs

We might expect all existent systems to tend more and more towards complete integration of their phonemes by a reduction in the number of the distinctive articulations but maintenance of the number of the phonemes. What opposes this tendency is, first, the necessity to alternate units of widely different aperture in the spoken chain, hence the general existence of two systems, consonantal and vocalic. Secondly, we have the asymmetry of the organs of speech. This means that the articulatory combinations of a certain type may be excellent, that is to say easy to pronounce and identify if they are produced at a certain point of the articulatory passage or with a certain degree of aperture of the passage; but they may be of poor quality when they are produced elsewhere or with a different degree of aperture. It thus seems natural to distinguish between a front retracted closed vowel /i/ and the back, rounded, closed vowel /u/, since nearly all languages present this opposition. But in combination with maximal aperture, retraction and rounding are procedures of little account, so that only a minority of languages distinguish between a front vowel /a/ and a back vowel /ɑ/.

It is this asymmetry which most of all explains why we nowhere find the vocalic system of 64 vowels sketched above. It is of interest to note that in one type of French, of common occurrence, eleven of the twelve features envisaged for this system are used: *ni, nu, nous* are distinguished by lip and tongue positions and form three distinct types (instead of the four envisaged). The vowel of *banc* is opposed to that of *bas* as nasal to non-nasal; *faite* is opposed to *fête* in virtue of its different quantity (short: long); *riz, ré, raie, rat* are distinguished by the degree of aperture in the second element. But the sum total of phonemes of the system, far from reaching 64 (or rather $2 \times 2 \times 2 \times 2 \times 3 = 48$), does not exceed 16, and this does not amount to any great degree of economy. There are, of course, systems whose yield appears to be much superior; e.g. the vowel system of Danish which has 20 units for only nine distinctive features. But a proportion of 16 to 11 is by no means unusual. It does not mean that we must look elsewhere than in economy for the principle which governs the articulation of phonemes into relevant features. What is meant is that the economy of phonological systems is a complex matter in which factors of different orders are at work.

6.32 Prior importance of linguistic facts

The difficulties experienced in identifying all the circumstances which may have influenced the genesis of a linguistic change should not deter the search for an explanatory analysis. In this, priority should always be given to that aspect of the causality of phenomena which takes account only of the language in question and the permanent framework, psychological and physiological, of every linguistic economy: the principle of least effort, the need to communicate and to express, the structure and functioning of the speech organs. In the second place, account should be taken of the facts of interference by one usage or language on another. Although the diachronist will never be blind to historical data of every kind, he will not have recourse to them except in the last resort, after having exhausted all the possibilities of explanation offered by an examination of the evolution of the structure itself and after study of the effects of interference.

Brief Bibliography

I FURTHER READING AND REFERENCES

Chapter 1 Ferdinand de Saussure, *Cours de linguistique générale*, Paris–Lausanne, 1916 (English translation: *Course in General Linguistics*, New York, 1959, pp. 7–20, 65–139); Robert Godel, *Les sources manuscrites du cours . . . de Saussure*, Geneva, 1957, pp. 23–25, 130–251.

Chapter 2 Problems of meaning: Eric Buyssens, *Les langages et le discours*, Brussels, 1943, pp. 5–96. Functional phonetics: André Martinet, *La description phonologique*, Paris–Geneva, 1956, pp. 11–33. General phonetics: K. L. Pike, *Phonetics*, Ann Arbor, 1944; Martin Joos, *Acoustic Phonetics*, Baltimore, 1948.

Chapter 3 André Martinet, 'Accent et tons' in *Miscellanea Phonetica*, II, London, 1954, pp. 13–24, and *La description phonologique*, pp. 34–101.

Chapter 4 André Martinet, *A Functional View of Language*, Oxford, 1962, pp. 39–65. For Kalispel, see Hans Vogt, *The Kalispel Language*, Oslo, 1940.

Chapter 5 F. de Saussure, *Course in General Linguistics*, pp. 191–211; A. Martinet, 'De l'économie des formes du verbe en français parlé', *Studia phil. et litt. in hon. L. Spitzer*, pp. 309–326, 'Diffusion of Language and Structural Linguistics', *Romance Philology*, VI, pp. 5–13, 'Dialect', *Romance Philology*, VIII, pp. 1–11, and *A Functional View of Language*, ch. 4, pp. 103–33. Bilingualism and interference: see Uriel Weinreich, *Languages in Contact*, New York, 1953.

Chapter 6 Linguistic economy: see Henri Frei, *La grammaire des fautes*, Paris–Geneva–Leipzig, 1929; George K. Zipf,

Brief Bibliography

Human Behavior and the Principle of Least Effort, Cambridge, Mass., 1949; and A. Martinet, *Économie des changements phonétiques*, Berne, 1955, and *A Functional View of Language*, ch. 5, pp. 134–60. Information theory: relatively easy introductions are offered by Pierre Guiraud in *Bulletin de la Société de linguistique*, L, pp. 119–33, and Vitold Belevitch, *Langage des machines et langages humains*, Brussels–Paris, 1956.

II STRUCTURAL LINGUISTICS

General survey: A. Martinet, 'Structural Linguistics', *Anthropology Today*, Chicago, 1953, pp. 576–86. The different schools and movements are represented in *Linguistics Today*, New York, 1954 (*Word*, 10, fasc. 2 and 3).

For the 'Prague School', the movement in which phonology in the modern sense originated, see *Travaux du Cercle linguistique de Prague* (= TCLP), nos. 1, 2, 4, 5 (2), 6, 7 and 8; TCLP 7 = N.S. Trubetzkoy, *Grundzüge der Phonologie* (French translation: *Principes de phonologie*, Paris, 1949).

For glossematics, see Louis Hjelmslev, *Prolegomena to a Theory of Language* (translated from the Danish), Baltimore, 1953.

'American linguistics' in the narrow sense of the term goes back to Leonard Bloomfield, *Language*, New York, 1933. A characteristic account is to be found in Zellig S. Harris, *Methods in Structural Linguistics*, Chicago, 1951. Less difficult for the beginner are H. A. Gleason, *An Introduction to Descriptive Linguistics*, 2nd ed., New York, 1962; and Charles F. Hockett, *A Course in Modern Linguistics*, New York, 1958. The dynamics of this school emerges clearly from *Readings in Linguistics*, Washington, 1957, a collection of articles by a number of authors with comments by Martin Joos.

A rather different approach is to be found in Kenneth L. Pike, *Language in Relation to a Unified Theory of the Structure of Human Behavior*, Glendale, 1955.

On binarism, a development of the *a priori* tendencies of phonology, see M. Halle and R. Jakobson, *Fundamentals of Language*, The Hague, 1956.

Brief Bibliography

III GENERAL WORKS

Edward Sapir, *Language*, New York, 1921, forms the starting-point for all researches into the classification of languages; Otto Jespersen, *Language*, London, 1922, contains useful information on the history of linguistics and the learning of language by the child. See also L. R. Palmer, *An Introduction to Modern Linguistics*, London, 1936.

On historical linguistics, a field which still shows few signs of the impact of structural researches, see Antoine Meillet, *Linguistique historique et linguistique générale*, 2 vols., Paris, 1921 and 1938; Walter von Wartburg, *Einführung in Problematik und Methodik der Sprachwissenschaft*, Halle, 1943 (French translation: *Problèmes et méthodes de la linguistique*, 2nd ed., Paris, 1963).

Genetic classification of languages in A. Meillet and Marcel Cohen, *Les langues du monde*, 2nd ed., Paris, 1952.

The following journals are either wholly devoted to general linguistics or give much space to it: *Transactions of the Philological Society*, London, 1854–; *Bulletin de la Société linguistique de Paris*, 1869–; *Language*, Baltimore, 1925–; *Norsk Tidsskrift for Sprogvidenskap*, Oslo, 1928– (general articles, mainly written in English and French); *Acta Linguistica*, Copenhagen, 1939– (at irregular intervals; French, German, English); *Cahiers Ferdinand de Saussure*, Geneva, 1941–; *Word*, New York, 1945–; *Lingua*, Amsterdam, 1947– (at irregular intervals; mainly English and French); *Studia Linguistica*, Lund, 1947– (mainly French, English and German); *Archivum Linguisticum*, Glasgow, 1949–.

Current bibliography: since 1939, *Bibliographie linguistique*, published by the Permanent International Committee of Linguists, Utrecht–Antwerp (French and English).

Index

Index

economy, linguistic, 6.5
endocentric, 4.34
energy, 3.24
equidistance between phonemes, 6.26
exocentric, 4.34
expansion, 4.30–33
expression, function of, 1.4
expressive function, 3.1

feature, *see* relevant . . .
first articulation, 1.8, 2.10
form, 2.8
frequency, 6.11–17
frequency of phonemes, 3.38
fricative, 2.15
front vowels, 2.14
function, 2.6
functions of language, 1.4
  of the phonic elements, 3.1–4
  of the monemes, 4.12
  primary, 4.18
fusion, 6.20

gap, phonological, 6.30
gender, feminine, 4.5, 4.23
glottis, 2.13
governed moneme, 4.18–19
grammatical moneme, 4.19

homonymy, 2.8
'hushing' sounds, 2.15

idiom, 1.5
information, 6.9–11
integration of phonemes, 6.30
intelligibility, mutual, 5.3
interdental, 2.15
interference, 5.28
inventories, limited and unlimited, 4.19, 4.38
intonation, 1.15–16, 3.25, 3.30

juncture, 3.6

labial, 2.15
labio-dental, 2.15

labiovelarized, 2.15
language, 1.1–4
language (*langue*), as the object of linguistics, 1.14, 1.18
lateral, 2.15
least effort, 6.5
lexeme, 1.9, 4.19
lexical moneme, 4.19
linear character of language, 1.10
lists, open and closed, 1.13
literary works, 6.18
load, 6.28
long vowel, 2.14

mark, of correlation, 3.15
meaning, 2.7–9
melody of speech, 1.15–16, 2.13, 3.25
message, 1.18
modifier, 4.19–20
moneme, 1.9
  autonomous, 4.10–11
  functional, 4.12
monoglot, 5.27
moods, 6.17
mora, 3.29
morpheme, 1.9, 4.19
morpho(pho)nology, 3.41
mother tongue, 5.27

nasal, 2.14–15
neutralization, 3.18–20
neutral vowel, 2.14
norm, active and passive, 5.6
noun, 4.43

open vowels, 2.14
opposition, 1.20, 4.8
order, in a correlation, 3.15
order of units, 1.10, 4.8–9

palatal, 2.15
palatalized, 2.15
paradigmatic, 1.20
parole, *see* speech
patois, 5.9–10
pause, virtual, 3.5

Index

The
Amazing
Life of
Moe
Berg

The
Amazing
Life of
Moe Berg

Catcher,
Scholar,
Spy

Tricia Andryszewski

The Millbrook Press
Brookfield, Connecticut

PG
Library of Congress Cataloging-in-Publication Data
Andryszewski, Tricia. 1956-
The amazing life of Moe Berg : catcher, scholar, spy / by Tricia
Andryszewski.
p. cm.
Includes bibliographical references.
Summary: Traces the life of a man who managed two successful
careers, as a baseball player and as a secret agent during World
War II.
ISBN 1-56294-610-2 (lib. bdg.)
1. Berg, Morris, 1902-1972—Juvenile literature.
2. World War, 1939-1945—Secret service—United States—
Juvenile literature. [1. Berg, Morris, 1902-1972. 2. Spies. 3.
Baseball players.] I. Title.
D810.S8B46925   1996
940.54'8673'092—dc20   [B]   95-8828   CIP   AC

Published by The Millbrook Press, Inc.
2 Old New Milford Road
Brookfield, Connecticut 06804

For my sister Julie

Contents

The
Amazing
Life of
Moe
Berg

Author's
Note

Moe Berg was a formidable puzzle even to the people who knew him while he was alive. Piecing together the story of his life now, years after his death, is a mind-boggling challenge for researcher and reader alike.

Berg was a great storyteller and a great source of stories for others to tell. Many of these stories, as they were told and retold, were stretched and embroidered and altered. As a result, it's extraordinarily difficult to sort out the truth from the tall tales about Moe Berg.

Worse still, key sources of information about Berg are suspect for several reasons. For example, the authors of the biography of Berg written shortly after his death (*Moe Berg: Athlete, Scholar, Spy* by Louis Kaufman, et al.) had the advantage of being able to interview many people who knew Berg. Presumably they *did* interview a great many of the people who are quoted in their book; unfortunately, they didn't detail the provenance of most of their quotes. Their book is also peppered with factual errors. Furthermore, Kaufman and his coauthors labored under a terrific disadvantage: Moe Berg's sister, Ethel Berg, who knew a lot about her brother and with whom Berg was sharing a house when he died, refused to cooperate with them and threatened to sue if they so much as mentioned her name in their book. (They didn't.)

Other sources have different shortcomings. Ethel Berg put together a thick book of her own: *My Brother Morris Berg: The Real Moe*, mostly a collection of photostated documents (such as Berg's letters to his family and papers connected with his government service) and a few documents that were apparently retyped (accurately, one hopes) by Ms. Berg when she assembled the book. Ethel Berg's emotional annotations and commentary on these documents are factually unreliable and sometimes bizarre. Nonetheless, the documents themselves are a unique window into her brother's life, and they allow us to hear Moe Berg's own voice, through his notes and letters and speeches.

A much more recent biographer, Nicholas Dawidoff (*The Catcher Was a Spy: The Mysterious Life of Moe Berg*) has done a Herculean job of sorting through fact, fiction, and formerly secret government documents. His carefully researched and well-written book is the single most reliable source of information about Berg.

Other sources provide useful information not only on Berg but also on the world in which he moved. A great many newspaper and magazine articles were written about Berg, especially in the 1930s, and these help flesh out his baseball career. As for his spying activities during World War II, Thomas Powers's *Heisenberg's War: The Secret History of the German Bomb* is a wonderfully readable book that supplies the context for much of what Berg did for the Office of Strategic Services (OSS) in Europe. Many books cover aspects of the U.S. war effort in general and the OSS and the Manhattan Project in particular (including General Leslie Groves's not-always-accurate memoirs). Readers interested in learning more about formerly classified wartime activities would do well to approach, in a skeptical frame of mind, several different sources at once to try to winnow out the truth that may lie somewhere among them.

As for what lies below: Everything included here is at least plausible—it all *could* have happened this way, and my research has left me willing to believe that it really did. Readers, however, should judge for themselves. Much of the story included in this book is told by Moe Berg and his contemporaries, in their own voices. Every quotation is annotated, and every source note specifies not only where I found the quote but also, whenever possible, where that source found the quote.

Chapter One

Early Years

Millions of immigrants made their way to America at the turn of this century. Among them was young Bernard Berg, who left Kippinya, a Jewish Ukrainian village, in 1894, and traveled west to New York City. "When my father saw the tenements in the Lower East Side he got sick," Sam Berg, Bernard's eldest son, relates:

> So intense was his outrage at the plight of American immigrants that he decided to try his luck in England. Fundless, he worked his way across the ocean as a cowhand on a cattle freighter bound for London. . . . Just as my father arrived, a money panic and mild depression began. Unable to find work, he tried to enlist in the British army, rationalizing that at least it was a job, but he was rejected because he was an alien. Rather than return to Russia or live in another foreign

country, he returned to the United States, this time working as a coal stoker on a freighter.[1]

Bernard Berg settled in New York. His fiancee, Rose Tashker, joined him in 1896 and became his wife. Their first child, Samuel, was born in the back room of the laundry Bernard ran by day while studying in the evenings to be a pharmacist. "My mother would do the washing and ironing," says Sam Berg, "and my father would iron and deliver. . . . My father studied from a bookstand when ironing shirts, but he scorched so many that my mother had to take over."[2]

A daughter, Ethel, was born, and then Morris, born on March 2, 1902. By the time Morris (soon and ever after nicknamed Moe) came along, the family had left the laundry and moved uptown to a cold-water tenement in Harlem. Bernard Berg by then was working in a pharmacy.

Soon the family moved to Newark, New Jersey, eventually settling in the Roseville section, where Bernard Berg bought a building with a pharmacy on the first floor. The Bergs lived in an apartment above the family store while Moe Berg was growing up.

Newark in the early 1900s was bustling with industry and bursting with immigrants. Newcomers from eastern and southern Europe, including tens of thousands of east European Jews like Bernard and Rose Berg, jostled earlier immigrants from Germany and Ireland. Many immigrants settled into neighborhoods already crowded with others of their own ethnic background—Russians living among Russians, Italians among Italians—but not the Bergs. Few Jews lived in Roseville, the middle-class neighborhood Bernard Berg chose.

Morris "Moe" Berg was born on March 2, 1902, in New York City.

Bernard Berg had chafed at the restrictions and expectations of his traditional Jewish upbringing. He left all that behind when he left his tiny village of Kippinya and went out into the wide world to seek his fortune. Unlike many Jewish immigrants at the time, he also seems to have left behind most of his Jewishness. Although he didn't try to hide that he was Jewish, Bernard Berg didn't attend synagogue in America, and he didn't allow Yiddish to be spoken in his home. His children were given no formal religious instruction.

The Berg household appears to have been a happy one. Years later, Moe's cousin Elizabeth noted, in a letter to Ethel Berg:

> It is really rare for children to be blessed with two parents who possess wisdom and employ it to create an atmosphere in which young bodies and minds are well nourished. Your parents accomplished this not only for their own children but for any who came their way. . . .
>
> How may I describe the Sunday dinners except by saying that it wasn't just the beautiful dining room . . . or even the glorious food. There was an ambience of warmth, being wanted, and the whole special thing of being part of the family.[3]

Bernard Berg worked long hours at his pharmacy, seven days a week. Rose Berg helped out by working behind the counter, and there must have been work that the Berg children could have done as well. But Bernard didn't put his children to work in the pharmacy; instead, he sent them to Roseville's well-respected public schools and expected them to study hard. All three Berg children did well in school.

Sam eventually became a doctor, and Ethel a teacher. Moe, however, became the star student of the family.

By the time Moe graduated from Barringer High School in 1918, he had earned a sheaf of honors and been voted "Brightest Boy" by his classmates. Moe especially excelled in languages, a talent he shared with his father. (When Bernard Berg settled in America, he understood his native Yiddish, Russian, Hebrew, English, French, and German.)

Moe's passion for learning, however, grew alongside a passion of a very different sort—a passion for baseball. From

Moe (last row, fourth from left) and the Barringer High School team.

earliest childhood, Moe played whenever he could, and he played well. At age seven he made his first baseball headlines, in a local newspaper, playing for Roseville Methodist under the less-Jewish-sounding name of Runt Wolfe. (Moe was then short and small for his age.)

Moe's father emphatically did not approve, but not because Moe hid his Jewishness to play with the church's team. As far as Bernard Berg was concerned, sports were childish games to be set aside as childhood waned. To his father's dismay, as Moe grew older his enthusiasm for baseball increased. He spent more and more time on neighborhood sandlots, honing his skills. Not even baseball, however, could keep Moe away from school, and his father never had cause to complain about Moe's grades.

Moe went straight from high school into New York University (NYU). His brother Sam was already studying there. Moe studied hard at NYU for two semesters—and he continued to play baseball. His grades were good enough for him to step up into the Ivy League at the end of the academic year—to Princeton University.

Moe Berg entered Princeton, as a freshman, in September 1919. "Things came very easily to Moe," his roommate Raymond Sutton recalls. "He had a retentive memory. He took copious notes. He never wasted any time."[4]

Berg's strongest subjects were languages, and he studied seven of them while at Princeton: Latin, Greek, French, Spanish, Italian, German, and Sanskrit. He took an unusually wide variety of other courses as well, and he even audited classes in which he wasn't enrolled. He attended biology lectures, for example, at the urging of his brother, who was by then a medical student.

Berg kept in close touch with his family. Princeton is only an hour or so by train from Newark, and he visited home often. In between visits, he wrote letters:

Dear Family,
At last I can stick my head out in the sun and talk to you.
Essays—exams—study—essays—exams—I hope I come out of the muck with a clean record. . . . Between this I have to eat and sleep . . . but still I enjoy it.
I will be home Monday night for supper surely.
How's everybody? I've got some good stuff for Pa to read when I get home.
I just thought of it—Sam takes Pa's scientific mind, I his literary, Eth his instructive and all love from Ma.
So long,
Moe [5]

Bernard Berg was thrilled that his son was studying at such a rigorous and prestigious school, but not cowed by it, and still full of fatherly advice. After his son brought home a less-than-perfect grade in English, Bernard Berg wrote:

I am not blaming you in particular. There is a general tendency on the part of American born youths to drift away from the pure old English into vernacular slangy mixture of gibbering that would stagger the old English authors. Instead of making a daily practice of selecting appropriate words to express themselves properly, they shift to the side of least resistance. . . .
How are you progressing with your application for scholarship?
With all your studies do not fail to take a good perspective of life in general; it is not good to have the

student's eyeglasses on all the time. Every phase of human activity—moral, material and spiritual—has many angles of perspective, and you cannot understand anything unless you look at it from different angles. . . . Our good help in matters of life is association and mingling with different people not so much with the aim of forming a friendship as to get acquainted with the difference of opinions. . . . Through association you gain knowledge of things that would be denied to you otherwise. It is a very good axiom; talk little, hear much and think and digest; this tends for a wholesome, healthy mind and able reasoning.[6]

While Moe Berg valued his father's advice and took much of it to heart, one thing he did not do, though it would have pleased his father immensely, was set aside baseball at Princeton. On the contrary, he played first base for an undefeated team during his freshman year, and in the following three years he started every game of the season at shortstop for the varsity Tigers. During Berg's senior year, the Princeton Tigers won eighteen games in a row.

Berg's strengths—and his shortcomings—as a ballplayer became clear at Princeton. No longer a runt, Berg had grown into a six-foot athlete. He was an able fielder, he could throw strongly and accurately, and he had a good feel for the game. He was only an adequate hitter, however, and a noticeably slow runner. His coach at Princeton, Bill "Boileryard" Clarke, joked that Berg would "get to first base just as fast wearing snowshoes."[7]

Berg's love of learning and languages spilled over into his baseball playing. He and his friend Crossan Cooper, who played second base, practiced Latin on the ballfield. "Sometimes we did it to confuse the opponents," Cooper

While at Princeton University, Moe was not only an excellent student, but also an able baseman and shortstop for the varsity team, the Tigers.

explains. "Moe and I would shout 'your turn' or 'my turn' in Latin so that the other side would not know which of us was going to cover second base on a given play. Of course, we assumed the first base coach for the other side didn't understand Latin."[8]

Cooper noted that Berg had few close friends at college. Perhaps this was largely because he was Jewish. Anti-Semitism was widely accepted in America at the time, and almost all of Berg's fellow Princetonians were white Anglo-Saxon Protestants. "There weren't many Jewish people at Princeton," Cooper later recalled. "As a group they were kind of looked down upon."[9]

Much of the social life at Princeton, which at that time was in a rural setting, away from city diversions, centered on the university's status-conscious "eating clubs." About two-thirds of Princeton students belonged to one or another of these clubs. Few Jews were invited to join, although Berg was. One club said it would welcome Berg—but only if he wouldn't push for any more Jews to be admitted. Berg decided not to accept the invitation, and he didn't join any of the eating clubs while he was at Princeton.

Being Jewish wasn't the only reason Berg didn't blend into the crowd at Princeton. Most Princeton students came from wealthy families, and Berg did not. Just how tight money was for him is made clear in a letter to his family, written in November of his first year at Princeton:

> I have to break some hard news. I just got a bill from the Princeton Univ. Store to the amount of $31.90. It's pretty high but it includes everything I have bought. . . . I paid for some in cash and brought it down to $31.90. But you can bet that I needed every bit of it and this is the last time I'll have a bill for a month of over a couple

of dollars. It requires a little bit to get started. So, Pa, if you will mail a check to me for $31.90, payable to the 'Princeton University Store,' everything'll be O.K. I hate like the dickens to write to you to do this but I have to. My expenses are curtailed now to a minimum. If I could leave to make the money I would.[10]

In the summers between his terms at Princeton, Berg worked at odd jobs, from delivering mail to counseling at a summer camp. At the end of his senior year, in 1923, about to graduate 24th in his class of 211 students, Princeton offered him a proper professional job teaching languages. Audaciously, Berg turned the job offer down. He had other things in mind.

More than anything else, the newly graduated Moe Berg wanted to travel to Europe, preferably to France. (French was his strongest language.) Travel abroad cost money, however, and Berg had little to spare.

More than anything else, Bernard Berg wanted his younger son to prepare for a respectable professional career by going to law school. Although Moe Berg still loved baseball, it was time, his father thought, to set it aside and become a responsible adult.

But baseball beckoned. Not one but two New York baseball teams—the New York Giants and the Brooklyn Robins (later called the Dodgers)—wanted Berg for the remainder of the 1923 season. The teams' managers were impressed with the skills Berg had demonstrated at shortstop for Princeton. Furthermore, management viewed Berg's Jewishness as a strong asset likely to draw more paying customers from New York's large Jewish population to the ballfield.

As Moe Berg mulled over what to do, advice from a former Yale University pitcher helped him to make up his mind. "Take the baseball career," Dutch Carter, then a successful lawyer, urged Berg. "The rest can wait. When I was your age I had a chance to pitch in the National League. But my family looked down on professional sports and vehemently opposed my accepting. I've always been sorry I listened to them, because it's made me a frustrated man. Don't you become frustrated. At least give it a try."[11]

Moe Berg signed on with the Brooklyn Robins. For the three months remaining in the 1923 season, Berg earned $5,000. This was a respectable sum in 1923—enough to allow him to pay for a long trip to France in the fall. The law, as Dutch Carter said, could wait.

Chapter
Two

One Foot
in Each
World

On June 27, 1923, Moe Berg suited up as a
Brooklyn Robin to play in his first major-league
baseball game. Only the day before, at Yankee
Stadium in New York, Berg had played his last
Princeton Tigers game, in which the Tigers had
lost the Big Three title to Yale, 5-1. Now, with
the Robins well ahead toward the end of the
game, Berg's new boss tried him out at shortstop. According to the papers the next day, Berg
did well. The *Brooklyn Daily Eagle* noted, however, "that like many other baseball performers,
and some of them the best, he is more agile than
fast. He can bob around quickly in scooting after wide hit balls, but is rather a slow runner on
the bases." [1]

Like many rookie ballplayers, Berg spent
most of the rest of the season on the bench.
When he did start in a few games, in August

*Moe played his first major-league game in 1923
with the Brooklyn Robins.*

and September, family members recall that his mother was thrilled. His father, predictably, was not.

At the end of the season, in October, Berg hung up his uniform and stepped back into student life. For the next several years, he kept one foot in the world of baseball, the other foot in the world of school and "respectable" work.

In fall and winter of 1923 he was in Paris, where he studied at the Sorbonne and lived in an apartment in the Latin Quarter. In a letter to his family, he called himself "the happiest one in the universe." [2]

Paris in the 1920s was truly a thrilling place to be. A new, modern Europe had emerged after the convulsions of World War I ended, and Paris was its cultural hot spot. Writers, artists, and performers of all kinds flocked there from America as well as from elsewhere in Europe.

Moe Berg was a very studious twenty-one-year-old. Not for him were the bright lights and nightlife of Paris. Instead he studied voraciously, taking no fewer than twenty-two classes at the Sorbonne in his year there. He was fascinated by how words come to be what they are, and much of his time in Paris was spent studying linguistics. He later told a sportswriter:

> My original interest was in discovering where the irregular spellings and endings crept into the various languages. For instance, the farther Caesar's legions trekked from Rome, the more the pure Latin became diluted with the words and idioms of the people they were trying to subjugate. In one sense it's a breakdown, but true philologists consider it an evolution. For example, the Latin word for twenty is, as you know, 'viginti.' The modern word in French for the same thing is 'vingt.' To

a philologist it's instantly apparent that the 'g' in vingt is in the wrong place. Tracing backwards we discover that before the Renaissance, 'viginti' had been corrupted or had developed into 'vint,' so far as the French were concerned. Scholars of the Renaissance, comparing the two, decided the word was being misspelled, and undertook to place the 'g' back in it. They simply got it in the wrong place, that's all.[3]

Not everyone—and certainly not every baseball player—found this sort of thing as fascinating as Berg did. According to Berg, his Brooklyn Robins buddy Charley "Boss" Schmidt teased him about going to Paris "to study about goddam words of a thousand years ago. Hell, Moe, don't you know what Paris is for?"[4]

Berg, however, thought he did know what Paris was for. "I don't let a thing go by,"[5] he wrote to his family, and where his classes were concerned, he surely didn't.

He also rarely let a newspaper go by. Newspapers for every point of view flourished in Paris in the 1920s, and Berg followed the news in perhaps a dozen different publications. Berg's habit of reading many different newspapers became a routine that he followed for the rest of his life.

"I read newspapers because they instruct me as to what is going on," Berg once explained. "There is, really, no alternative to them, and I seek none. There is a majesty about the printed word. There is life to it. I consider a newspaper a friend. My only demand is that it report to me well. Great writing is not essential, but the truth is."[6]

Fresh off a boat from Europe, Berg didn't exactly shine in spring training in 1924. The Brooklyn Robins' management decided to option Berg to the minor-league Minneapolis Millers who in turn, in August, sent him to the Toledo Mud Hens. Berg played a lackluster season. A major-league scout, Mike Gonzalez, filed a merciless but accurate four-word report on Berg's performance that year: "Good field, no hit."[7]

The following winter Berg attended graduate-school classes at Columbia University. By spring 1925 he was itching to play ball again, and that year he really did shine. His hitting and fielding, now for the Reading (Pennsylvania) Keystones, was much better than it ever had been—some of it was spectacular. By the end of the season, two major-league teams—the Chicago Cubs and the Chicago White Sox—wanted him. The Sox got him.

But first came another round of school. It was time, Berg felt (and his father certainly agreed), to lay the groundwork for a respectable professional career. Columbia Law School was where Berg chose to do that. He told the White Sox that he'd have to skip spring training and the early part of the baseball season in order to complete his first year of law school. Most players offered a slot in the major leagues would drop everything else and concentrate on the game, but Berg's priorities were different. "I have always considered the game only as a means to an end, because of its uncertainty," he wrote to a Princeton alumni coordinator at about this time, "and the means are very important to me at this stage of life. It was a faster and more enjoyable way than any other to enable myself to finish my academic education and now a profession."[8]

The White Sox weren't happy about it, but Berg got away with his unusual, even outrageous decision. He put on the team uniform in May 1926, after law school was done for the year—and spent most of the season sitting on the bench. When he did get a chance to play, his playing was only adequate.

The colorful baseball legend Casey Stengel once sharply summarized Berg's qualities at shortstop: "Now, I'll tell ya, Moe was a graceful shortstop; great arm, threw the ball like a bullet. He looked real marvelous. But I'll tell ya somethin' else. He couldn't run. Bad legs. A turtle could beat him to first base. If Moe got a two-base hit, why the kid was in a marathon to get to second."[9]

The following winter Berg was back in law school. In February 1927, he asked the White Sox's owner, Charles Comiskey, for permission once again to join the team after law school classes and exams were done for the year. Comiskey was not pleased. He wrote,

My Dear Young Man,

I am in receipt of your kind letter of recent date and was very pleased to hear from you. Last year you asked for permission to report late, stating that a leave of absence was essential due to your starting your education, and it would not be necessary to ask for same again. The time has come when you must decide as to the profession you intend following. If it is Baseball, then it is most essential and important to the club and yourself that you report for spring training along the same lines as all the other players do. If you do not intend to remain in Baseball, then, of course, the future is one for you to decide for yourself. Therefore, if you will be good enough to advise me of your intentions, we can make our plans accordingly. Whether or not you decide to play Baseball, the Chicago Club must continue, so you may rest assured that whatever action you take, will make no difference to us.

Trusting you have been spending a pleasant winter and with kind regards . . . .[10]

Berg stuck by his decision to finish the school year; by the time of his correspondence with Comiskey, it was too late to do anything about the current academic year short of quitting school, which Berg refused to do. He worried, however, about how he could continue to juggle sports and schooling. Fortunately, a baseball-loving professor helped Berg arrange extra classes the following fall and a leave of absence from the end of his final year of law school beginning February 1928.

Comiskey apparently found these arrangements acceptable. Berg finished out the spring 1927 semester, rejoined the White Sox, and once again spent much of the season sitting on the bench as a backup shortstop. Then, accidentally, his major-league career was launched in earnest.

After a freakish series of accidents and injuries, White Sox manager Ray Schalk found himself mid-game on August 5 with not a single catcher fit to play. Berg, in the dugout, said, "You've got a big league catcher sitting right here," meaning Earl Sheely, a backup first baseman who had played catcher in the minors. Schalk misunderstood—he thought that Berg was talking about himself.

"All right, Berg, get in there," Schalk said, much to Berg's astonishment.

Berg, who hadn't played catcher since he was a child, got in the game. Although he was probably scared stiff ("If the worst happens, kindly deliver the body to Newark," he reportedly said), Berg played just fine.[11]

*In spring of 1927, Moe was playing shortstop for the
Chicago White Sox until manager Schalk suddenly needed a
catcher. The next day, Moe caught again when team
member Ted Lyons struck out the Yankee legend Babe Ruth.
Moe's famed major-league career as a catcher began.*

The next day, the White Sox faced the formidable Yankees, in New York. According to pitcher Ted Lyons, "Our manager had imported a catcher from Philadelphia and as it was my turn to pitch and the Philly catcher wasn't in too good shape, I asked for Moe to catch."[12]

Years later, Berg himself told a story about what happened that day when Yankee legend Babe Ruth first came to bat.

"Moe," Ruth said, "you're going to be the fourth wounded White Sox catcher by the fifth inning."

Lou Gehrig trots back to plate after hitting a home run for the Yankees. Catcher Moe Berg looks on.

"I . . . said," Berg recalled, "that I would only call for inside pitches and we'd keep each other company in the hospital. We both laughed and then Lyons struck the Babe out."[13]

Lyons finishes the story: "[Moe] caught like he had been behind the plate for years, did a great job and we won the game . . . as a result of a super play by Mr. Berg at the plate to cut off the tying run. So Moe caught from that time on."[14]

Berg got serious about baseball. The following February he took his leave of absence from law school, spent several weeks working himself into shape at a lumber camp in the Adirondack Mountains, then reported to Shreveport, Louisiana, for a full run of White Sox spring training. He learned the tricks of the catching trade, and even his hitting improved. The White Sox in 1928 had a dismal season, but Berg did well. By fall, he was their starting catcher.

Law school that year, however, didn't go so well. Trying to squeeze in extra classes before taking yet another leave of absence in the spring, Berg failed a course on the subject of evidence. He didn't graduate with the class of 1929, although he did manage to pass the New York State bar exam that spring.

Berg followed this worst season of his academic career with the very best season of his baseball career, even as the White Sox stumbled through another less-than-stellar summer. (After one particularly humiliating defeat, 17–2, a reporter for a local paper fumed: "The White Sox are no longer comical, they are pathetic."[15]) Berg caught well and batted .288 that year. He was at the peak of his physical powers.

Although Berg was a careful player who made few errors, he did make one terrible mistake in 1929—the worst and most memorable blooper of his career—playing against the Senators, in Washington, with the score tied 1–1. White Sox pitcher Tommy Thomas recalls the story:

> I got the next batter to hit a high foul near the home bench and Moe had to run a long way toward it and he made a darned good catch. I had run to cover home plate so that the runner on third wouldn't attempt to run home after the catch. Then something happened that I've never seen before and probably won't happen again. As soon as Moe caught the ball, he flipped it behind his back toward the pitching mound. He failed to realize that there were only two outs. And while the ball was resting on the unattended mound the Washington runner on third base ran home to give the Senators a 2–1 lead, and that's the way the game ended. The look on Moe's face as the winning run scored should have been recorded for posterity. Moe felt terrible, of course, and he never forgot that play.[16]

Berg wouldn't have been allowed to forget such a play even if he'd tried. After all that time in school, the players and sportswriters jeered, Berg still hadn't learned how to count to three.

Fortunately, this spectacular error was a fluke. Berg was usually a steady player, and pitchers, especially Ted Lyons, liked to have him at the plate. "Moe caught the damnedest game," Lyons recalled. "He was a big man and made a fine target. He had good actions and a strong arm and great hands. His signal calling was flawless and in the years he was to catch me I never waved off a sign; few pitchers did.

He became clinical in studying batters, knew their weaknesses and strengths. He took full advantage of this and pitchers simply felt confident with Moe doing the catching. He was a remarkable handyman. He lacked only speed."[17]

And batting power. Berg's career batting average was a lackluster .243, and he was often teased about his hitting: He could speak so many languages but couldn't hit in any of them. Once, as Berg returned to the bench after striking out for the second time that day, fellow White Sox catcher Frank "Buck" Crouse drawled, "Moe, I don't care how many of them degrees you got. They ain't learned you to hit that curve ball no better than me."[18] But though Berg's hits were few in number, they often came when they were needed most.

Berg did well back in school that fall. He passed his evidence course and, on February 26, 1930, received his LL.B. degree. Practicing law would have to wait, however. Berg reported for a full run of White Sox spring training. He was to be the team's starting catcher that season.

On April 6, Berg and the White Sox played an exhibition game in Little Rock, Arkansas. Berg, leading off first base, caught his cleats in the dirt. His leg twisted sharply, tearing a ligament in the knee.

A damaged knee takes time to heal. Berg checked into a hospital where—gloomy as he must have felt—he nonetheless made a great impression on the nurses. (One, a nun, wrote to him years later: "I'll continue to pray for you and for the Red Sox," which was Berg's team by that time.[19]) After leaving the hospital, Berg worked out a regimen of heat treatments with his brother, who was by then a practicing physician. Although he showed up for work

Moe, nursing his injured leg at Mercy Hospital.

with the White Sox in mid-May, his badly damaged knee wasn't fully healed, and he played in only twenty games that year.

His knee never completely recovered, and it made the already-slow Berg an even slower runner. White Sox management concluded that Berg's best playing days were behind him, and they dropped him.

In October 1930 it was time, finally, for the law. Berg joined the prestigious New York law firm of Satterlee and Canfield as a corporate lawyer and practiced law through the winter.

He hadn't abandoned baseball, though. In spring of 1931 Berg was with the Cleveland Indians. The team already had three adequate catchers, so Berg was a mild gamble. If he turned out to be better than the rest of the pack—if he played as well as or better than he did in 1929—the gamble would pay off. If his knee was too weak, or if he decided to give up baseball to practice law, the Indians wouldn't lose much.

Berg's knee had little opportunity to give him trouble that season. He came down with pneumonia and ended up playing very little.

While Berg was making less and less of a splash on the ballfield, he was making more and more of an impression as an unusual character. It was strange for a ballplayer to be so ostentatiously educated and to try to keep up a professional career—as a lawyer, no less—in the off season. Berg's Jewishness set him apart as well, although he neither emphasized nor attempted to hide it.

Berg developed a well-known array of purely personal eccentricities. By the early 1930s, whenever he wasn't in uniform Berg always dressed exactly the same way: dark gray dress suit, white shirt, black tie, black shoes. His teammates teased him about never changing his clothes, but in fact Berg traveled with a closetful of identical suits, shirts, and ties.

And then there were the newspapers. Berg kept up the habit of reading a wide variety of papers, and when he traveled with the team he carried a separate suitcase just to hold them all. If he got behind in his reading, he'd keep the papers stacked up until he had time to go through them. He said they were "alive" until he read them, and no one was allowed to touch his papers until he'd finished with them. (After he'd read them, the papers were "dead.")

Berg loved newspapers, and the reporters who wrote for them loved Berg. Even if he was no star on the field, Berg was intelligent, colorful, and full of entertaining stories. Reporters faced with writing about a dull game often decided to fill up their columns with Moe Berg anecdotes.

John Kieran, a longtime columnist for the *New York Times*, was especially fond of writing about Berg, and Berg fully appreciated the value of Kieran's affectionate publicity. "You kept me in the big league for years," Berg wrote toward the end of his life to Kieran.[20]

In 1932, the Indians released Berg. He went to the Washington Senators, and he played pretty well that year. He batted .236—hardly spectacular, but many of his hits came when they were badly needed. His catching was solid, and he made not a single error that year. The Senators finished in third place, one game out of second in the American League, and decided to keep Berg on.

Chapter Three

Japan— and the World

By the end of the 1932 baseball season, Moe Berg had settled into the less-than-starring role of an aging third-string catcher with a weak knee. He played less and less but became useful to his team in other capacities—warming up pitchers and providing a steadying influence for talented younger players. Berg knew baseball, and he was an entertaining storyteller. He could, and did, talk about virtually any subject—from the fine points of the game to obscure aspects of linguistics to all manner of trivia. Players, management, and news reporters alike enjoyed his company.

Berg's unique talents made him ideally suited for an unusual enterprise during the 1932-33 off season. Japan had fallen in love with baseball, and an American ex-ballplayer turned entrepreneur, Herb Hunter, had made it his business to bring U.S. baseball know-how to Japan. Hunter in 1931 had organized an all-star American team's

*In 1932, entrepreneur Herb Hunter (first row, far left),
batter Lefty O'Doul (third from left), ace pitcher Ted Lyons
(fifth from left), and Moe Berg (second row, second from
right) traveled several weeks by ocean liner to Japan to teach
baseball to students at universities there.*

tour of Japan, with the American pros playing seventeen exhibition games against Japanese college teams.

For 1932, Hunter decided to bring just a handful of American ballplayers to teach baseball clinics at Japanese universities. Lefty O'Doul, the National League's best batter, would teach the finer points of hitting, fielding, and base running. Ted Lyons, an ace pitcher, would work with Japanese pitchers. And Moe Berg, who alone among the three American pros could be expected to learn to speak at least some Japanese, would work with the catchers.

Today, by jet airplane, American travelers can get to Japan in hours. In 1932 the journey was made by ocean liner, and it took several weeks for Berg and his colleagues to reach their destination. Berg spent much of his travel time studying a Japanese grammar book. By the time he arrived in Japan, Berg had learned enough Japanese to begin to try it out on native speakers. Since most English speakers find the Japanese language very difficult to learn, and few in 1932 even tried to speak any of it, Berg's efforts made him immensely popular in Japan.

Sotaro Suzuki, a Japanese baseball enthusiast who met Berg during the 1932 tour, recalled him vividly and fondly many years later in a letter to a Berg biographer:

Moe was respected as a fine gentle and highly educated intelligent American by everybody who came in contact with him. Suzuki took him as the games finest mathematician in plays. Moe is the first baseball man to teach Japanese players the technic of 'Runner on scoring position,' 'Winning runner' and 'Tying runner,' etc. Japanese baseball learned lots of 'inside baseball' from Moe.[1]

"Baseball fields were everywhere and the love of the game was incomparable," pitcher Ted Lyons recalled years after the tour. "And Moe combined his instruction with vigorous study of the Japanese language. He pursued it as if he were taking his doctorate. The athletes were intrigued by his gifted linguistic ability and understood him perfectly. He was always probing them about the language. No matter where we went in Japan, Moe had a Japanese newspaper in his hand. He bought every paper in sight."[2]

Berg not only learned to speak some Japanese but also picked up the basics of *katakana*—Japan's phonetic written alphabet. He used this knowledge in a restaurant one evening to play a trick on Lefty O'Doul. While O'Doul was trying to order dinner, Berg wrote some *katakana* characters on a napkin, and the waitress read them back, obviously not understanding what she was saying: "O'Doul is the ugliest mug I have ever seen," she read. "He is also a lousy baseball player. Someday he will get hit with a fly ball and get killed."[3]

Berg had a terrific time in Japan. In 1932, Japan was very different from the way it appears today, and it was certainly worlds apart from anything Berg had ever seen. He wrote home describing it all vividly and at great length. He wrote from the Imperial Hotel, in Tokyo:

Dear Famille,
I have never enjoyed a visit or anything any more in my life than this one—Tomorrow will be the third week here and it is marvelous—new, novel, instructive and interesting. Please excuse me for not writing from Tokyo till now. We disembarked late afternoon Octo-

ber 20 at Yokohama—90% of the people to greet the voyageurs were in native, Japanese garb, that is kimonos, etc. No matter how much you read about this, it is a great surprise to see people in the streets with kimonos on—beautiful. Our party had a special car to take us to Tokyo, about ¾ of an hour from Yokohama—so this was the Orient—saw rikshaws . . . at the boat but the auto is driving them out—on the way, smelled some of the distinctive odors of Japan—the ride was a page out of a dream—streets narrow, lined with shops, thousands of people going home from work on bicycles, street cars packed with people, everybody moving—in fact, there are no Japanese loafers—everybody seems to work—have not seen one beggar yet. . . .

    We were met at the boat by a dozen or so Japanese newspapermen and others connected with the University Baseball League here—they are a fine bunch of fellows, very accommodating and are constantly with us to show us all favors and anything we want to do.[4]

Berg's 1932 language is not always what a 1990s reader would consider politically correct. His warmth, enthusiasm, and obviously genuine respect for Japanese customs, however, earned him great popularity among the Japanese—popularity that persisted for many years. Although he came to know many Japanese as individuals, and became close friends with a few of them, in this letter he generalized:

    The Japanese are a very courteous race of people—no shaking of hands in greeting among themselves; they bow almost at right angles 3 or 4 times and while

Moe, with the help of an interpreter, explaining to students at Waseda University in Tokyo the best use of the hands when catching.

bowing they talk about the weather, how everybody is at home and then bow some more—very intriguing and interesting—I greet all my Japanese friends with bows now. They bow to say "hello" and again for "good-bye."

The meals here are excellent. . . . In order to show one's appreciation of the meal, especially the hot tea, you must inhale it with the noise of a steel-mill at full blast, sound your p's and q's, dot your i's and cross your t's and then when the food or drink has passed your gullet, you exhale a sound of satisfaction—and so your host or hostess knows you are enjoying the food. . . .

Contrary to what is generally believed, the Japanese are a very clean race, especially the women—they bathe in extremely hot water, once or twice *every day*—and the women always look fresh, clean and there are some beautiful girls here—they all walk pigeon-toed like Mama and me—believe me, Mama would make a great Japanese lady in every way—fine black hair, about the right size and a good disposition like all these ladies here—everybody smiles here . . . .

The Ginza (GINZA) nicknamed by me GINZBERG is a fine broad street, the main street here . . . a motley of colors—oriental and western dress and very few foreigners.[5]

Together with the other American ballplayers, Berg taught American-style baseball to Japan's top players. According to Berg, here's how it went:

On account of rainy weather before we arrived, the league season here was continued. Games are played about 3 or 4 times a week until November 20. We coach sometimes morning, sometimes afternoon and it is very interesting. The colleges here play the best baseball in Japan—there is no professional baseball—the six universities in Tokyo (all in the surrounding and outlying districts) play a two game series with each other—spring and fall—we are in the fall season. . . . O'Doul coaches the hitters—I the catchers—Lyons the pitchers and after a couple of days, we play a game and stop it to correct faults as they come up—we are at each school 5 or 6 days—put on uniform at the hotel and drive to ballgrounds in a car—the league games are played at Meiji Shrine grounds and, believe me, there is plenty of interest here—I have seen 40,000 at a game here already.

Moe made several good friends in Japan. Here he is with Takizo "Frank" Matsumoto, professor at Meiji University. Both men are wearing the traditional Japanese kimono. Moe learned to write and speak the language and to follow many of the Japanese customs.

. . . Women go to the games—kimonos and all but western dress predominates at ball game—they have cheering sections like at our football games—no doubt about it, baseball is the national pastime here.[6]

At one of the universities visited by the American ballplayers, Berg became friends with Takizo Matsumoto, who helped Berg with his Japanese. "MATSUMOTO," Berg wrote, "my age, teacher of English at Meiji Univ. is my close friend and teacher—I teach him French."[7] Matsumoto was as keen about going to America as Berg was about being in Japan; several years later, Berg helped Matsumoto to enroll at

Harvard Business School. After the baseball tour ended, Berg traveled throughout Japan with his new friend, soaking up the culture.

Berg didn't hurry home after touring Japan. Instead, he embarked on a grand world tour, seeing as much of Asia, the Middle East, and Europe as he could cram into a few months of travel. Berg's first stop was Manchuria, a region of what is now China. China in the early 1930s was governed by a confusing welter of authorities: Factions of native Chinese, several Western governments interested in Asian trade, and imperial Japan all vied for control in various regions. Japan, especially, was an increasingly aggressive presence. In 1931 the Japanese military had occupied Manchuria and set up a Japanese-controlled government there called "Manchukuo." In a long letter written to his family on New Year's Eve from Bangkok, Berg chronicles the turbulent politics of the places he has just visited:

> Dear Folks,
>   Happy New Year! . . . The last time I wrote you in detail was Manchuria I believe . . . snowing and very cold [when I arrived there]—two gentlemen greeted me—am always meeting people, and leave them or have their company as I please . . . . They showed me everything in Mukden. After the Japanese-Russian war of 1904–05, the Japanese were given a lease on the territory of the South Manchuria Railway—it runs down a central strip of territory . . . through Mukden . . . well, to make it brief, all you see along the railroad is Japanese military—they have construed the lease to mean whole territories adjoining the r.r. too and are administering whole cities like Mukden. . . .

Saw no bandits, but the air is rife with uncertainty. Swords and guns all over and you never know where trouble is going to strike.

The old walled Chinese city [within Mukden] is interesting. You must use Chinese stamps to mail letters from within that because the Chinese (if the letter travels via China) will not recognize Manchukuo.

Took a train to Dairen [another city in Manchukuo] (midnight to 8 A.M.)—spent the morning there—the Japanese have built the newer part into a modern city—a fine sea-port.

Left noon . . . for Tientsin, China [governed by the Chinese Nationalists] (arrived 3 P.M. next day)—pleasant and enjoyable trip on a rather small boat—from the second morning till Tientsin, up a stream from . . . the first small port of China I saw—all mud houses there. Tientsin, with its tall buildings, looked like a part of U.S.—

To know China, you must remember that parts of almost all the cities are concessions to foreign governments. These governments have administrative power over the concessions, but China is supposed to own the land. . . .

Peking, now Peiping [today Beijing] . . . the old capital of China . . . a beautiful city, all walls. . . . Since the Boxer rebellion about 1900, brought about by the Chinese in Peking as a protest against foreign invasion (British, American, etc.—and you'll see it again), all the embassies here have their own separate and beautiful, modern quarters and guards, soldiers of the respective countries, guns on their shoulders in front of the embassy gates. . . .

In Peiping about 3 days—then, the Shanghai Express, leaves Peiping early evening and arrives Shanghai 48 hours later—I travelled in a vapor-lit coach . . .

Shanghai is a modern city. . . . Many tall buildings, bank, shipping, commercial etc. on the [waterfront]. . . . I saw two great big warships, English and American, [and] a Japanese ship . . . there'll be trouble here some day—

Visited . . . the district that the Japanese ruined here [in Shanghai] early this year—the Japanese tried to stop a Chinese boycott on their goods with force and murder and I don't think they succeeded.[8]

Berg traveled southward from China. His first destination was Saigon, now the capital of Vietnam, then the hub of the French colony of Indochina. His letter continues:

Left Shanghai on S.S. Clemonceaux Dec. 17 for Saigon, French Indo-China . . . to Hongkong [along the way] on Tuesday Dec. 20—spent from early morning till 3 P.M. there—an island belonging to Great Britain—all the English and Americans live on the side of a great hill here—picturesque—the [hot] climate a distinct change from Peking and Shanghai—men in shorts, no shirts, the girls, as in Shanghai wear tight-fitting skirts with slits up the side, above the knee some of them— very fashionable. . . .

The 23d in Saigon—extremely hot—nobody moves except me—cafes on the sidewalk just like Paris. . . .

From Saigon to Pnom-Penh by auto-bus (French company), no r.r.—5 A.M. X-mas morning, arrived 11 A.M. . . .

Pnom-Penh to Angkor [Angkor Wat], former capital of Cambodia . . . the most thrilling sight I saw in the Orient—beautiful, immense palaces deserted in the middle of a forest and rediscovered about 70 years ago . . . .

Then to . . . Siamese city on the border (Siam-Cambodia) by auto in time to catch early morning train to Bangkok—

This is all wild animal country—was invited to hunt tigers, but told the Frenchman who invited me I didn't eat meat—wild elephants, tigers, all snakes, rhinoceros, panthers everything—was told this was the mating season for tigers and they journeyed even to the edge of villages (usually keep away from lights) so I did not promenade at night.[9]

Berg outlined where he planned to go next:

Now on my way inland to India—Calcutta through Benares, Agra, Delhi—then to Egypt and Palestine, then Athens and then Europe—have decided to see it all at not much extra expense—may never have the chance to see it again. . . .

Will be in Athens about January 21 . . . then Vienna, Berlin, and Paris . . . where I will be late January or early February—will sail home early February—will give you details later. . . .

I am having wonderful time in every way studying the people, etc. . . . Love, Moe[10]

Berg *did* just about see it all. He climbed a pyramid in Egypt, and he crossed the Sea of Galilee and visited the River Jordan in Palestine (now Israel and the West Bank). He arrived in Berlin just after the Nazi leader Adolf Hitler became chancellor of Germany. He also probably visited his beloved Paris. And then he sailed home.

Chapter Four

More Baseball— and More of Japan

Moe Berg made it home in time for spring training. The Senators had a great year in 1933 (they
won the pennant); 1934 was a disaster. Berg
played steady though not spectacular ball through
the two seasons. He broke the American League
record by playing without a single error for 117
games in a row.

But it took him two years to do it. By this
time, Berg wasn't being put in to play very often;
however, it didn't seem to matter to him. "Isn't
this wonderful," he once said. "Work three hours
a day, travel around the country, live in the best
hotels, meet the best people, and get paid for it."[1]
Berg's love of travel life shines through this 1932
telegram he sent from Salt Lake City to his father back in Newark:

JUST LIKE A DREAM TWO PASSENGER
MAIL PLANE SINGLE MOTOR SPED LIKE A
GOD OVER AMERICAS GOOD EARTH

FARM LAND AND MORE FARM LAND ILLINOIS
THE MISSISSIPPI IOWA THE MISSOURI NEBRASKA
FARMS AND SANDHILLS DINNER CHEYENNE NIGHT
RIDE SALTLAKE LEAVING SIX THIRTY MORNING
LOSANGELES

M.[2]

Washington, during the years he played for the Senators, made a congenial home base for Berg, whose exceptional language skills, educated demeanor, and graciousness with the ladies earned him invitations to countless embassy dinners and receptions. Baseball not only paid his salary but also made it possible for him to hang around the ballpark watching ball games, catching from time to time, encouraging his teammates, and talking with whomever else happened to be hanging around.

Fortunately the Senators' manager, Joe Cronin, valued Berg for his usefulness off the field. Cronin recalls:

He was a living university in a baseball uniform. He loved the game and was a smart ballplayer. That's why I wanted him on my team. He had a great influence on a club, knew how to handle men. Moe was the only man I know of who could sit on the bench for two months, then be brought into a game and catch perfectly. I would wave him in from the bullpen. Moe would approach me in the dugout and ask if the rules of the game were still the same and if everyone still got three strikes due them. Then, with a big smile on his face, he would get behind the plate hollering encouragement to the players.[3]

As the Senators skidded through their miserable 1934 season, however, both Cronin's and Berg's time with the team ran out. During a mid-season management shakeup that August, the Senators dropped Berg from their roster.

Within days, the Cleveland Indians once again picked him up. By now, Berg was hardly a hot prospect, and he didn't play often for the Indians. "When I was catching with Cleveland," Berg later told a group at Princeton, "and [Al] Schacht was in town with the Washington Senators he asked me to go out with him and drink a few beers. Now, Walter Johnson was manager of the Indians at the time and he was a stickler for training rules. So I said, 'Why Al, you know how Johnson is, everybody in by eleven-thirty.' But Schacht came back with 'Why, I'm sure Walter won't mind, Moe, as long as I don't keep any of the ballplayers out.' "[4] Berg finished the 1934 season at Cleveland as he'd begun it for the Senators—playing well enough, though not very often, and rarely brilliantly.

The 1934–35 off-season was far more exciting for Berg than the previous summers had been. Herb Hunter tapped him for an all-star team he was assembling to tour Japan and play a series of exhibition ballgames against a team of Japan's best. The American team was to feature Babe Ruth, whom Japanese baseball fans had been clamoring to see for years.

Just before they sailed for Japan, Ruth asked Berg: "You're such a linguist; do you speak Japanese?"

"No, I never had occasion to learn it," Berg lied, setting up a joke. On board ship, Berg once again studied the language, and when they arrived in Japan, Ruth overheard him speaking it to someone at the dock.

"Wait a minute," Ruth said. "You told me you didn't speak Japanese."

"That was two weeks ago," said Berg.[5]

Berg was thrilled to return to Japan, even though relations between Japan and the United States were strained by 1934 and Japan was increasingly becoming a totalitarian state. The Japanese military had tightened its control over Manchukuo and was extending its reach deeper into China. Western nations, including the United States, disapproved, but did nothing that effectively countered Japan's

Herb Hunter's All-American team toured Japan to play seventeen exhibition ball games against Japan. Moe is in the first row, far right. Lou Gehrig is standing, second from right. Babe Ruth, a favorite in Japan, is sixth from right.

aggression. As diplomatic relations frayed, hostility and even contempt toward the West grew among the Japanese people.

Diplomatic tensions notwithstanding, many Japanese loved baseball, and they received the American baseball team enthusiastically. Huge numbers turned out everywhere they played. Berg played little, however, appearing in only six out of seventeen games. Nonetheless, as a baseball-playing linguist and scholar, Berg was popular with the Japanese press and the public.

He was even asked to make a speech at Meiji University. Berg, speaking in English, told the Japanese audience:

> Two years ago I had the honor of coaching your base-
> ball team in conjunction with the other five universi-

ties of Tokyo. And now I am particularly happy to be your guest again at Meiji University because of all that that great name brings up. It is particularly fitting for us to be here in our role of baseball players because I believe the Emperor Meiji, for whom your great university was named, would have been happy to see foreign commerce and intercourse spread to the world of sports. Those who know ever so little of Japanese history do know that it was during the prosperous era of Meiji that Japan bloomed into a world nation. . . . And now added to your desire to trade with us and other nations you have done us the honor of adopting our national game as yours. There is no greater leveller, no greater teacher of humility than competitive sports, and I sincerely hope that our innocent junket thru Japan

The All-American team in Hawaii for an exhibition game, en route to Japan in 1934. Moe Berg and Babe Ruth are standing at center. Lou Gehrig is standing at far right.

will serve to bring the countries whom we represent unofficially closer together.[6]

Berg's attempts at unofficial diplomacy cut both ways. In addition to speaking to the Japanese students, he spoke over the radio from Tokyo to the United States. "It would be a revelation to you folks back home," he said, "to see what a marvelous influence a representative all-American ball team can have in cementing and furthering the good relations and overthrowing the barriers of race, language, politics, and customs of our widely separated nations—we are playing against the best Japan has to offer on three of the four islands and having a fine time doing it. I hope an innocent adventure like ours will turn out to be a scoop of diplomacy without portfolio."[7]

During his time in Japan, Moe Berg pulled off an extraordinarily audacious stunt. Berg had brought a movie camera with him to Japan, apparently to be used in fulfilling a contract he had signed to film highlights of his trip for a U.S. newsreel producer. Although by 1934 the Japanese government was very leery of foreigners with cameras (and the Japanese press frequently hissed about purported foreign spies), Berg got away with taking pictures wherever he wanted, which was just about everywhere he went. Berg knew, however, that even he could push this too far—and that's just what he decided to do.

On November 29, Berg didn't show up for a baseball game. Few people noticed that he was missing, and those who did didn't think much of it. "I remember Moe being missing from the ballpark that day," says Lefty Gomez. "He had disappeared and no one on the team knew where the hell he was. Of course Moe was a mysterious guy all his

In 1934, the Japanese were concerned about foreign spies and cameras, but that didn't stop Moe from documenting the trip with his movie camera.

life. He looked the same at six in the morning, eight in the evening or at midnight. He was always moving about. He was always coming from some place or other. No one ever knew where he lived or what he did with his time. He'd spend some time with the guys but overall Moe Berg was total mystery. You could expect anything as far as Moe was concerned."[8] The Americans' first-string catcher caught the whole game, and they clobbered Japan 23-5.

Berg, meanwhile, was miles away, in Tokyo, taking pictures that the Japanese government certainly would not have permitted. Incredibly, Berg had slicked back his hair, dressed up in traditional Japanese clothes, picked up a bouquet of flowers, walked into St. Luke's Hospital, and asked where he might find the daughter of the U.S. ambassador, Elsie Lyon, who had just given birth to her first child. At six-feet-one-inch, large-framed and muscular, Berg must have made a startling picture in his kimono. Still, the hospital's front desk directed him to the fifth floor.

Berg rode the elevator to the fifth floor, got off, dropped the flowers in a trash can, then re-boarded the elevator without visiting Mrs. Lyon. He rode up two more flights to the top floor, climbed a spiral staircase into St. Luke's belltower, and then pulled his camera out from under his kimono.

St. Luke's Hospital was built on the outskirts of town, right on Tokyo Bay. At that time no building built in Tokyo could be taller than the emperor's palace. St. Luke's was just far enough away that the height restriction didn't apply, but close enough so that its belltower commanded a clear view of all of the city.

Berg slowly panned his camera over the entire panorama spread out below him. When he had finished, he hid the camera beneath his kimono once again, then climbed back down the staircase and left the hospital.

Years later Berg claimed, or others claimed for him, that his film had been used by the U.S. armed forces to plot bombing raids over Japan during World War II. Certainly Berg gave his film to the U.S. government, but by wartime better and more current pictures were available, so it's unlikely that the U.S. military had any real use for Berg's film footage.

At the time the film was made, however, it must have seemed quite a daring stunt to Berg. He got away with it, and the experience both tested and demonstrated his capacity for invention, steady nerves, and audacity.

Two days later Berg was back in uniform at the final Japanese game of the tour. The American team, and Berg, then sailed to Shanghai for an exhibition game, then to the Philippines for two more.

After the team disbanded, Berg once again went traveling on his own. He was keen to try out the fabled Trans-Siberian Railroad; years later he was still telling stories about the six-day trip:

> My real introduction to modern Russia was the first call to the dining room on the trans-Siberian train on leaving the border of Manchukuo. It was evening, and they were serving *breakfast*. . . . Of course, I had to ask the reason why, and the waiter looked askance at me. Pulling out his watch, and addressing me in his haughtiest Red Russian, he said, "Comrade, in Moscow, the capitol of the Union of the Soviet Socialistic Republics, it is morning, and we do not change our watches for meals in Siberia."[9]

Berg traveled with the camera he'd used in Japan, but his photo-taking luck didn't hold. In Moscow, Berg was detained for taking pictures and had his film confiscated. In April, he returned home.

The Cleveland Indians had dropped Berg from their roster while he was in Japan, but Berg wasn't through yet with baseball. His old buddy Joe Cronin, who had been let go by the Senators and became coach for the Boston Red Sox at the end of 1934, learned that Berg was available and offered him a catching contract. Berg headed up to Boston as the Sox returned from spring training in April.

In the spring of 1935, the United States was mired in the Great Depression—the hardest economic times in the nation's history. Millions were out of work, jobs of any kind were hard to find, and good jobs were rare indeed. Berg's brother, Sam, remembers "during the depression standing outside the pharmacy talking with my father. We were discussing income and how difficult it was for everybody in the country. And then we referred to Moe. I said, 'Well look, Pa, after all Moe's making a living. He's a baseball player.' And my father said, 'A sport,' then turned his head and feigned spitting. He did not like it."[10] Whether his father—who never once came to see his son play pro ball—liked it or not, baseball was a very good living for Moe Berg, one that gave him a life that he loved.

Berg played adequately for Boston, though less and less often—and that seemed just fine with him. He didn't seem to have a great drive to be the very best (which would have been beyond his reach at this point in his career); he just wanted to be on the team. And he knew he was welcome with the Red Sox. Reporter Harold Kaese tells a story about Berg at spring training one year:

> The Red Sox had a rookie catcher in George Lacey. The first day of spring practice, Berg was on the field working like a horse. The second day, he was on the training table, reading a paper. "What's the idea, Moe? You're supposed to be out there winning a place on the team." "I was out yesterday, looked over the opposition, and saw I had nothing to worry about."[11]

Berg knew that, at his age and with his bad knee, he wasn't up to the rigors of playing often. Rick Ferrell, a young Red Sox catcher during Berg's years with the team, recalls that "Joe Cronin's locker was two down from mine. We'd play a doubleheader in Boston and Moe'd come over to my locker after the first game and say, 'Rick, you're the greatest catcher in the American League. Joe, let's not change the lineup.' So I'd catch two games. I didn't care. He didn't want to play unless he had to."[12] More and more, Berg's role was to train younger catchers, warm up pitchers, and report on the progress of up-and-coming players.

Baseball was still only one part of Berg's life, not the whole thing. He continued to plow through heaps of news-papers, as well as stacks of books. "I remember one trip we went on," says teammate Eldon Auker. "Moe got on the train. He was all excited. He had a book about four feet thick. The title was *The Holy Bible in 1,000 Languages*. It must have weighed twenty pounds. He couldn't wait to sit down and open it up. He'd found it somewhere in Boston. It made his day and, I guess, most of his year."[13]

Berg's improbable literary and academic interests not only attracted the attention of his teammates but also continued to inspire reporters. John Kieran, perhaps desperate for colorful copy on a dull December day, passed along this report from a fellow Berg watcher:

It may be hard to catch the learned catcher. He moves mysteriously. The last report of his whereabouts [placed] Professor Berg in the audience down at Princeton University a week or so ago when Dr. Thomas Mann, the eminent exile [from Germany], was delivering a lecture on Goethe's Faust. Mr. Bushnell [Kieran's source for this story] lost track of him after the lecture, but thinks Professor Berg went looking for Dr. Albert Einstein for the purpose of discussing critically Professor Archibald Henderson's monograph on the internal bisector problem offered lightly as "A Classic Problem in Euclidean Geometry." It is known that this is a subject that Professor Berg has had on his mind since he read Professor Henderson's monograph during a double-header between the Red Sox and the Detroit Tigers in Detroit one day late last Summer.[14]

When he wasn't haunting lecture halls and ballparks, Berg was something of a ladies' man. He was rather secretive about the women he dated and kept this part of his life separate from his teammates. He was, however, often seen out for the evening with an attractive woman on his arm, none of whom became a habit with him—until he met Estella Huni.

Estella Huni was a delicately beautiful, witty, and vivacious young woman when Moe Berg met her in New York, probably in the mid-1930s. An accomplished musician, she earned her living giving recitals and piano lessons. Although Berg didn't share Huni's passion for music, the two had several key common interests: she read as widely and deeply as Berg did and, better yet, she shared his love of languages and the origins of words.

Further, both loved to go out on the town and did so often, in New York and in Boston, where Huni would visit Berg during the baseball season. Huni herself lived in New York, and when Berg was in town he stayed at her Upper East Side apartment. It was unusual, even scandalous for an unmarried couple to live together openly at that time. Berg's father did not approve of the arrangement and re-

fused to meet Huni. Berg's brother, sister, and mother, however, all became fond of her.[15]

In the entire 1938 season, Berg caught in only ten
games—an idle season even by Berg's relaxed standards.
"Professor Berg, the Red Sox catcher . . ," John Kieran joked
after the season was over, "officiates only in the second games
of double-headers and not even then if it is a hot day."[16]

In 1939, however, what Berg did or didn't do on the
field wasn't pressingly important to Red Sox management;
he had become worth his salary for an entirely novel reason. During the off-season, in yet another bizarre twist in
his career, Berg had become a national sensation and an
unofficial goodwill ambassador for baseball in general and
the Sox in particular—as a radio trivia wizard.

Moe and "Black" Jack Wilson, during spring training in Florida.

He Tags 'Em Out at Second in Sixteen Languages

In the 1930s, radio swept the United States the way that television would do in the 1950s. Nearly everyone listened to the radio—for music, of course, but also for news and for the sort of entertainment Americans now get from television: comedy programs, programs that tell a dramatic story, and game shows. One of the most popular radio game shows, "Information, Please," quizzed a panel of experts on all manner of trivia.

Berg for years had been amusing teammates and reporters alike with his apparently unlimited command of trivia. It seemed he knew something about everything, and in particular was famous for rattling off information about places that came up in the course of casual conversation. One reporter recorded this exchange Berg had had with the temperamental rookie Red Sox catcher Ted Williams, at spring training: " 'So you come from San Diego, eh, young man?' said Mr. Berg, who, if he pooled his information with Einstein's, would have all but about 2 per cent of the information there is. 'So what?' said Mr. Williams suspiciously. 'San Diego,' mused Mr. Berg. 'County seat of San Diego County, about 15 miles north of the Mexican border. An excellent harbor. Largest naval and marine base west of Chicago.' " [17]

John Kieran appeared regularly on "Information, Please," and it was almost certainly Kieran who suggested that Berg be invited on the program as a guest expert. On February 21, 1939, the program's announcer introduced Berg to its national audience: "Professor Berg catches for the Boston Red Sox. In addition, he's got a string of degrees long enough to hang yourself. A philological baseball player is something new on this program. Okay, Mr. Berg. I'll pitch 'em, you catch 'em." [18]

Berg was a hit, correctly answering one obscure query after another. Reporters trailed him all summer long, peppering him with trivia questions which he answered gamely, and usually correctly. Boxes of letters from fans piled up at NBC, the radio network that produced "Information, Please," demanding that Berg be brought back on the air. Berg appeared on the program twice more, in October and November of that year.

Not even Moe Berg could catch forever. Newspapers reported in February 1940 that Berg had been dropped from Boston's playing roster and would become a coach for the team. "Of course," John Kieran noted, "the term 'coach' was not sufficiently academic under the circumstances. . . . In the case of Professor Berg, who had prepped at Princeton, the Sorbonne and Columbia law, 'instructor' should have been the starting title, with a full professorship coming in due time."[19]

Berg settled in as a bullpen coach and spent 1940 and 1941 pretty much as he had spent his last few years on the playing roster. In 1941, *Atlantic Monthly* asked Moe Berg to write an article about baseball. The eight-page essay Berg produced, "Pitchers and Catchers," distilled his two decades of baseball experience into one of the canniest primers ever written on the teamwork needed to play the game well:

> We know that the pitcher studies the strength and weakness of every hitter and that the hitter notes every variety of pitch in the pitcher's repertory; that the big-league hitter is resourceful, and quick to meet every new circumstance. . . .
>
> [The catcher] signals the pitcher what to throw, and this implies superior baseball brains on his part. But a pitcher can put a veto on a catcher's judgment by shaking him off and waiting for another sign. The game cannot go on until he pitches. . . . Of course, no player monopolizes the brains on a ball club. The catcher gives the signals only because he is in a better position than the pitcher to hide them. . . .
>
> The whole club plays as a unit to win. The signs that the pitcher and catcher agree on reflect the collective ideas, the judgment of all the players on how to get the opposition out. . . . The players know how the pitcher intends to throw to each opponent. They re-

view their strategy before game time, as a result of which they know how the battery is going to work, and they play accordingly. . . . The players are not interested in the score, but merely in how many runs are necessary to tie and to win. . . . The idea is to win.[20]

By the time Berg wrote this, he had drifted far from the center of the ballpark's action, but that didn't seem to bother him. "I seek no other man's shoes," he later told sports columnist Arthur Siegel. "If I've misdirected my priorities, and I'm confident that this is not so, I've had a pretty fair time in lost country. There are no regrets."[21]

Chapter
Five

Latin
America

On September 1, 1939, Nazi Germany invaded
Poland, unleashing World War II. In the spring
of 1940, German troops marched through Nor-
way, Denmark, the Netherlands, Luxembourg,
and Belgium. In June, the French government
surrendered Paris to Nazi occupation. "Europe is
in flames," Berg told a sportswriter, "withering
in a fire set by Hitler. All over the Continent men
and women and children are dying. Soon we too
will be involved. And what am I doing? Sitting in
the bullpen telling stories to the relief pitchers."[1]

The escalating war in Europe and the threat
it posed to America weighed heavily on Berg.
"Moe was from an era and background that held
strong loyalties to the country," his brother Sam
noted. "Our parents were fiercely loyal and proud
of America. This trait was reflected in Moe."[2]

Berg had faith that good would ultimately
triumph over the evil of fascism. In a 1940 speech
at a book fair in Boston, Berg said:

As I looked about this Book Fair today, I thought of Paris, the Paris when it was still France, where a few years back, I first enjoyed browsing at the bookstalls along the Seine. These days will come back, they always do. . . . Spirit, ideas, triumph over force. There are wall-builders and book-burners still rampant today, but they cannot win over *our* great wall, the wall of ideas as crystallized in the books you see around you tonight. And so all those walls and fortifications are fleeting; only thought within the covers of a book is indestructible.[3]

As 1940 stretched into 1941, the war spread. On December 7, 1941, Japanese bombers attacked the U.S. military base at Pearl Harbor in Hawaii. America was now in the war.

Only weeks later, Moe Berg left baseball to join the fight against fascism, quitting the Red Sox to work for Nelson Rockefeller, who was then coordinator of the Office of Inter-American Affairs (OIAA). (An old friend of Berg's had arranged an interview for him at the office.) The OIAA's mission was to bolster the war effort by encouraging friendly relations between the United States and its neighbors—now allies—in Central and South America during World War II.

U.S. relations with Latin America labored under a legacy of heavy-handed U.S. interference. Nazi propaganda played on long-standing Latin American resentment of old U.S. military interventions and wariness of Yankee imperialism. Although all of the nations of Latin America (except for Argentina) broke off official relations with the fascist powers soon after the United States entered the war, fascism retained many Latin American sympathizers who posed a threat to the American war effort.

In 1941, with America at war, the Red Sox catcher quit his job to begin another career.

Berg's retirement from baseball to join the OIAA was nationwide news in January 1942. With his eyes on the future, rather than on exploiting his faded baseball glory, Berg told a hometown Newark newspaper: "I have no intention of making a so-called goodwill tour in the hemisphere countries to the south. This program goes much deeper. It may take in, for instance, health and athletics, nutrition and diet, and a study of the best means of promoting good will between the hemisphere countries."[4]

And what did Bernard Berg think of his younger son setting aside baseball—at long last—to take part in the war effort? He never found out about it. Bernard Berg had been ill for some time, and he died that month without knowing about his son's career change.

Moe Berg loved his father. Just how important his father was to him, and how fond he was of the old man, comes through in a letter Berg wrote for his father's birthday the year before his father died:

> Dear Pa,
>
> Congratulations on your birthday. You must realize what a tower of strength, an oracle you have been to all of us. And we appreciate, Ethel, Sam and I, more than we have ever told you, what you have meant to us at all times, through thick and thin—and, thank God, because of your early teachings, it has been mostly on the happy side for all of us. You have imbued us with a firm grasp of the human side of life, you have given us a sense of values from the earliest time that we can remember. You, yourself, grasped the meaning of life, its true value, early, and because it wasn't easy, you have been able all these years to sit still, like the Chinese philosopher who said "Be like a rock."—you did and the world, through books and keen insight, came to you. We have, too, seen much, and we value what you mean to us all the more.[5]

Moe Berg was sworn in at the OIAA on January 21, but he didn't go to Latin America right away. His first contribution to the war effort, in fact, had to do with neither the OIAA nor even the Western Hemisphere. Instead, the fledgling U.S. Office of Strategic Services (OSS) tapped Berg to make a propaganda speech, in Japanese, that was broadcast late in February by radio to Japan. By that time, the Japanese military was overrunning great swaths of the Far East, and the United States and its allies were not yet fully mobilized to push them back.

I speak to you as a friend of the Japanese people, as one who has studied the origins of your language, your history, your civilization, your progress, your adaptability, your culture, and I have found much to admire. . . .

It may seem presumptuous of me to speak to you, the Japanese people, while we are at war with you, but may I recall that I was greeted by thousands of you on two other and happier occasions . . . .

I am able to talk to you somewhat in your own language, because I studied it in order to know you better. I lived among you, and traveled with intimate Japanese friends, to see your historic sites and appreciate your cultural history.

I have admired the exquisite delicacy of your art, the woodprints of Hokusai, Toyokuni and Hiroshige.

I stood on the bridge, sacred to you, in Kyoto, where Ushiwakamaru fought his famous battles.

I journeyed to and admired the temples of Nikko and the falls of Kegon No Taki. . . .

Just ten years ago I watched, with thousands of you, the return of your Emperor from military maneuvers on his way across the Nijubashi. And my head too was lowered in reverence.

Even in those days, when an excess of nationalism seized upon many of you, still there were innumerable

Moe visits me a few days before departure for overseas.

Before leaving for Latin America in 1943 to work for the Office of Inter-American Affairs (OIAA), Moe visited his brother Sam in California.

delightful contacts possible. You loved us enough to copy our national game—baseball. We appreciated it when thousands of you gave our all-American baseball team a great reception in 1934, waving American flags. . . .

I ask you, what sound basis is there for enmity between two peoples who enjoy the same national sport? . . .

This war is no great surprise to me. Exactly ten years ago I could see that war was imminent unless you, the Japanese people, could rise up and break the power of the warlords. . . .

I know your glorious history, about your samurai, the Cult of Bushido, your love of the Confucian classics. I was impressed by your hospitality and customs—all these things I still admire. But you betrayed your friends—you made a sneak attack on Pearl Harbor while your Ambassadors Nomura and Kurusu were carrying out diplomatic conversations with us; you have lost face and are committing national *seppuku* [ritual suicide].

We assumed you were civilized even in battle—we thought we saw that when we taught you our national game and watched you play it. We thought that you played and would fight according to rules.

But you have outraged us and every other nation in the world with the exception of two—two that are tainted with blood, Germany and Italy. They welcome you as friends.

But your temporary victories will bring you only misery.

You cannot win this war. We and the twenty other republics of America are unified—we are united.

Your leaders have betrayed you. They have misinterpreted democratic freedom and debate for weakness. The Matsuokas, your Jingoist army and navy officers, and your Axis partners, Hitler and Mussolini, have misjudged us, have misled you. . . .

Believe me when I tell you that you cannot win this war. I am speaking to you as a friend of the Japanese people, and tell you to take the reins now. Your warlords are not telling you the truth.

The people of the United States and the people of Japan can be friends as they were in the past.

It is up to you![6]

Berg's speech likely touched the hearts of Japanese whom he had met during his two visits to Japan, but it obviously did not subvert the war effort. Furthermore, sadly, a passion for baseball soon ceased to be a bond between Japanese and Americans: The Japanese government disapproved of the game of its enemy and discouraged baseball playing during the war.

As Berg focused temporarily on Japan, the OIAA mulled over what sort of work he should do next. By April 1942, his assignment was clear: Tens of thousands of U.S. troops were stationed at bases throughout Latin America, and Berg's mission would be to visit the troops and report back to the OIAA on ways to improve their living conditions and boost their morale. He would also (no matter what he had told the newspapers earlier) serve as something of a goodwill ambassador—and he'd keep his eyes and ears open for any information that might be useful to U.S. intelligence operations.

Berg spent several months, mostly in Washington, preparing for his new work before heading south. By summer's end his buddy John Kieran could report: "Professor Berg, former instructor of foreign languages and international economics in the Red Sox bullpen, is no longer in baseball. He is now a diplomat in the South American field."[7]

Berg's Latin American itinerary was dizzying: a week in Panama, then a stop at an aircraft warning station in Costa Rica, followed by a runway on the Pacific coast of Peru, the Galápagos Islands, Ecuador, Guatemala, Honduras, Panama again, bases in Colombia, Aruba, Curaçao, Venezuela, then on to Trinidad and Dutch Guiana. By mid-October, Berg was traveling in Brazil, where he would remain through December.

Berg's reports to OIAA chief Rockefeller not only detailed conditions on U.S. military bases but also addressed much broader, longer-range issues of U.S.-Latin American relations. He wrote:

> The place to stress our democracy and democratic principles, and to teach away non-constitutional dictatorships of any kind and degree—the bitter lesson must now be clear to all freedom-loving people that the slightest touch of dictatorship poisons our life—is in the school, the university. The young student is impressionable. Exchange of students and teachers is vital for firsthand information about us and our democratic way of life. The teacher, with convictions, will, himself, scrutinize the texts and his fellow-teachers. The question of non-intervention in other sovereign nations' affairs, internal meddling, will not arise. Our example will be strong enough. More understanding North Americans ought to mingle with the Latins, speak their language and stress democracy in their talk and actions. We must let the real democrats, in the generic sense of the term, know where we stand, selfishly because it is vital to us and, unselfishly, as a matter of good neighborliness.[8]

Moe Berg's education in languages and law prepared him for his new career as goodwill ambassador and diplomat for the OIAA—and for his career eventually as a spy for the OSS.

During Berg's time in Brazil, his mission changed. All of the sports and other equipment for U.S. troops either had been delivered or was on its way, and Berg had no more bases to visit. So he turned to gathering intelligence. January found him traveling from Rio de Janeiro to São Paulo, then back to Rio again by the middle of the month, where he learned, via an ex-consul from Brazil's embassy in Italy, that Benito Mussolini, the fascist dictator of Italy, "is degenerating both physically and spiritually, that his son-in-law, Count Ciano, is gaining in popularity, especially because, says the ex-consul, Ciano was never for the war, and that Germany [Italy's ally in the war] has practically occupied Italy, with 50,000 German troops in Rome."[9]

From sources within the Brazilian military, Berg learned that anti-American sentiment was hampering support for the war effort. Among the details he learned and reported to Rockefeller:

> Bulletin #26 issued by the Brazilian Chief of Staff, secretly published on December 30 or 31, 1942, [was] to be read to all officers of the Brazilian Army within ten days and then destroyed, the contents and substance as follows:
> 1) The United States promised Brazil such and such but has given or are giving Brazil only so much.
> 2) (To mitigate this indictment of the United States in failure to carry out a promise) Brazil itself is not producing what it should for the war effort.
> This bulletin comes from the official war headquarters of a country allied with us in a war, criticizing us. The impression the general [Berg's source] wanted to give is that this bulletin reflects the attitude of the authors, some of Brazil's chief generals, toward the United States and what we are fighting for.[10]

Further on in this report, Berg notes: "In all my visits and talks with the above Brazilians I made clear that although I was making an official trip my status with them was unofficial and off the record."[11] Berg, by his own design, had in effect become a spy.

By mid-February Berg had returned to Washington, where he wrote up a lengthy and detailed final report of his mission. Rockefeller responded to Berg's report with a letter of generous praise:

> I want to take this opportunity to tell you how much I appreciate all you've done for this Office and for the Government. Your work in assisting the Army to orient more effectively their units in South America to the various local problems has contributed greatly to the inter-American programs. Only someone with your experience and knowledge of international as well as human problems could have handled this situation with such tact and effectiveness.[12]

His job, well done, was now behind him, and Berg found himself at loose ends. Latin America, it was clear by now, wasn't going to be overrun by Nazis or invaded by Japanese. The war's real action was elsewhere, and Berg wanted to be a part of it. In June, he resigned from the OIAA and sought work with the OSS.

Chapter Six

A Spy for the OSS

The darkest days of the war against fascism in Europe had come in 1942, when German troops or regimes supportive of the Nazis occupied most of the continent. By early 1943, however, the tide had begun to turn, and Axis troops were falling back in Russia and North Africa.

The Americans were well into the war by now, and one part of the American war effort was the OSS—Office of Strategic Services, forerunner to today's CIA. Authorized by President Franklin Delano Roosevelt in 1942 as a wartime necessity, and run by the swashbuckling "Wild Bill" Donovan, the OSS was a glamorous organization that attracted a diverse assortment of talented and colorful characters. Although OSS agents indulged in a lot of cloak-and-dagger silliness—dashing flamboyantly, haphazardly, and sometimes far too obviously secretively around war-riven Europe—they nonetheless often unearthed information that greatly aided the war effort.

Moe Berg was an appealing candidate for the OSS for several reasons. He was intelligent and broadly educated, and he was an experienced and resourceful traveler who could land in a strange city, find and work with whoever was needed for the task at hand, then leave town smoothly and unattached when the job was done. "Moe was absolutely ideal for undercover work," fellow OSS agent Michael Burke recalled years later:

> Not by design; just by nature. One, because of his physical attributes. He could go anyplace without fear. He had stamina. . . . In addition, he had an alert, quick mind that could adapt itself into any new or strange subject and make him comfortable quickly. He was immensely involved intellectually and active in international affairs through reading and travel. He had the capacity to be at home in Italy or France or London or Bucharest. He was on familiar ground in all those places. He also possessed a great capacity for being able to live comfortably alone, and could do this for long periods of time. The life of an agent sometimes is a lonely one and some people aren't suited for that.[1]

Berg's knack for languages, too, must have strongly appealed to the OSS. On his OSS job application, Berg characterized his French, Spanish, and Portuguese as "fair," but this may have been too modest. His French, although rusty, had been excellent when he lived in Paris, and his Spanish and Portuguese must have become quite polished during his recent travels in Latin America. Berg also noted on his application that his knowledge of Italian, German, and Japanese was "slight," and he made no mention of the many other languages that he had dabbled in at various times throughout his life: Russian, Polish, Mandarin Chinese, Arabic, Latin, Sanskrit, Old High German, Bulgarian, Yiddish, and Hebrew.

The OSS seemed anxious to bring Berg on board. By the end of the summer of 1943, Berg had been sworn into the organization, completed his basic training, and been assigned to the OSS's Secret Intelligence branch. His first work was at the Balkans desk in Washington.

Toward the end of the year William Horrigan, an OSS man who had been working in Algiers, came to Washington to recruit an operative for a special assignment. "I didn't need a muscle-boy, a guy who could jump out of parachutes or take submarines," Horrigan recalled years later. "I needed a bright, competent fellow. They wanted me to see a bunch of people around the world. That's why I got Moe. I brought Moe in, and they were very happy with him. At that time, what they were talking about was the greatest mystery of life"[2]—the secret of nuclear fission.

In 1943 the Manhattan Project—America's crash program to build the world's first nuclear weapon—was in full swing. In a Chicago laboratory in December 1942, U.S. scientists had engineered, for the first time, a controlled nuclear chain reaction. Now the race was on to construct a working weapon.

And a race it was. American scientists and policy makers feared that the Germans, whose scientists had been leaders in nuclear physics before the war, might get there first. Chief among the German scientists whose expertise the Americans feared was Werner Heisenberg, one of the

Moe Berg, on the lake in Geneva, Switzerland, Easter Sunday, 1945.

founders of the field of quantum theory and one of the world's most brilliant theoretical physicists.

General Leslie Groves, head of the Manhattan Project, in 1943 launched the Alsos mission—an effort to locate Heisenberg, to find out how his and other German scientists' research was progressing, and thereby to discover how far along the Germans were toward manufacturing a nuclear bomb. Soon thereafter Azusa, a parallel effort seeking the same information, was begun under OSS auspices, and Berg joined this mission toward the end of 1943. Notes about the mission that Berg later wrote stress how high the stakes were: "They can beat us at a minute to midnight—in my own lingo, that meant 'don't take the game for granted until the third man is out in the ninth inning.' This was for keeps. It was the toppest secret in World War II, maybe the greatest in any war ever waged. Could and would the Nazis make the atom bomb? That was what they asked me to find out."[3]

Berg's job, initially, was to go to Italy. Mussolini had been overthrown in mid-1943, and Italy was now occupied partly by the Germans, partly by the Allies. Berg was to meet with Italian scientists and try to find out from them where German physicists were located and what they were doing. He no doubt was itching to get to Europe, but his travel orders were delayed, then delayed for still longer. The U.S. Army commanders in charge of the Italian theater of war, it seems, were reluctant to give a green light to the Azusa mission.

Berg took advantage of the delay to learn as much as he could about nuclear physics in general and about Heisenberg's work in particular. He pored over technical texts in libraries, and he visited American scientists to pick their brains.

During the delay, General Groves received a report from British intelligence that concluded that the Germans had no hope of constructing a nuclear bomb. This was not an unreasonable assessment, given how badly the war had by then ravaged Germany's manufacturing capabilities. But Groves refused to concur. "In this conclusion it is felt the British are skating rather thin," he noted, discounting the report.[4] Groves would take no chances; the Azusa mission would go forward.

On May 4, 1944, Berg at long last left Washington for Europe. His travel documents, signed by "Wild Bill" Donovan himself, permitted him to travel to London, Portugal, Algiers, and then Italy.

Berg spent much of May in London, which was then the U.S. Army's headquarters for the European Theater of Operations. There he met with various American intelligence personnel. Colonel H. K. Calvert, head of the Manhattan Project's liaison office in London, recalls that Berg—then as later in the war—"would appear suddenly out of the blue and then disappear just as mysteriously. He was a loner and was always on the move."[5] Berg's movements after he left London that May are shadowy: He turned up in a trench coat on a plane from Casablanca to Algiers, and he may have spent time in Istanbul.

By the beginning of June, however, Berg was in Italy. On June 5 he was at dinner with two American generals in Bari, on the Adriatic Sea, when word arrived that U.S. troops had liberated Rome from the Germans. It was crucial that the OSS make contact with the Italian scientific community in Rome immediately. Berg explained enough about his mission to the generals to convince them to speed him to Rome right away.

Berg soon made his way through the crowded, ecstatic streets of liberated Rome to the home of the eminent physicist Edoardo Amaldi. Over the next several days, Berg heard what little Amaldi had learned, while at his university post in fascist Italy, about German nuclear bomb research. Amaldi, who had had no direct contact with German physicists since 1941, believed that Heisenberg—though he was a brilliant theoretical physicist—didn't have the experimental skills needed to create and run a bomb-construction effort. If the Germans were working on a bomb (and Amaldi believed that they were), someone else was directing the effort.

While he was in Rome, Berg became friendly with another physicist, Gian Carlo Wick, who had years before been a student of Heisenberg. "He has a great love for, and a sentimental interest in, Heisenberg as his former teacher and as a brilliant physicist," Berg wrote in an OSS report.[6] The two scientists had kept in touch, and Berg acquired from Wick a postcard that Heisenberg had sent to him. Dated January 15, 1944, the card reports that Heisenberg's research institute in Leipzig had been destroyed by Allied bombing, although another facility, the Kaiser Wilhelm Gesellschaft, in Berlin, "is still standing." Better still, Wick knew at least approximately where Heisenberg was then based: in "a woody region" in southern Germany. Wick would not be more specific. Berg speculated in his report to Washington on this meeting that Wick was afraid that he might bring "harm to Heisenberg."[7] Imprecise as it was, the report on Wick was useful intelligence, and when Bill

Donovan passed through Rome late in June he praised Berg highly for his work.

Berg visited more than a dozen scientists as well as many other sources that seemed promising to him during his time in Rome. He kept his eyes and ears open for information, and he sent valuable reports to Washington on matters ranging from German radar technology and wind-tunnel experiments to Italian military equipment. He befriended Antonio Ferri, a scientist specializing in supersonic wind flow who had led anti-fascist guerrilla fighters during the war in Italy. (Eventually, with Berg's help, Ferri and his family moved to the United States, where he helped to develop U.S. supersonic flight technology after the war.) Berg also made several excursions outside Rome, including an extended (though not terribly fruitful) trip to just-liberated Florence.

In September, Berg returned to London, where he lingered through the fall having a wonderful time, the persistent German rocket bombing of the city notwithstanding. The OSS had little for him to do, so Berg was able to prowl around town, browsing in bookstores by day, attending dinner parties by night. He caught up on his letter writing: "Have a wonderful job and enjoy doing it," he wrote to his family.[8]

While Berg was puttering around London, the OSS not only pinpointed Werner Heisenberg's location (he was living in Hechingen, near the Black Forest) but also uncovered more evidence that the Germans had no nuclear weapon and no hope of acquiring one in the near future. General Groves remained dissatisfied; as long as there was a shadow of a possibility of a German A-bomb, Groves wanted to keep the Azusa mission alive.

For a while, plans were afoot to send Berg to Hechingen for reconnaissance and, perhaps, to kidnap Heisenberg. When General Groves heard about the plan, however, "I immediately stopped it," he recalled years later, in his memoirs, "realizing that if [Berg] were captured, the Nazis might be able to extract far more information about our project than we could ever hope to obtain if he were successful."[9] Instead, in December, Berg was dispatched to Paris (Allied troops had by then liberated France), where he received a full briefing on his next OSS assignment. Werner Heisenberg was expected to deliver a lecture in mid-December in Zurich. Switzerland had remained neutral during the war, a tradition it had maintained through two centuries of other European wars, so Axis as well as Allied citizens could visit Zurich. Moe Berg was to travel to Zurich and attend the Heisenberg lecture—with a gun in his pocket.

Berg's mission to Zurich—and his nuclear bomb intelligence work generally—was such a closely held secret that even other U.S. intelligence officers knew little about it. Gerhard Van Arkel, an aide to Allen Dulles, the OSS station head in Switzerland, recalled:

I had the notion he traveled around a good bit, but nobody knew exactly what the hell he was up to. I did, at the time, see the cables, with few exceptions, that went through our office. And I saw the cables that Moe was sending from Zurich and other spots around Switzerland. His cables were Greek to me. They were full of terms which at the time didn't mean a damn thing to me; terms such as isotopes and thorium and uranium and so forth. I hadn't the vaguest inkling of what was going on, but after I'd heard about the atomic bombs being dropped on Japan and had read the reports on them, I understood what Moe had been doing—counterintelligence on the A-bomb.[10]

Years later, long after the war was over, Berg told a fellow former OSS operative exactly what his mission in Zurich had been. Earl Brodie said that Berg told him "he'd been drilled in physics, to listen for certain things. If anything Heisenberg said convinced Berg the Germans were close to a bomb then his job was to shoot him—right there in the auditorium."[11]

Posing as a Swiss physics student, Berg attended Heisenberg's lecture in Zurich on December 18. (At forty-two years of age, this was rather an unlikely cover for Berg, but he apparently got away with it.) Berg's limited knowledge of German and of nuclear physics must have allowed him only a hazy understanding of what Heisenberg was saying. His notes on the lecture concentrate on appearances rather than on substance—what Heisenberg wore, for example, and that he looked small and frail.

If Heisenberg had reported any German nuclear breakthrough, the news would have hit the auditorium like a bombshell. No such bombshells exploded. Berg's orders were to fire only if he was convinced that development of a German bomb was imminent. Unconvinced, Berg held his fire.

After the lecture, Berg approached Paul Scherrer, director of the Swiss institute at which the lecture had taken place and a very secret, very valuable OSS source. Scherrer told Berg not only that Heisenberg had not developed a bomb but that he wasn't even working on such a project. Heisenberg's current work focused on cosmic rays.

Moe Berg and Professor Paul Scherrer, director of the Swiss institute where Heisenberg lectured and a valuable OSS ally. He and Moe became great friends.

Furthermore, Scherrer convinced Berg that Heisenberg was anti-Nazi. And, indeed, at a party a few days later at Scherrer's house Heisenberg affirmed: "I am not a Nazi but a German."[12] Heisenberg also acknowledged that evening that the war was lost for Germany. Berg followed Heisenberg out of the party and walked with him into the cold, dark night. It would have been a perfect opportunity for assassination, but once again Berg held his fire. He was convinced that Heisenberg posed no threat to the Allied war effort. The two parted company and never saw each other again.

Berg did, however, see a lot more of Scherrer. Paul Scherrer maintained contact with many German scientists, so he was well situated to pick up news about German nuclear research. He was also an immensely valuable source of other strategic information. Berg settled in at Zurich as Scherrer's lone contact with the U.S. government.

Berg and Scherrer became great friends. Scherrer, like Berg, loved newspapers, good books, and good food. He also loved everything American. Berg taught him baseball, and Scherrer taught Berg science. Berg became friendly not only with Scherrer but also with his family, accompanying them on skiing expeditions in the Alps and on warm-weather holidays at a lakeside vacation home.

Scherrer's family guessed that Moe Berg was a sort of bodyguard sent by the Americans to whisk Scherrer out of Switzerland in the event the Nazis invaded. They never guessed that Berg was a spy. They never even knew that Paul Scherrer had taken the enormous risk of passing information to the Americans until years after his death, long after the war was over.

By April 1945, the war in Europe was accelerating toward its conclusion, with British and American troops pressing toward Berlin from the west, Russians from the east. Berg left his friend Scherrer in the care of another OSS operative and reported to Paris, where he met Bill Donovan for breakfast on April 13. President Roosevelt had died suddenly, of a stroke, just hours earlier on April 12, and both Berg and Donovan were stunned. Berg was deeply touched when Donovan told him, "FDR knew what you were doing." Years later Berg wrote in a notebook: "And what I was doing was known to few."[13]

As American troops drove deep into Germany, the OSS and other U.S. intelligence operatives scoured the countryside to pick up the pieces of the German scientific establishment so as to deny Soviet Russia these spoils of war. So aggressive were the American agents—sometimes moving ahead of the liberating troops—that even U.S. military leaders came to call them "the body snatchers." Captured German scientists (Heisenberg included) were shipped off to confinement in England, captured scientific equipment was scavenged or destroyed, and captured documents were examined carefully.

Moe Berg hitched onto this mopping-up operation, traveling from Paris to Wiesbaden, then through Weimar to the famous laboratories at Gottingen. By then it was obvious from captured evidence not only that there would be no German bomb but also that the Germans had never even been close to developing one.

Berg's anti-Nazi mission had ended. He headed west through Paris and London to Newark, New Jersey, where the catcher-turned-spy sat down to dinner at his mother's house on April 25, 1945.

Moe and his mother, Rose, in the 1950s.

Chapter Seven

Into the Cold War

Bill Donovan liked to surround himself with interesting people, and when he traveled from Washington to London to Paris in May 1945, Moe Berg was asked along more for his companionship than for any specific OSS mission. Donovan wasn't the only person whom Berg entertained. When the OSS group visited a field hospital in eastern France, Berg found himself watching some American troops playing catch with a baseball. "Let's see the ball," he finally said, then threw it. "You're a pro," one of the G.I.s said. Berg threw the ball again, and the young man guessed, "You're a catcher." One more throw, and the soldier concluded, "And your name is Moe Berg."[1]

Berg parted company with Donovan in Europe and undertook a brief mission at Groves's behest. In June, he carried a letter from his friend Paul Scherrer to the eminent physicist Lise Meitner. Meitner had worked closely with the

German experimental physicist Otto Hahn in the late 1930s on breakthrough experiments that involved bombarding uranium with slow-moving neutrons. It was Meitner who, correctly, interpreted the results of these experiments: Her mathematical calculations showed that uranium atoms had been split, that nuclear fission had for the first time been achieved in a laboratory. By the time Berg caught up with her, Meitner, an Austrian of Jewish descent, was living in exile in Sweden, having fled Nazi persecution years earlier.

Scherrer knew that Meitner was finding it difficult to locate the resources to continue her work, and he proposed, in the letter Berg carried, that she pursue her research at his institute in Zurich. Berg and Meitner talked at length, and she gave him a letter to take back to Scherrer, describing her current work and agreeing to consider a move to his institute.

In July, Berg accompanied Scherrer on a trip to the United States—a visit that Scherrer had long wanted to make and one that Berg had helped to arrange. Berg and Scherrer met with OSS officials in Washington to discuss how to prevent Meitner and other European physicists from assisting the Russians. As the war in Europe wound down, the long-standing mutual suspicion and rivalry between Communist Russia and the capitalist West had re-emerged and would soon escalate into the decades-long Cold War arms race. The Soviet Union in 1945, devastated by war, was far from being able to produce nuclear weapons. But it would not remain so forever.

Berg next traveled with Scherrer to California, where the physicist visited Cal Tech and the Aerojet company. While Berg and Scherrer were still in the United States, the mushroom-shaped clouds of the world's first nuclear bombs erupted, first over the Manhattan Project's Nevada nuclear test site, on July 16, then on August 6 and 9, 1945, over Japan.

Everything changed after Hiroshima and Nagasaki. The war ended, and the United States became the world's first nuclear superpower. Around this time, the U.S. government seriously debated placing nuclear technology under international control to avert a new arms race, this one with the Soviet Union. But no effective controls were agreed upon, and the great Cold War arms buildup began.

In September 1945, President Harry S. Truman terminated the OSS, ordering it to clean up loose ends—and cut personnel—under a new name: Strategic Services Unit (SSU). Berg received a welter of instructions from the SSU. He was told to visit Lise Meitner, then told he should instead visit Rome to encourage physicists he had met there not to cooperate with the Russians. He was also hounded by bureaucrats in Washington to account for thousands of dollars of cash advances he'd taken from OSS accounts to cover his expenses during his wartime travels.

Berg hitched onto yet another mission undertaken for Leslie Groves. The Red Army had by late 1945 occupied Eastern Europe, and the Russians were busily recruiting scientists there. Lieutenant Colonel H. K. Calvert, still in Europe working for Groves, later recalled that "we had already picked up the top ten German atomic scientists and interned them at Farm Hall, England. We had won the prizes. The Russians, on the other hand, did not have a . . . team like ours during the war; they did not have body snatchers."[2] So now they were making up for lost time.

Berg and several other agents headed east to assess the situation. They drove from Vienna to Prague to firebombed

Dresden to the Soviet sector of Berlin. There they ascertained that the Russians were in fact still recruiting lesser scientific lights. If bribery didn't convince a targeted scientist to move to Russia (and in war-devastated Eastern Europe bribery could be a potent temptation indeed), he would simply be carted off by force.

Berg slipped quietly into the American-occupied sector of Berlin, then continued his intelligence-gathering journeys throughout Europe, dipping into special government accounts to pay his way. (He continued to avoid writing up a formal account of his expenses.) He investigated a French physicist who was suspected of being Communist, spent two weeks in Rome, and in January revisited Lise Meitner, who assured him that she would not work for the Russians. Ultimately, she chose to remain in Sweden permanently and became a Swedish citizen in 1949.

Berg also checked up on the famous physicist Niels Bohr. Bohr, who had contributed mightily to the Manhattan Project before returning to Europe in 1945 to work on peaceful applications of nuclear energy, had come to the conclusion that the only way to avert a terrifying nuclear arms race between Soviet Russia and the West was to have no more secrets concerning nuclear science. Toward the end of 1945, Leslie Groves had been chagrined to learn that Bohr, in Copenhagen, had been visited by a Soviet agent. Berg saw Bohr at the end of January 1946 and determined that Groves's fears were groundless: Bohr was not in the business of passing nuclear secrets to the Russians.

The SSU's commanding officers were pleased with Berg's work, and they gave him a raise in salary. The accountants, however, still wanted to know exactly how Berg had been spending government expense-account money.

Throughout the first half of 1946, Berg continued to gather information all over Europe, mostly writing his own agenda. At the end of July, he was ordered home.

Sitting at a desk among bureaucrats in Washington must have been disheartening to Berg after the exciting and peripatetic life to which he was accustomed. In August he resigned from the SSU. The accountants ordered him to explain $21,439.14 of government-funded expenditures, in writing, by October.

While government accountants hounded him, grateful officials higher up the government ladder worked to give Berg the recognition that was properly his. On October 10, Moe Berg was awarded the Medal of Freedom—a high honor indeed. Since Berg's intelligence work remained classified, his award citation was a monument of intentional vagueness:

> Mr. Morris Berg, United States Civilian, rendered exceptionally meritorious service of high value to the war effort from April 1944 to January 1946. In a position of responsibility in the European Theater, he exhibited analytical abilities and a keen planning mind. He inspired both respect and constant high level of endeavor on the part of his subordinates which enabled his section to produce studies and analyses vital to the mounting of American operations.[3]

Berg turned down the Medal of Freedom, stating: "I regret that I must refuse to accept and I reject the medal awarded me. I do this with due respect for the spirit with which it is offered." In a letter to the SSU's Lieutenant Colonel William Quinn, Berg added: "I am grateful to those War De-

Moe Berg was awarded the Medal of Freedom in October 1946. He turned it down.

partment officials who were kind enough, under the circumstances, to offer this award for my very modest contribution. But I cannot accept it."[4] A famous storyteller, Berg may have been reluctant to accept an honor that he wouldn't be permitted to explain to anyone. Being disgusted by the demands of the accountants might also have contributed to his decision to reject the award. And it's possible that Berg resisted accepting an award that would have appeared to cap his career as a spy, when he really didn't want that career to end.

His accounting problems were soon over. A government lawyer looked over Berg's file and determined that, far from owing money, Berg probably was due a payment from the government. "I don't want any of your money," was Berg's angry response.[5] The SSU decided in April 1947 to close Berg's account. "Berg's services were of great value," a memo in Berg's file notes, "inestimable in dollars and cents, but in all probability far exceeding the cost to the government for Mr. Berg's two and a half years of service."[6] Career ended, case closed.

Moe Berg was one of millions of Americans mustered out of military or other war-related government service at the end of World War II. Most Americans were eager to get on with their lives after the war. Some, however—Berg among them—found it difficult to adjust. Berg had loved his work for the OSS, and he'd especially loved the glamorous and exciting life it allowed him to lead. He didn't want to come home and settle down. He wanted to be a spy.

Although the new Central Intelligence Agency (CIA) had carried onto its payroll only 1,300 OSS/SSU employees (the OSS had employed 13,000 in 1945),[7] there was no shortage of espionage in the 1950s. America's spying, however, had developed a very different focus from what the OSS had done during the war. They weren't shooting at Nazis anymore; instead, the enemy was communism, and the fight was a Cold War.

The CIA also developed a very different style of management and operation from the thrilling atmosphere the OSS had created during the war. "The difference between the two organizations, basically," recalls Richard Helms, an OSS veteran and later CIA director, "was that the CIA, since it was operating in peacetime, had to set up far more regulations on what people and agents were doing."[8] Regulations never sat well with Moe Berg. He was unpredictable and didn't always follow orders, preferring to write his own itinerary. Blazing his own trail during the war, Berg had sometimes brought unexpected and valuable results. Fitting Berg into the more tightly managed CIA was another matter altogether. On one occasion, nonetheless, the CIA decided that Moe Berg's unique talents were needed, and they contracted with him for a special mission.

It was 1952. The Soviet Union was already building and testing nuclear weapons, China had recently gone Communist, and the Red Scare was at fever pitch. Many in the American government—and, more widely, among the American people—worried obsessively about who might be passing what atomic secrets to the Communists. Moe Berg proposed to the CIA that he revisit his contacts in Europe, to see what he could find out from them about the state of Soviet and East German nuclear physics research. This seemed like a good idea to the CIA, so off Berg went to Europe in July, armed with a $10,000 contract and an expense account.

Berg traveled throughout Europe in the luxurious and secretive style to which he was accustomed, racking up hefty hotel bills and allowing the bureaucrats back in Washington to wonder where he was much of the time. He visited his old friend Paul Scherrer in Zurich, looked up old contacts in Rome, and spent a good bit of time in London and in Germany.

After several months, Berg returned to Washington. According to a CIA officer who interviewed him at that time:

> We said to him, "Who did you see, what did they have to say?" [Berg's reporting] was not very solid. It was, well, flaky. He was tantalizing. He'd talk about schemes

Moe Berg, while visiting friend and colleague Paul Scherrer in Switzerland.

and people with great enthusiasm and you'd say, "Moe, tell me about this," and it disappeared in a cloud of fluff. I sometimes felt that when Moe told things, some of it might have been embroidering.[9]

Worse still, Berg was no tidier about accounting for his trip's expenses than he had been during the war. No one accused him of doing anything improper with his expense accounts, but the trouble Berg caused the accountants and his failure to produce useful information were together too much for the CIA. They continued to keep him under contract for a while, but they gave him no more assignments. In 1954, the CIA terminated Berg's contract.

Chapter Eight

Cut Adrift

Berg's life after the government cut him loose became aimless and rather sad. He never married. He and Estella Huni had drifted apart during the war; by the time he returned to the United States, she had married someone else.

Berg never owned a house, or even kept an apartment of his own. After the war, he moved into the house in Newark, New Jersey, where his brother, Dr. Sam, lived and practiced medicine. He didn't bring much with him, just several of his famous gray suits, some old catcher's mitts, and his books.

He never owned a car—in fact, he never even learned to drive. A tireless walker, Berg could and did cover mile after mile of city streets even in his fifties and sixties.

He never had much money. In 1933, Berg had invested in Novelart, a stationery and film production company. The firm, through no fault

After his career as a government spy ended in the mid-50s, Moe Berg had a hard time adjusting to a quiet, civilian life.

of Berg's, went belly-up at the end of the war, leaving Berg thousands of dollars in debt for an ill-considered contract his partner had signed with the U.S. government. Eventually Berg reached a compromise with and made partial payment to the government, but the whole prolonged mess "depressed him deeply—yet he did not speak of it," his sister, Ethel, told a friend.[1]

Not long after the war, the White Sox offered Berg a coaching position, but Berg turned them down. He didn't apply for teaching positions or seek to join a law firm. He didn't even list himself in the phone book. From time to time he did odds and ends of consulting and liaison work, but during all the long years after his career as a spy ended Berg never held a real job.

Instead, Berg traveled, living off the generosity of friends scattered across the country. Most people found Berg's company irresistibly charming, and Berg had made and retained many friends over many years. His friendship with Crossan Cooper, for example, dated back to Princeton in the 1920s and continued long after Berg's ballplaying and spying days were through. "One day he called me and said he was in town," Cooper, who lived in Baltimore at the time, later recalled. "I said to come on over and have dinner and spend the night with us. He came, had dinner, spent the night and stayed for six weeks. He was always good company. He knew about almost anything. Moe was a very cultivated gentleman. He would never talk about his OSS exploits. I'd try to get him to talk about them, but he wouldn't."[2]

Some of Berg's former teammates recall a gloomier aging Moe Berg. Ed Rumill saw him in 1967, and by then "Moe seemed to prefer staying in the background of things.

He had withdrawn, and was going through the motions. That marvelous exhilaration he generated was gone."[3]

Berg's eccentricities—the newspapers, the secretiveness, the unchanging somber wardrobe, and more—became more pronounced as he grew older. He was fanatical about bathing (even when camped among soldiers during the war he'd managed to rig up a shower for himself), and whenever possible he took no fewer than three baths a day. Although this must have been a terrific inconvenience for his

Moe's love of books and newspapers made him a difficult houseguest.

hosts, apparently many people thought Berg was worth the trouble. A teammate recalls a visit Berg made to his home in Pennsylvania Dutch country:

> Moe came during a drought. It hadn't rained in months. And, God, he took his standard three baths a day! Moe was the cleanest man in the world. He took a bath at eight-thirty in the morning, four-thirty in the afternoon, and eleven-thirty at night. He bathed for an hour at a time. We ran out of towels in the house and, worse, we ran out of water.
>
> My wife, Alice, was fascinated by him. We'd sit on the porch and Moe would point out the galaxies and constellations. The dippers, Ursa Minor, Ursa Major, Orion, the Milky Way. Stars captivated him. We'd have friendly little arguments and Moe would use the idiom of Dutch country, saying, "Now, Tommy, listen to me out. Listen to me out."[4]

Books remained close to Berg's heart and, shaky finances notwithstanding, he collected them voraciously. According to Sam Berg,

> Moe filled every available space in my house with his books and newspapers. There was a virtual confrontation between his massive book collection and my medical books. And my books were being overwhelmed. The place was overrun with literature. It was difficult to navigate. You had to move sideways. Having guests at the house was out of the question. They would have had to sit on books stacked high on every chair. . . .
>
> Further, after arriving home each night, the first thing Moe would do is take a shower, don a Japanese

kimono, come down to the library, where he often spent the entire night reading, underlining passages. Often he would leave the library in his kimono, his head buried in a book and walk past some of my patients, who couldn't believe their eyes. Moe would have been right at home in a Roman toga.

These books and magazines and papers that filled up my house were a source of conflict between us. Moe moved a few blocks away. I asked him to do that. It was the only way to resolve the problem. Moe had thousands of books. We put the books in one hundred huge cartons and loaded them onto a truck. The truck had to make three trips to move the books alone. It took another truckload to move the newspapers he had collected.[5]

Moe Berg moved from his brother's house to his sister's house in 1964. Brother Sam and sister Ethel were difficult personalities, and they nurtured old grievances. Although they lived just blocks away from each other, they hadn't spoken to one another in years. The situation must have been uncomfortable; Moe Berg, however, ducked out and spent as much time traveling as possible.

In May 1972, Moe Berg, then age 70, fell out of bed at his sister's home, bruising his torso badly. He shrugged off seeing a doctor about it, then found he couldn't eat. After several days, he checked into Clara Maass Medical Center, in Belleville, New Jersey. Berg's symptoms were confusing, and it took a day or so to figure out what was wrong with him—an abdominal aortic aneurism. By the time Berg was diagnosed, he was well on his way to bleeding to death.

On May 29, Berg asked a nurse: "How are the Mets doing today?"[6] He died before learning the answer.

Newspapers across the country ran features on the extraordinary catcher, scholar, and spy. Perhaps the *Boston Globe* said it best: "So long, Moe. We're going to miss you in at least 12 different languages."[7]

Moe Berg was unique. His accomplishments were diverse, his eccentricities mostly harmless, even endearing, and his company charming. "He was different because he was different," said Berg's friend Ted Lyons. "He made up for all the bores of the world. And he did it softly, stepping on no one."[8]

Source
Notes

Chapter 1: Early Years

1. Kaufman, Louis, Barbara Fitzgerald, and Tom Sewell, *Moe Berg: Athlete, Scholar, Spy* (New York: Ballantine Books, 1974), p. 16.
2. Kaufman, p. 17.
3. Letter dated October 15, 1975, apparently retyped by Ethel Berg when she printed it in Ethel Berg, *My Brother Morris Berg: The Real Moe* (published privately by author, 1976), p. 357.
4. Kaufman, p. 25.
5. Undated handwritten note reproduced in Ethel Berg, pp. 11-12.
6. Letter, apparently retyped, reprinted in Ethel Berg, p. 13.
7. Undated news clipping found in Princeton University alumni files, quoted in Nicholas Dawidoff, *The Catcher Was a Spy: The Mysterious Life of Moe Berg* (New York: Pantheon Books, 1994), p. 33.
8. Kaufman, p. 26.

9. Jiro Hirano et al., *The Spy Who Loved Japan* (1979 documentary film for NHK, a Japanese television company), quoted in Dawidoff, p. 30.
10. November 1919 letter quoted in Kaufman, p. 23.
11. Arthur Daley, *New York Times*, date unspecified, cited by Kaufman, pp. 30-31.

Chapter 2: One Foot in Each World
1. *Brooklyn Daily Eagle*, June 28, 1923, quoted in Dawidoff, p. 40.
2. Berg letter dated November 5, 1923, quoted in Dawidoff, p. 43.
3. *Boston Herald* sports columnist Bill Cunningham, date unspecified, quoted by Kaufman, p. 34.
4. Kaufman, p. 32.
5. Berg letter dated Dec. 2, 1923, quoted in Dawidoff, p. 44.
6. Kaufman, p. 32.
7. Dawidoff, p. 50.
8. Undated Berg letter to Asa (no last name), reproduced in Ethel Berg, p. 31.
9. Kaufman, p. 33.
10. Letter from Comiskey to Berg, dated February 10, 1927, reproduced in Ethel Berg, p. 29.
11. Dawidoff, pp. 55-56, citing several accounts of this story.
12. Undated letter from Lyons to Ethel Berg, apparently retyped, printed in Ethel Berg, p. 42.
13. Kaufman, p. 39.
14. Undated letter from Lyons to Ethel Berg, apparently retyped, printed in Ethel Berg, p. 42.
15. *Chicago Tribune*, June 6, 1929, quoted in Dawidoff, p. 61.
16. Kaufman, p. 42.
17. Kaufman, p. 39.
18. Arthur Daley, *New York Times*, December 2, 1964.

19. Undated letter from Sister M. Protese, reproduced in Ethel Berg, pp. 85-86.
20. March 1972 letter from Berg to Margaret and John Kieran, apparently retyped, printed in Ethel Berg, p. 308.

Chapter 3: Japan—and the World
1. Letter from Sotaro Suzuki, dated August 26, 1973, to Louis Kaufman, reproduced in Ethel Berg, pp. 40-41.
2. Kaufman, p. 3.
3. Arthur Daley, *New York Times*, December 2, 1964.
4. Letter dated November 9, 1932, reproduced in Ethel Berg, pp. 49-60.
5. *Ibid.*
6. *Ibid.*
7. *Ibid.*
8. Letter dated December 31, 1932, reproduced in Ethel Berg, pp. 63-72.
9. *Ibid.*
10. *Ibid.*

Chapter 4: More Baseball—and More of Japan
1. Undated news clipping, quoted in Dawidoff, p. 100.
2. September 1932 telegram reproduced in Ethel Berg, p. 33.
3. Kaufman, p. 45.
4. Kaufman, pp. 50-51.
5. Dawidoff, p. 90, citing several sources.
6. "Speech to Meiji University Students—November, 1934," typewritten page, apparently Berg's notes for his speech, reproduced in Ethel Berg, p. 97.
7. "Delivered over radio Tokyo to United States, November, 1934," typewritten page, apparently Berg's notes for his speech, reproduced in Ethel Berg, p. 98.
8. Kaufman, p. 53.

9. Typed text of speech Berg delivered to a book fair in Boston in 1940, reproduced in Ethel Berg, pp. 135-138.
10. Kaufman, p. 74.
11. Harold Kaese, "Goodby Moe Berg in any language," *Boston Globe*, June 4, 1972.
12. Dawidoff, p. 100, quoting telephone interview with Ferrell.
13. Dawidoff, p. 103, quoting telephone interview with Auker.
14. John Kieran, "An Obscure Baseball Item," *New York Times*, December 8, 1938.
15. All of the information about Estella Huni comes from Dawidoff, mostly pp. 143-145.
16. John Kieran, "It Must Be Catching," *New York Times*, January 31, 1939.
17. John Lardner, undated *Newark News* clipping reproduced in Ethel Berg, p. 108.
18. Dawidoff, p. 114, quoting a recording of the program.
19. John Kieran, "Nightlife in the Big Leagues," *New York Times*, February 14, 1940.
20. Moe Berg, "Pitchers and Catchers," *Atlantic Monthly*, September 1941.
21. Kaufman, p. 182.

Chapter 5: Latin America
1. *New York Times* sportswriter Arthur Daley, undated, quoted by Kaufman, p. 79.
2. Kaufman, p. 83.
3. Typed text of speech Berg delivered to a book fair in Boston in 1940, reproduced in Ethel Berg, pp. 135-138.
4. *Newark News*, January 16, 1942, cited in Dawidoff, p. 130.
5. Handwritten letter dated August 9, 1940, reproduced in Ethel Berg, pp. 141-146.
6. Berg's February 24, 1942, radio address to Japan, quoted in its entirety in Kaufman, pp. 98-102.

7. John Kieran, "Rain-Maker for Rent," *New York Times*, September 17, 1942.
8. Berg report to Rockefeller, date unspecified, quoted in Kaufman, pp. 109-110.
9. "Confidential and Secret Memorandum" from Berg to Rockefeller, dated February 27, 1943, discussing January 17 meeting, reproduced in Ethel Berg, pp. 172-178.
10. *Ibid.*
11. *Ibid.*
12. Letter from Rockefeller to Berg, dated April 14, 1943, reproduced in Ethel Berg, p. 183.

Chapter 6: A Spy for the OSS
1. Kaufman, p. 112.
2. Interview with Horrigan quoted in Dawidoff, p. 156.
3. Undated notes handwritten by Berg, reproduced in Ethel Berg, p. 330.
4. Groves notation on a December 22, 1943, Manhattan Project document, quoted in Dawidoff, p. 165.
5. Kaufman, p. 121.
6. Berg report, filed at the CIA, quoted in Thomas Powers, *Heisenberg's War: The Secret History of the German Bomb* (New York: Knopf, 1993), p. 307.
7. Powers, p. 308, includes a complete translation of the postcard as well as excerpts from Berg's OSS reports.
8. Berg letter quoted in Dawidoff, p. 189.
9. Leslie Groves, *Now It Can Be Told* (New York: Harper & Brothers, 1962), p. 217.
10. Kaufman, pp. 149-150.
11. 1990 interview with Brodie quoted in Powers, p. 393.
12. Interview with eyewitness quoted in Powers, p. 402.
13. The Donovan quote is reported in many sources; the quote from Berg's notes is in Dawidoff, p. 216.

Chapter 7: Into the Cold War

1. Interview with an eyewitness, related in Dawidoff, p. 220.
2. Kaufman, p. 161.
3. "Citation for Medal of Freedom," reproduced in Ethel Berg, p. 327.
4. Berg letter to Quinn, dated December 12, 1946, in which Berg himself quotes his earlier letter to Col. Skinner formally rejecting the medal, quoted in Kaufman, p. 171.
5. Telephone interview with Larry Houston, to whom Berg said this, quoted in Dawidoff, p. 233.
6. Memo in Berg's CIA file quoted in Dawidoff, pp. 233-234.
7. Dawidoff, p. 240.
8. Interview with Helms quoted in Dawidoff, p. 240.
9. Interview with CIA officer quoted in Dawidoff, p. 245.

Chapter 8: Cut Adrift

1. Letter from Ethel Berg to Sam Goudsmit, dated May 11, 1973, quoted in Dawidoff, p. 240.
2. Kaufman, p. 184.
3. Kaufman, p. 190.
4. Kaufman, p. 184.
5. Kaufman, pp. 185-186.
6. Dawidoff, p. 329, which cites several sources.
7. Harold Kaese, "Goodby Moe Berg in any language," *Boston Globe*, June 4, 1972.
8. Quoted in Ethel Berg, p. 358, source unspecified.

Index